Austria-Hungary's Last War, 1914-1918

Vol 2 (1915)

Leaflets and Sketches

Compiled by
The Austrian Federal Ministry of the Army and War Archive

Under the Direction of
Edmund Glaise-Horstenau

Edited by
Josef Brauner, Eduard Czegka, Jaromir Diakow, Friedrich Franek,
Rudolf Kiszling, Eduard Steinitz, and Ernst Wisshaupt

Translated by Stan Hanna

Legacy Books Press

Published by Legacy Books Press
RPO Princess, Box 21031
445 Princess Street
Kingston, Ontario, K7L 5P5
Canada

www.legacybookspress.com

This edition first published in 2024 by Legacy Books Press
1

ISBN: 978-1-927537-85-5

First published as *Österreich-Ungarns Leitzter Krieg, 1914-1918,* by Publisher of Military Science Releases, Vienna, in 1931.

This book is typeset in a Times New Roman 11-point font.

Title: Austria-Hungary's last war, 1914-1918 / compiled by the Austrian Federal Ministry of the Army and War Archive under the direction of Edmund Glaise-Horstenau ; edited by Eduard Czegka, Maximilian Hoen, Rudolf Kiszling, Viktor Meduna-Riedburg, Eduard Steinitz, and Ernst Wisshaupt ; translated by Stan Hanna ; introduction by Sir Hew Strachan.
Other titles: Österreich-Ungarns letzer Krieg, 1914-1918. English
Names: Austria. Bundesministerium für Landesverteidigung, compiler.
Description: All volumes are accompanied by companion volumes with title Leaflets and sketches. | Volume 2 edited by Josef Brauner, Eduard Czegka, Jaromir Diakow, Friedrich Franek, Rudolf Kiszling, Eduard Steinitz, and Ernst Wisshaupt. | Includes bibliographical references and index. | Content: Vol 2 (1915). From the battle of Limanowa-Lapanow Finale to the capture of Brest-Litowsk -- Vol 2 (1915). Leaflets and sketches | Includes some text in German.
Identifiers: Canadiana 20230439314 | ISBN 9781927537855 (v. 2, companion ; softcover)
Subjects: LCSH: World War, 1914-1918—Campaigns. | LCSH: World War,1914-1918—Austria. | LCSH: World War, 1914-1918—Hungary. | LCSH: Austria—History, Military. | LCSH: Hungary—History, Military.
Classification: LCC D539 .A97 2023 | DDC 940.4/13436—dc23

Table of Contents

Publisher's Note Regarding Leaflet 14

The contents of Leaflet 14 has been published in translation on pages 347 onwards in Volume 2 of *Austria-Hungary's Last War*. As such, it has not been reproduced here.

Leaflets

Österreich-Ungarns letzter Krieg II

Tabelle 1

Übersicht über die Menschenbewegung an der Front
von Kriegsbeginn bis Anfang 1915

	Nordfront		Balkanfront		Gruppe GdK. Rohr		Zusammen		Donaubrücken- köpfe	
	Verpflegs-	Feuer- gewehr-	Verpflegs-	Feuer- gewehr-	Verpflegs-	Feuer- gewehr-	Verpflegs-	Feuer- gewehr-	Verpflegs-	Feuer- gewehr-
					Stand in Tausenden					
Feldarmee	1612	810	468	240	.	.	2080	1050	.	.
Neu formierte Landsturmtruppen — zu den Armeen . . .	138	110	72	65	.	.	.	.	.	.
zur Gruppe GdK. Rohr (italienische Grenze)	.	.	.	.	45	30	288	227	.	.
bei Gruppe GdK. Rohr gebildet und zur Feldarmee verschoben	22	14	11	8	.	.	.	.	.	.
Donaubrückenköpfe .	.	.	.	.	.	.	.	.	48	32
II.,III.,IV.u.halbe V.Marschbaone.	460	385	160	134	.	.	620	519		
Bis Ende Dezember an die Front abgegangen	2232	1319	711	447	45	30	2988	1796	48	32
Verluste bis Ende Dezember 1914[2])	979	979	271	271	.	.	1250	1250	.	.
Somit Stand zur Jahreswende .	1253	340	440	176	45	30	1738	546		
Anfang Jänner 1915 kommt 2.Hälfte d.V.Marschbaone.hinzu	80	70	46	41	.	.	126	111		
Somit Stand Ende der ersten Jännerwoche	1333	410	486	217	45	30	1864	657	48	32

[1]) Bei den Kampfständen sind auch die Truppenstäbe, die Maschinengewehrabteilungen, Artillerie und die technischen Truppen inbegriffen, während bei den Feuergewehrständen ausschließlich die mit der Handfeuerwaffe unmittelbar in der Front stehenden Mannschaften der Infanterie und Kavallerie gezählt sind.

[2]) Die Verlustziffern beziehen sich richtigerweise auf den Gesamt- also Verpflegsstand, sie setzen sich in weitaus überwiegendem Maße aus den Verlusten beim Feuergewehrstand zusammen. Aus diesem Grunde und weil Unterlagen für eine zutreffende Verteilung der Verluste auf die drei Standesarten nicht vorhanden sind, wurde die Gesamtsumme bei allen drei Ständen eingesetzt, obgleich sich in Wahrheit eine kleine Abstufung bei den Kampf- und Feuergewehrständen ergeben müßte.

Tabelle 2

Feuergewehrstände an der Nordfront am 31. Dezember 1914
Deutsche Truppen, durch [ ] bezeichnet, in den Summen nicht inbegriffen

1.		2.		3.		4.		Armeegruppe GdK. Pflanzer-Baltin	
				Armee					
ID. (Gruppe)	Gewehre	ID. (Gruppe)	Gewehre	ID. (Gruppe)	Gewehre	ID. (Gruppe)	Gewehre	ID. (Gruppe)	Gewehre
5.	6.780	31.	7.526	von 6.	2.000	37. IBrig.	4.800	Rónai-Horváth	9.800
46.	9.621	32.	5.100	28.	2.600	82. IBrig.	5.700	Hofmann	10.600
25.	6.274	16	7.102	17.	3.700	3.	3.600	Durski	4.420
33.	4.822	35.	4.400	20.	2.810	8.	4.600	Haller	1.600
37.	11.120	27.	6.100	2.	6.670	[47. Res.]	[10.600]	Schreitter	2.800
4.	6.506	[35. Res.]	[5.800]	24	4.053	bh. IR. 1	2.000	Schultheisz	10.800
14.	9.680			34.	3.200	11.	2.200		
Kletter	8.965			56.	4.000	30.	4.000		
				XVIII. Kps.	8.530	38. IBrig.	7.200		
				44. IBrig.	2.400	86. IBrig.			
				SchR. 5	1.890	15.	3.300		
						38.	7.500		
						200. IBrig.			
						201. IBrig.			
						39.	6.500		
						45.	3.500		
						6.	4.500		
						10.	4.350		
						13.	3.550		
						26.	3.500		
						43. IBrig.	2.100		
						12.	5.850		

Summe der Armeen rund, ohne deutsche Truppen (35. und 47. Res.=Div.)

63.700	30.200	41.800	78.700	40.000

Summe rund 254.400 Gewehre

Hiezu Reiter und Fußabteilungen der Kavalleriekörper

2.500	2.200	5.700	4.400	1.600

Summe 16.400 Gewehre

In den Festungen — Krakau 16.600 Gewehre

Przemyśl 51.800 Gewehre

Status tables

Tabelle 3

Gesamtverluste bis Ende Dezember 1914

			tot	verwundet	krank	gefangen	vermißt	ohne Zergliederung	Summe
Nord- front	Kampf- truppen der Feld- armeen	Offiziere . .	2.099	4.580	5.062	2.095		873	14.709
		Mann	84.909	231.024	160.833	180.448		58.960	716.174
		Zusammen .	87.008	235.604	165.895	182.543		59.833	730.883
	Armeeunmittelbare und aufgelöste Formationen		Offiziere und Mann zusammen						264.000
	Zusammen								994.883
Balkan- front	Offiziere		1.069	3.211	2.599	66	656	.	7.601
	Mann		27.216	118.911	44.117	1.980	73.988	.	266.212
	Zusammen		28.285	122.122	46.716	2.046	74.644	.	273.813
Summe nach Aufteilung der „ohne Zer- gliederung", dann bei den „armeeun- mittelbaren und aufgelösten For- mationen" ange- gebenen Zahlen auf die einzelnen Verlustgruppen.	Offiziere . . .		4.100	10.050	10.200	3.560			27.910
	in %		14.7	36.0	36.5	12.8			100
	Mann		150.700	470.409	275.273	344.404			1,240.786
	in %		12.1	37.9	22.2	27.8			100
	Zusammen . .		154.800	480.459	285.473	347.964			1,268.696
	in %		12.2	37.9	22.5	27.4			100

Anmerkung: Die Prozente beziehen sich auf die Gesamtverluste innerhalb der betreffenden Kategorie

Status tables

Tabelle 4

Standesbewegung zwischen Heimat und Heer

Friedensstand	Offiziere und Beamte	36.000
	Mann	414.000
	Zusammen . . .	450 000
Bei Mobilisierung eingerückt	Offiziere und Beamte	54.000
	Mann einschließlich des Rekrutenjahrganges 1914 (Geburtsjahrgang 1893) *und 66,000 Zivilarbeiter*	2,846.000
	Zusammen . . .	2,900.000
Somit standen zu Kriegsbeginn in aktiver Dienstleistung.		**3.350.000**
Mit den Feldarmeen gingen an die Front.		2,080.000
Somit verblieben im Hinterlande zunächst		1,270.000
Dazu	die im Oktober vorzeitig gemusterten und gleich eingezogenen Rekruten des Jahrganges 1915 (Geburtsjahrgang 1894) sowie die Nachgemusterten der aktiven Jahrgänge 1890 bis 1893 . . .	361.000
	im Ausland Gemusterte aller dienstpflichtigen Jahrgänge	6.000
	aus der Front zurückgekehrte Verwundete und Kranke bis Ende Dezember 1914 genesen	200.000
Somit nach Ausmarsch der Feldarmee bis Ende 1914 im Hinterland verfügbare Kräfte . .		1,837.000
Bis Ende Dezember zu den Armeen ins Feld gestellt	II., III., IV. und ein Teil der V. Marschbaone	620.000
	Neuformationen des Landsturmes	288.000
	Zusammen Menschennachschub für die Feldarmee	908.000
Im Hinterlande standen in den Donaubrückenköpfen ~~und an der italienischen Grenze (Gruppe GdK. Rohr)~~ an mobilen, aber örtlich gebundenen Kräften		48.000
Es befanden sich daher Ende Dezember im Hinterlande *verfügbar*		881.000
Weitere Gestaltung der Lage zu Beginn des Jahres 1915	Die bereits marschbereite zweite Hälfte der V. Marschbaone. (1. Jännerwoche ins Feld)	126.000
	Für Ende Jänner in Aufstellung begriffene VI. Marschbaone. . .	170.000
	Somit würden verbleiben Ende Jänner	585.000
	Im Laufe des Jänner rückten genesene Verwundete und Kranke ein schätzungsweise	50.000
	Im Laufe des Jänner und Februar rückten die in den Monaten November und Dezember gemusterten (Geburts∗) Jahrgänge 1878 bis 1890 ein	619.000

Status tables

Beilage 1

Tabelle 5

Die aktiven und die Reserveoffiziere und die Offiziersaspiranten sowie die Mannschaftspersonen nach ihrer Sprachzugehörigkeit

	Unter 1000				
	aktiven		Reserve-		Mannschafts-personen
	Offizieren	Offiziersaspiranten	offizieren	offiziersaspiranten	
	waren				
Deutsche	761	648	568	514	248
Magyaren	107	170	245	255	233
Tschechen	52	76	106	120	126
Slowaken	1	1	1	2	36
Polen.	27	18	33	47	79
Ruthenen	2	2	5	9	78
Slowenen	5	4	8	15	25
Kroaten und Serben	27	60	19	23	92
Rumänen	10	17	7	7	70
Italiener.	8	4	8	8	13

Status tables

Tabelle 6

Übersicht über die Zahl der ein=, zwei= und mehrsprachigen Truppenkörper im k. u. k. Heere[1]

	Infanterie und Kaiser-jäger-jäger-regimenter	Feldjäger-bataillone	Kavallerie-regimenter	Feld- und Gebirgsartillerie			Festungsartillerie		Pionier-bataillone	Train-divisionen
				Feld- und Gebirgs-artillerie-regimenter	Schwere Haubitz-divisionen	Reitende Artillerie-divisionen	Re-gimenter	Bataillone		
Einsprachige Truppenkörper										
Deutsch	12	4	3	7	.	.	.	1	1	.
Magyarisch	14	1	16	5	1	2	.	.	1	3
Tschechisch	5	.	2	1	.	.	.	.	.	.
Slowakisch	2	1	.	1	.	.	.	.	.	.
Polnisch	6	1	2	1	.	.	.	.	.	.
Ruthenisch.	4	1	1	2	.	.	.	.	.	.
Slowenisch	2	1	.	.	.	.	.	.	.	.
Kroatisch, serbisch, serbokroatisch	12	2	2	3	.	.	.	.	1	1
Rumänisch.	3	1	.	.	.	.	.	.	.	.
Zweisprachige Truppenkörper										
Deutsch und — magyarisch	4	1	.	4	.	.	2	1	3	.
tschechisch	14	8	9	10	1	1	1	1	4	4
italienisch	4	.	.	.	.	.	.	.	.	.
eine der übrigen Nationalsprachen .	3	.	1	8	.	.	1	1	1	2
Magyarisch und — rumänisch	7	1	.	3	.	1	1	.	.	.
ruthenisch, kroatisch-serbisch, slowakisch	4	2	.	3	.	.	.	.	.	3
Andere zweisprachige Mischungen	9	2	6	4	2	2	1	.	2	2
Mehrsprachige Truppenkörper										
Deutsch und — magyarisch und — tschech., slowak. kroat.=serb., rumänisch . .	1	.	.	4	.	.	1	.	2	.
tschechisch und — polnisch, ruthen. slowakisch . .	1	1	.	2	.	.	1	1	1	1
Sonstige dreisprachige Truppen-körper ohne deutsch und un-garisch	3	.	.	.	.	.	.	.	.	.

[1] Nach dem Militärstatistischen Jahrbuch für das Jahr 1911 (Wien 1912). Später aufgestellte Truppenkörper sind daher nicht berücksichtigt.

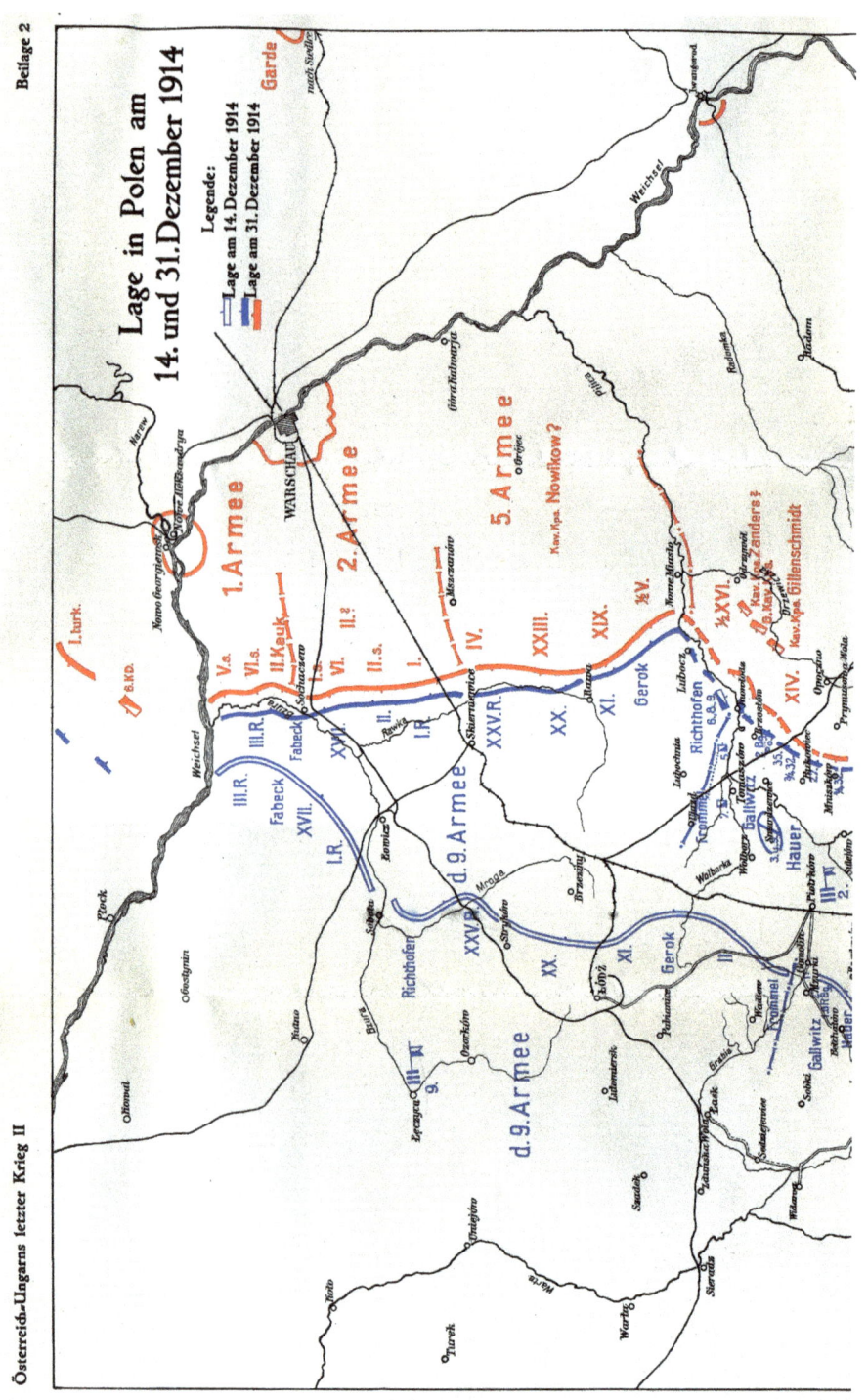

Situation in Poland on

December 14 and 31, 1914

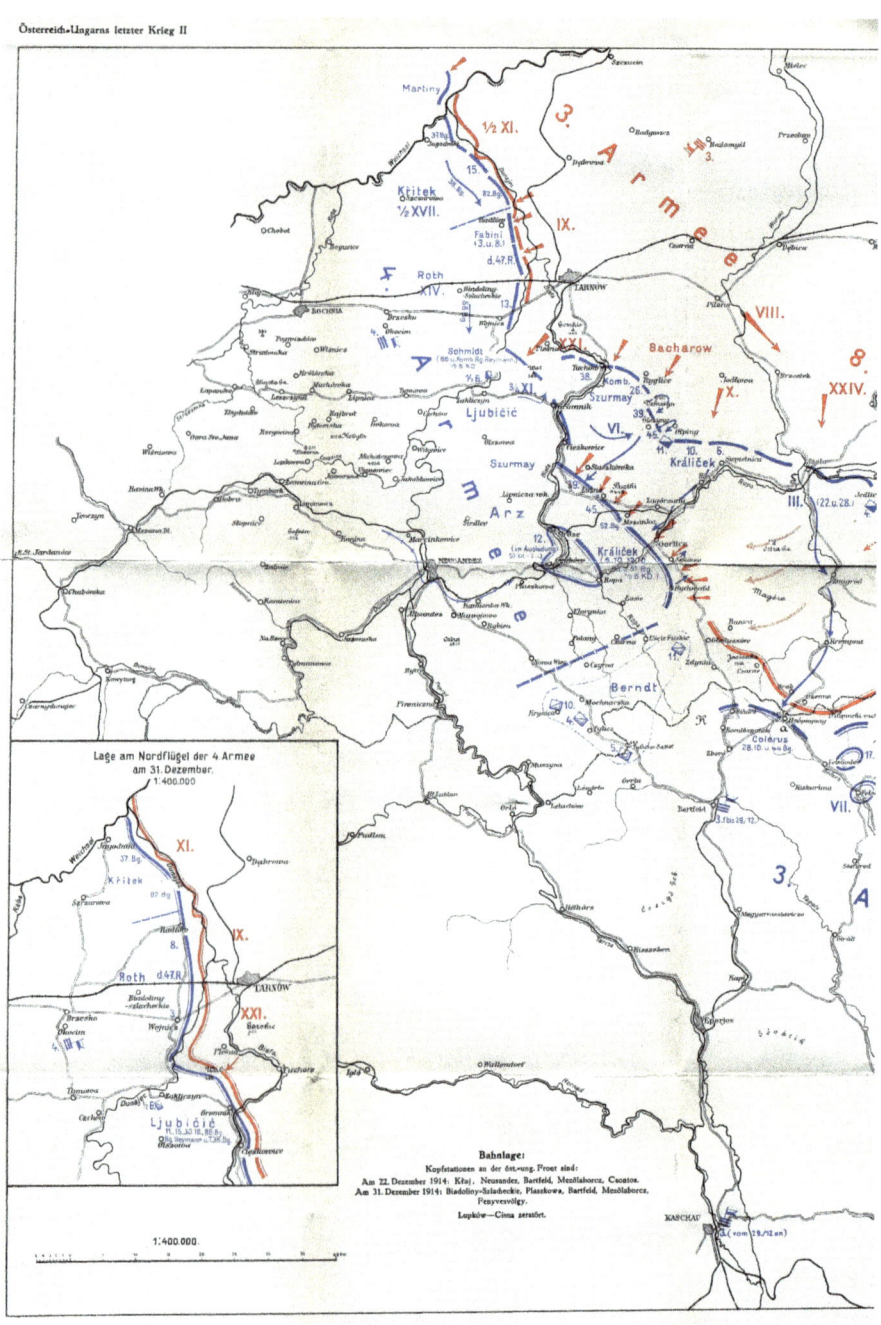

Situation of the 3rd and 4th Armies

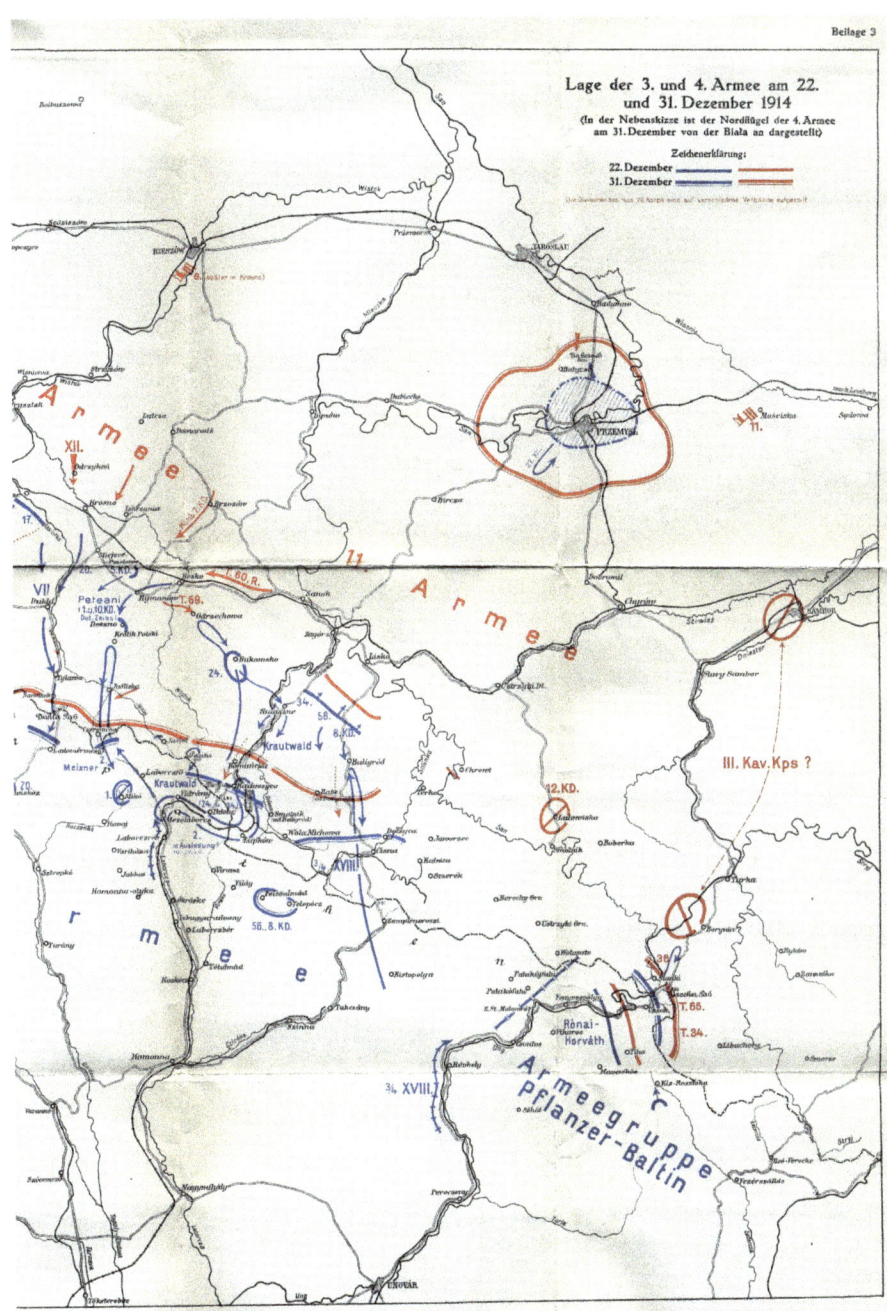

on 22 and 31 December 1914

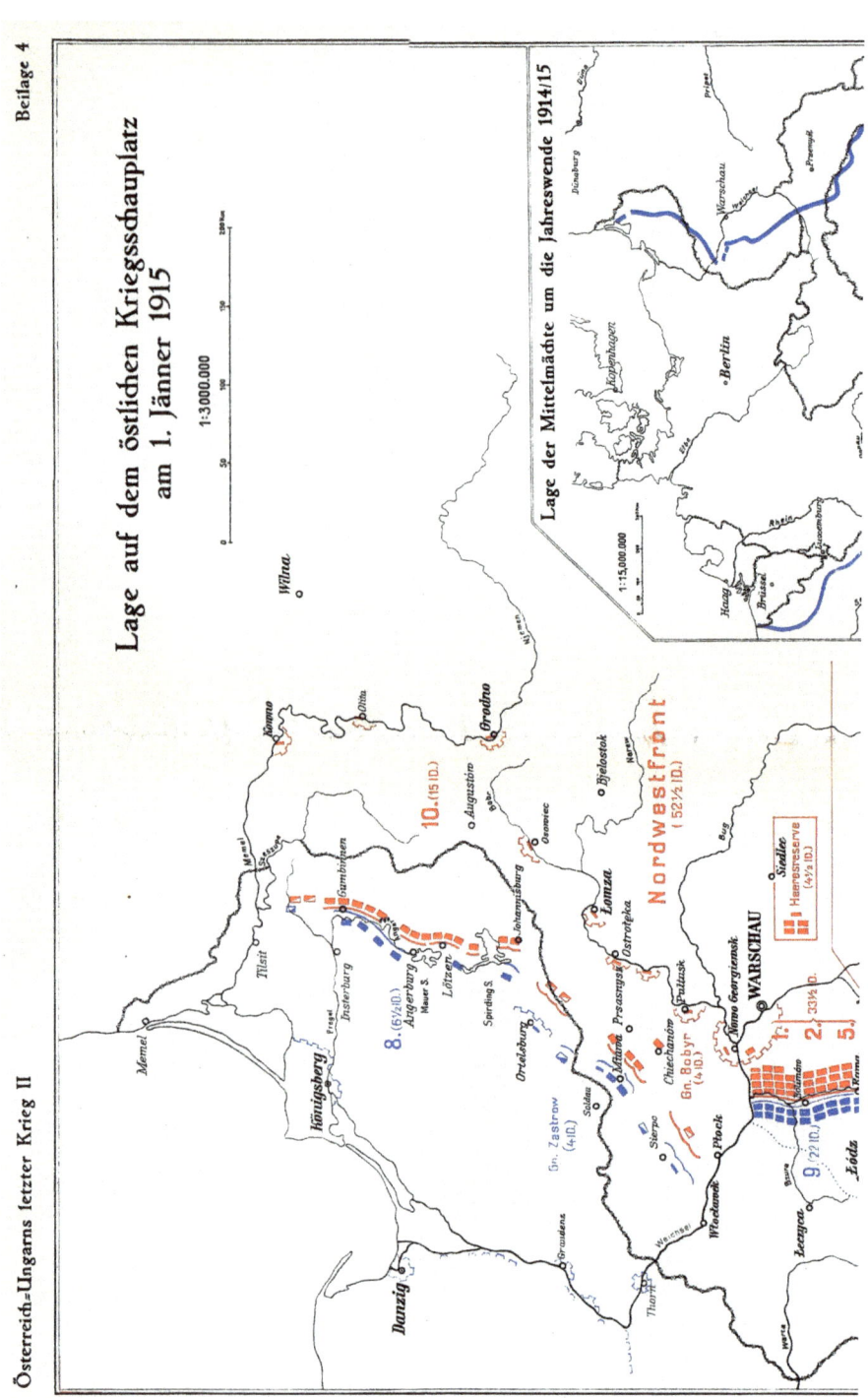

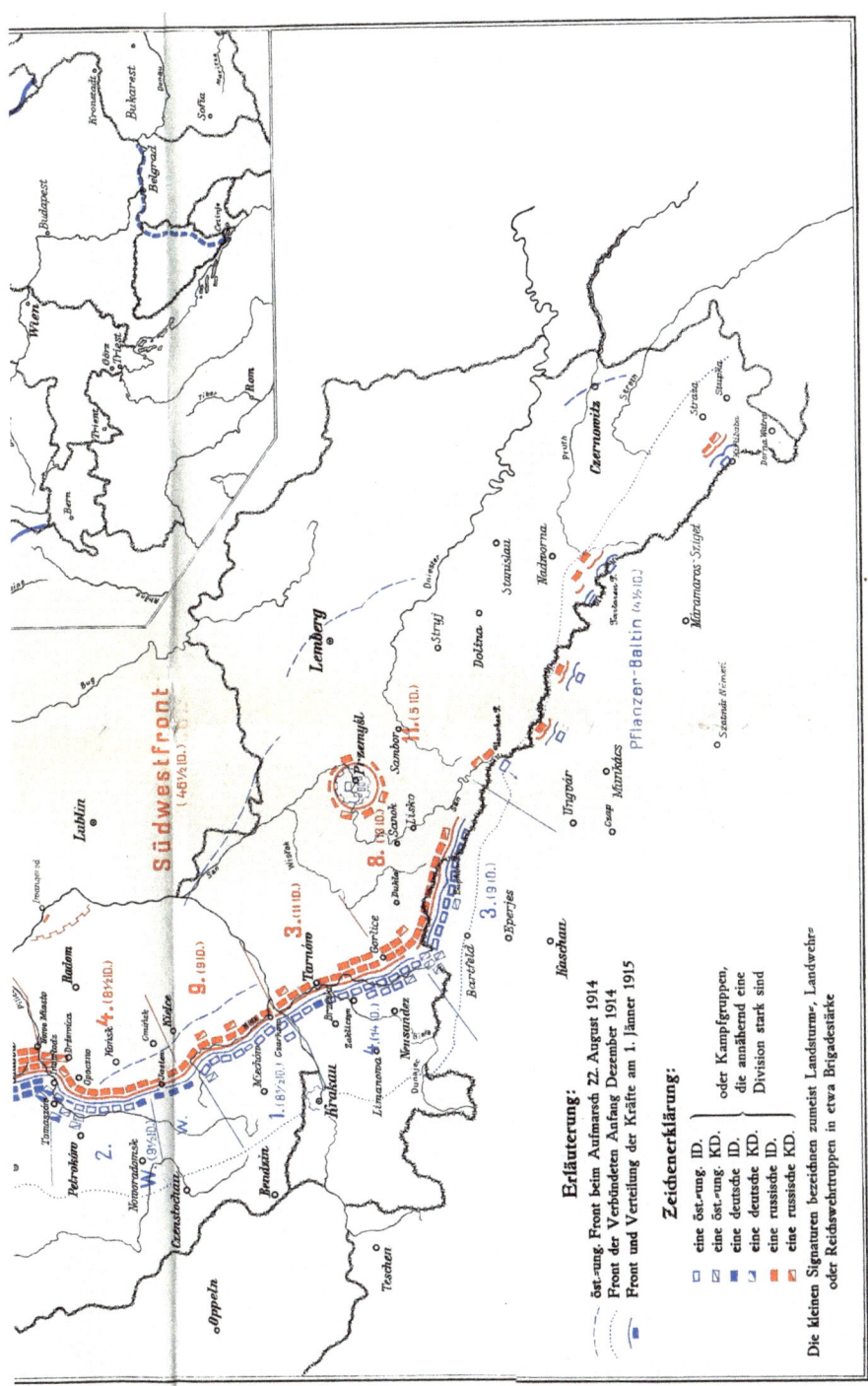

of war on January 1, 1915

Position south of the

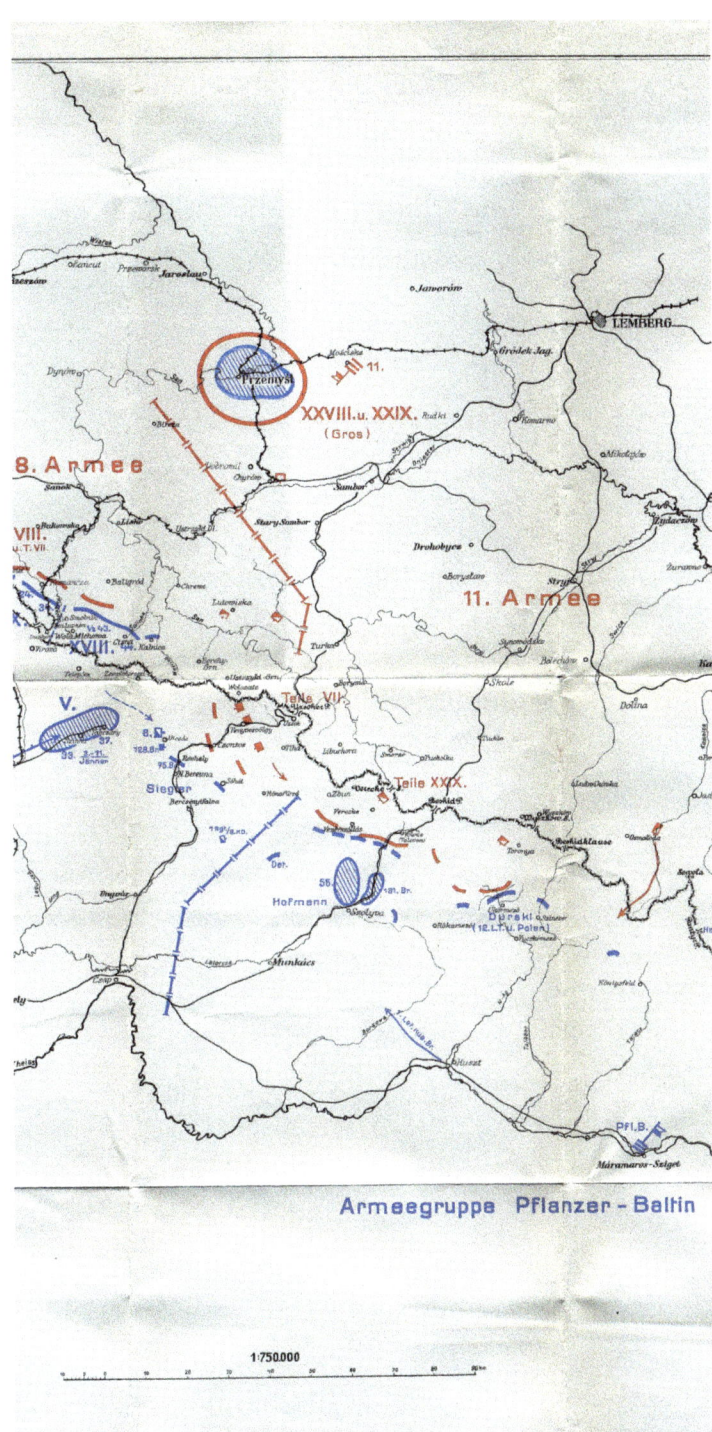

Vistula on January 5, 1915

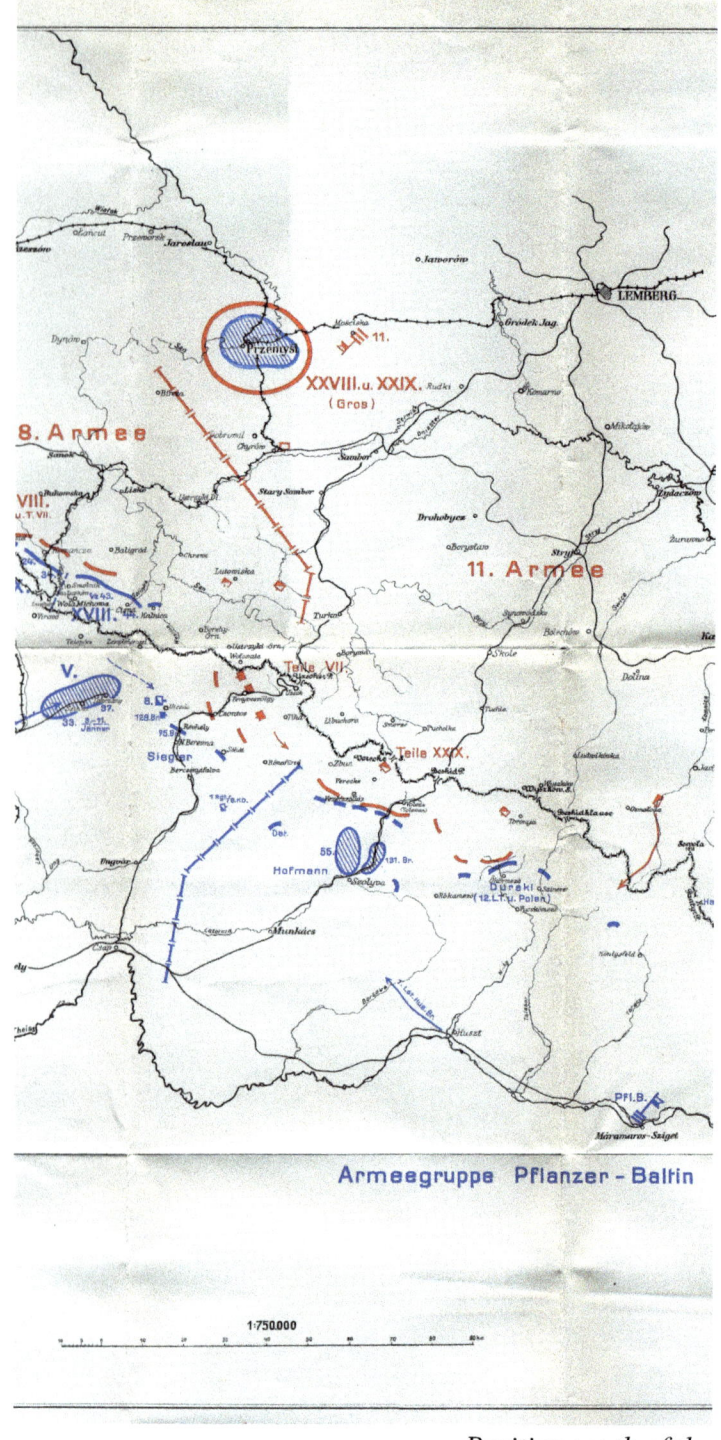

Position south of the

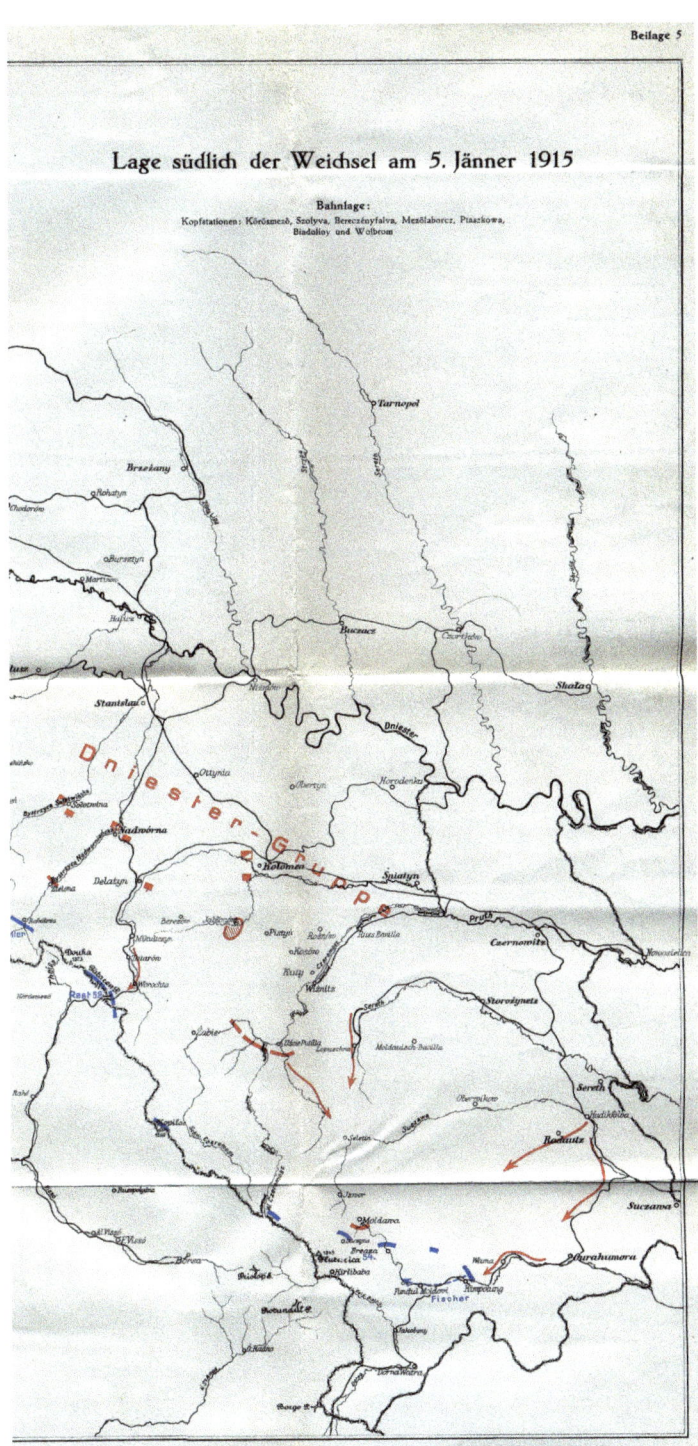

Vistula on January 5, 1915

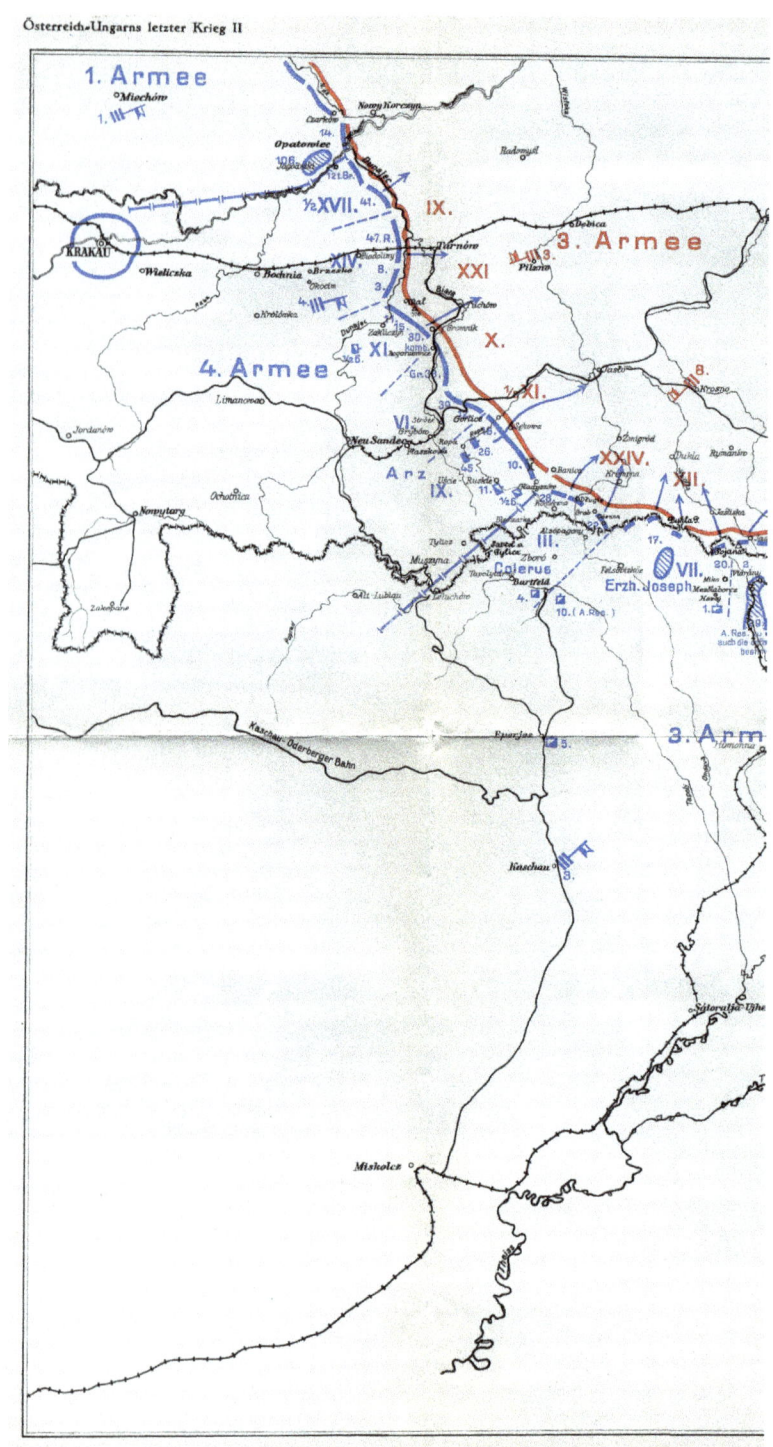

Plan of operations for the offensive across the

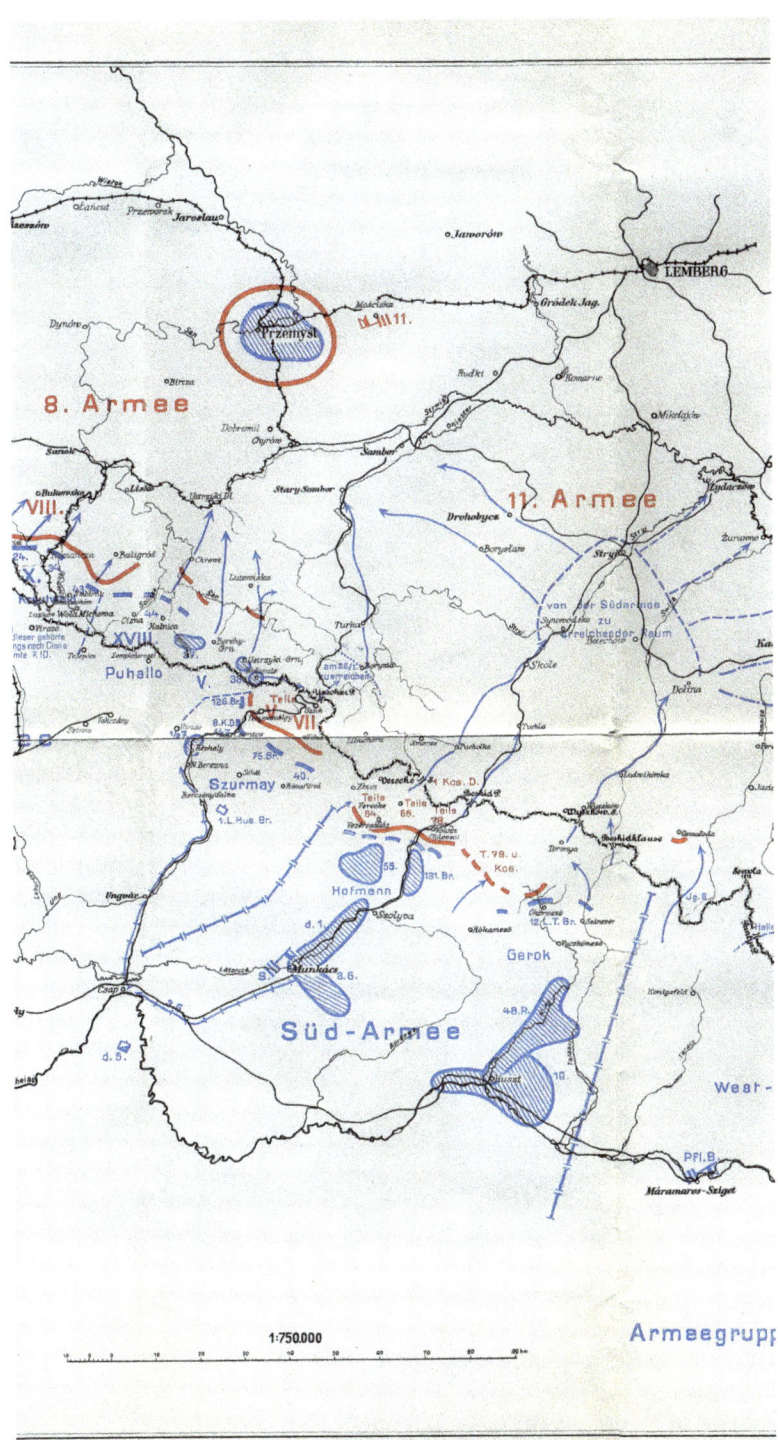

Carpathians and situation on January 22nd 1915

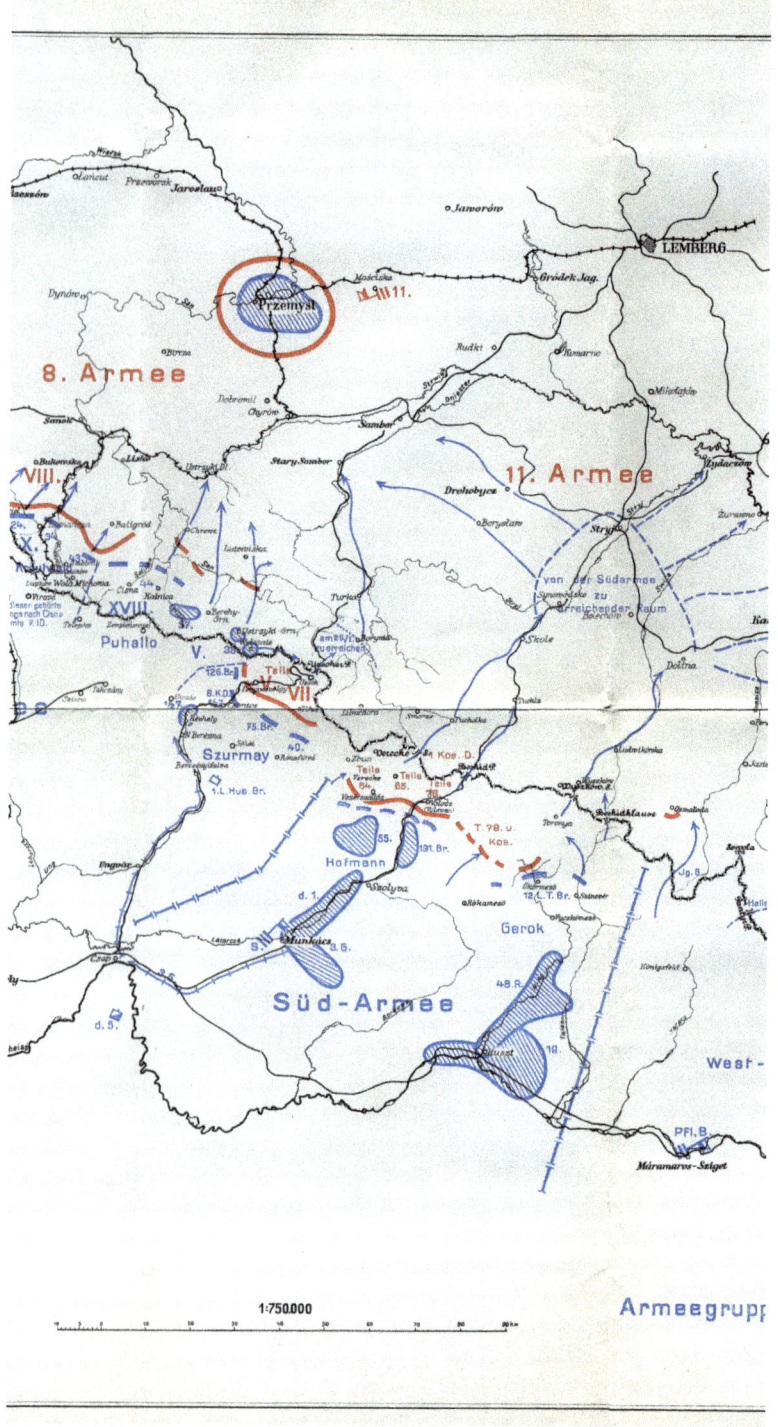

Plan of operations for the offensive across the

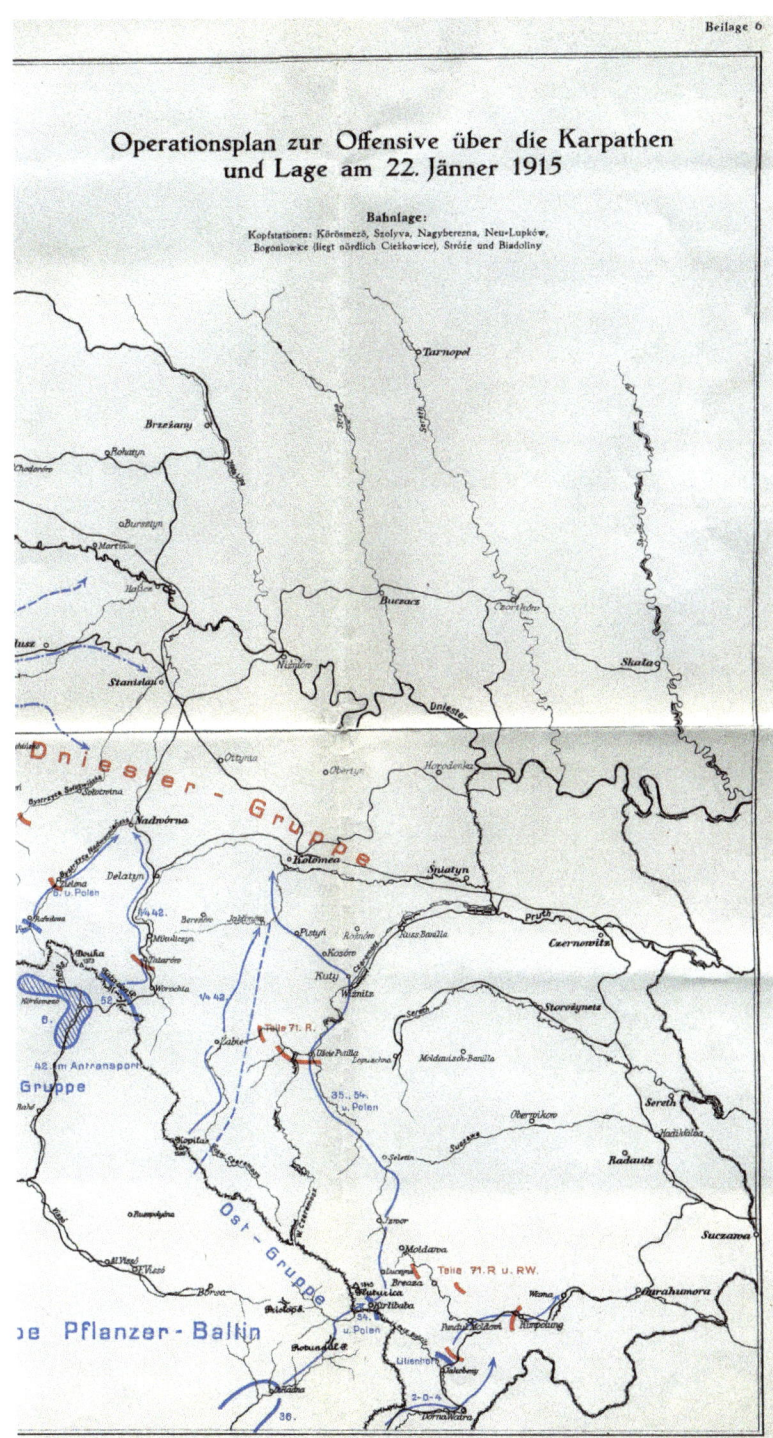

Carpathians and situation on January 22nd 1915

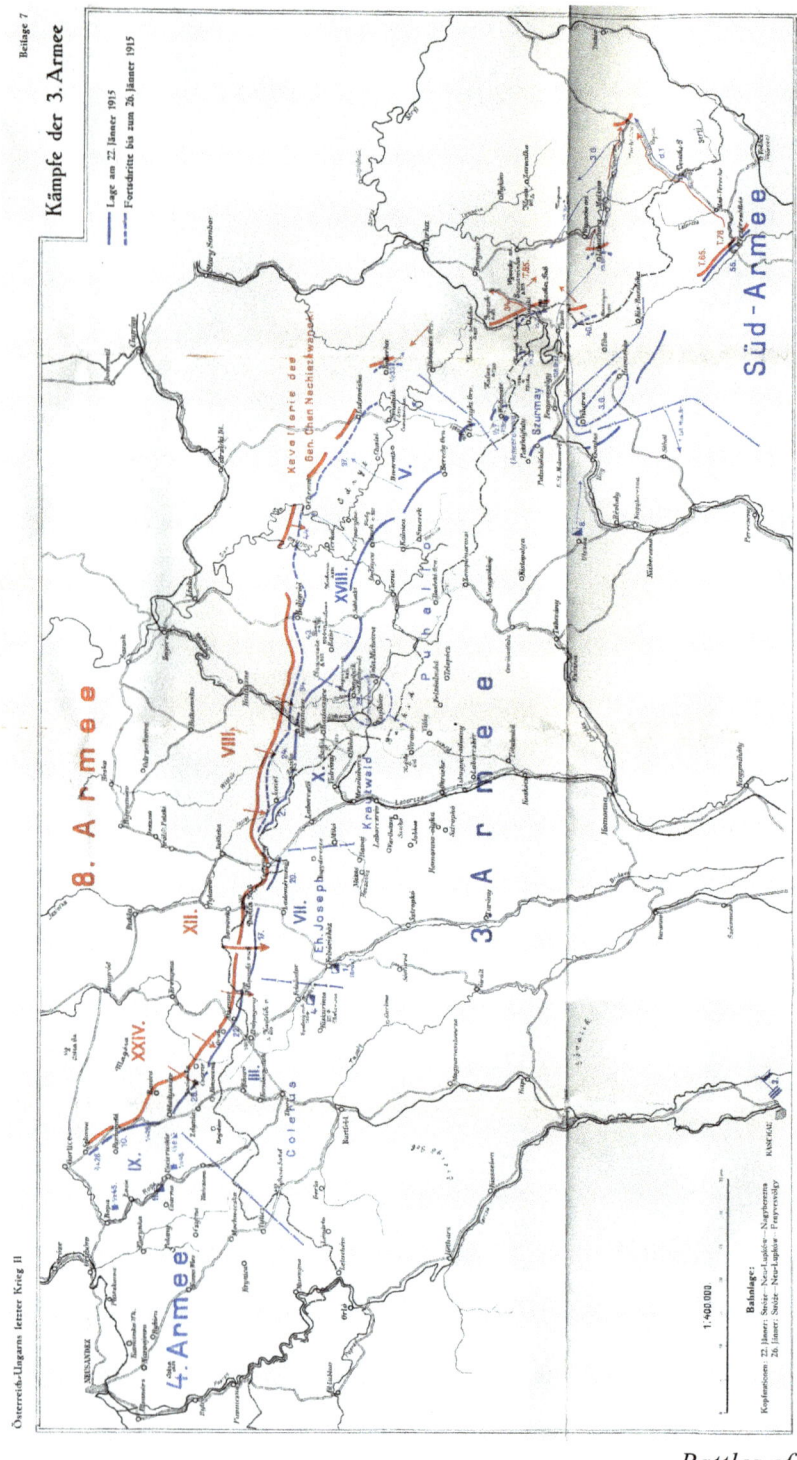

Battles of

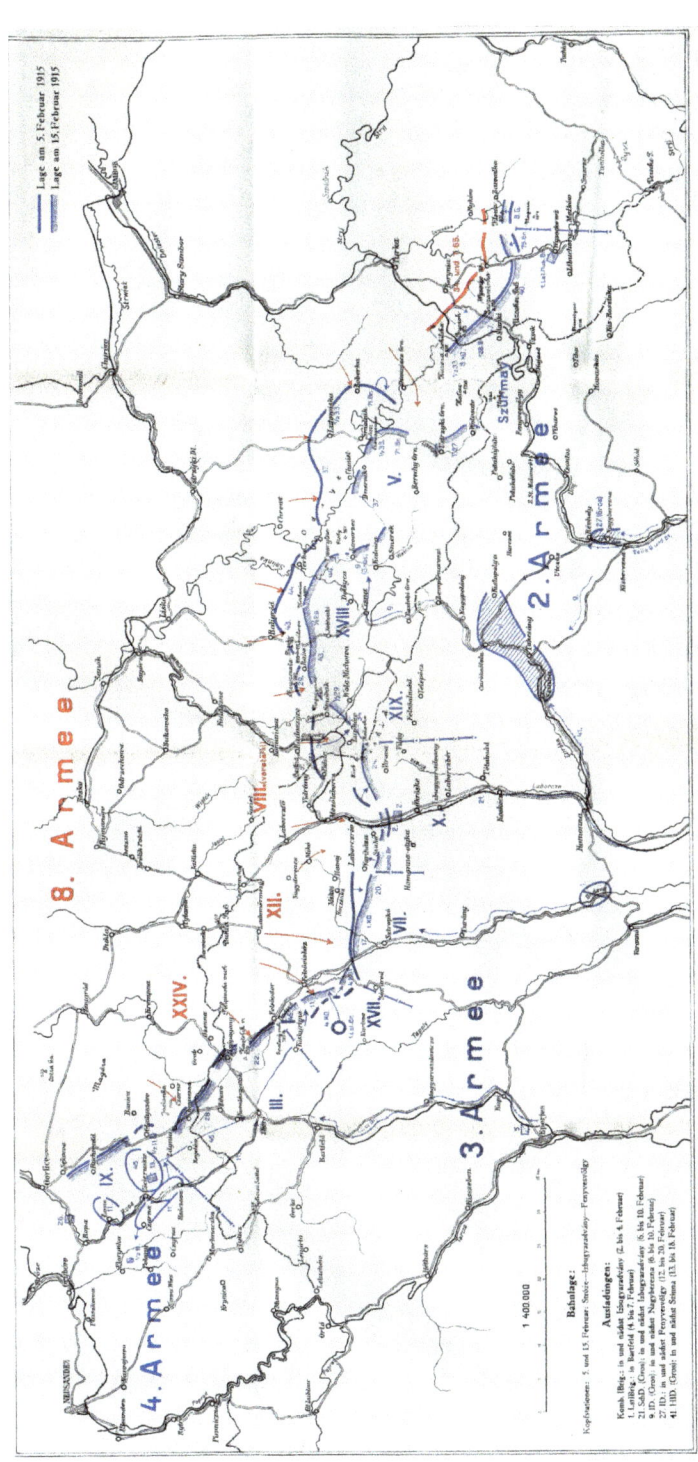

the 3rd Army

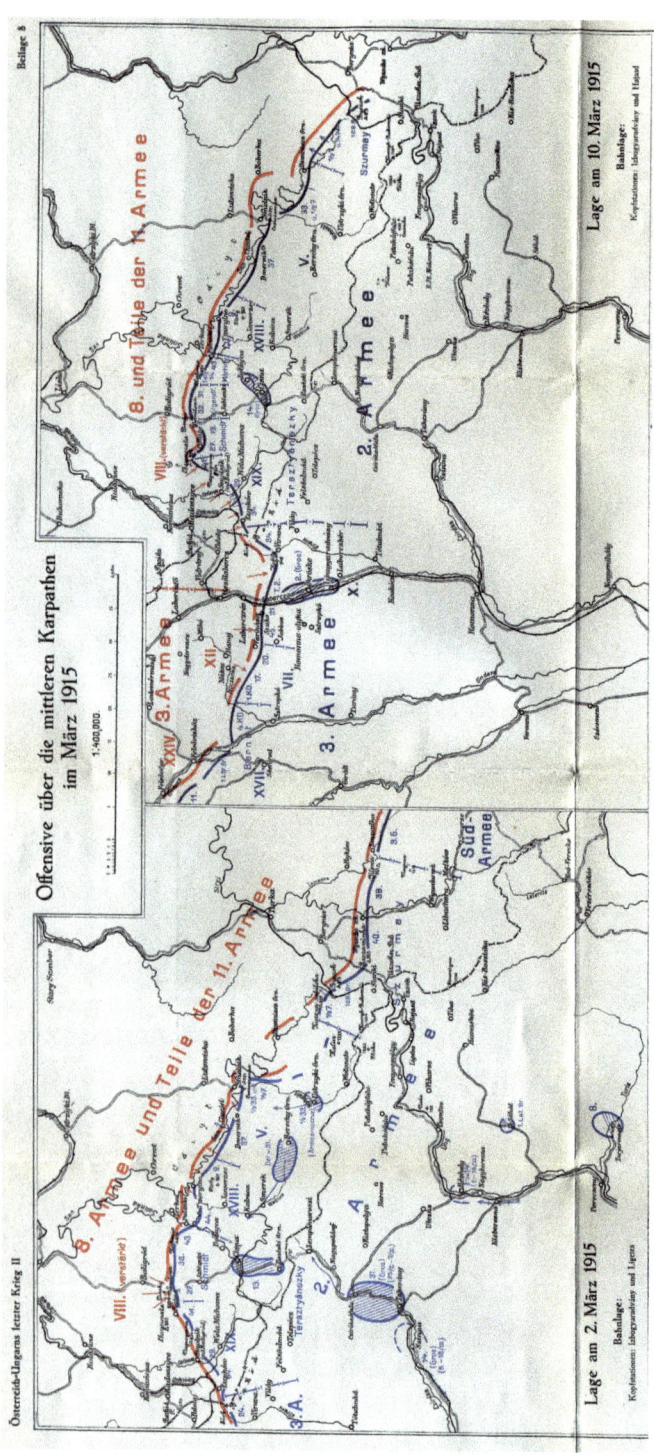

Offensive across the central

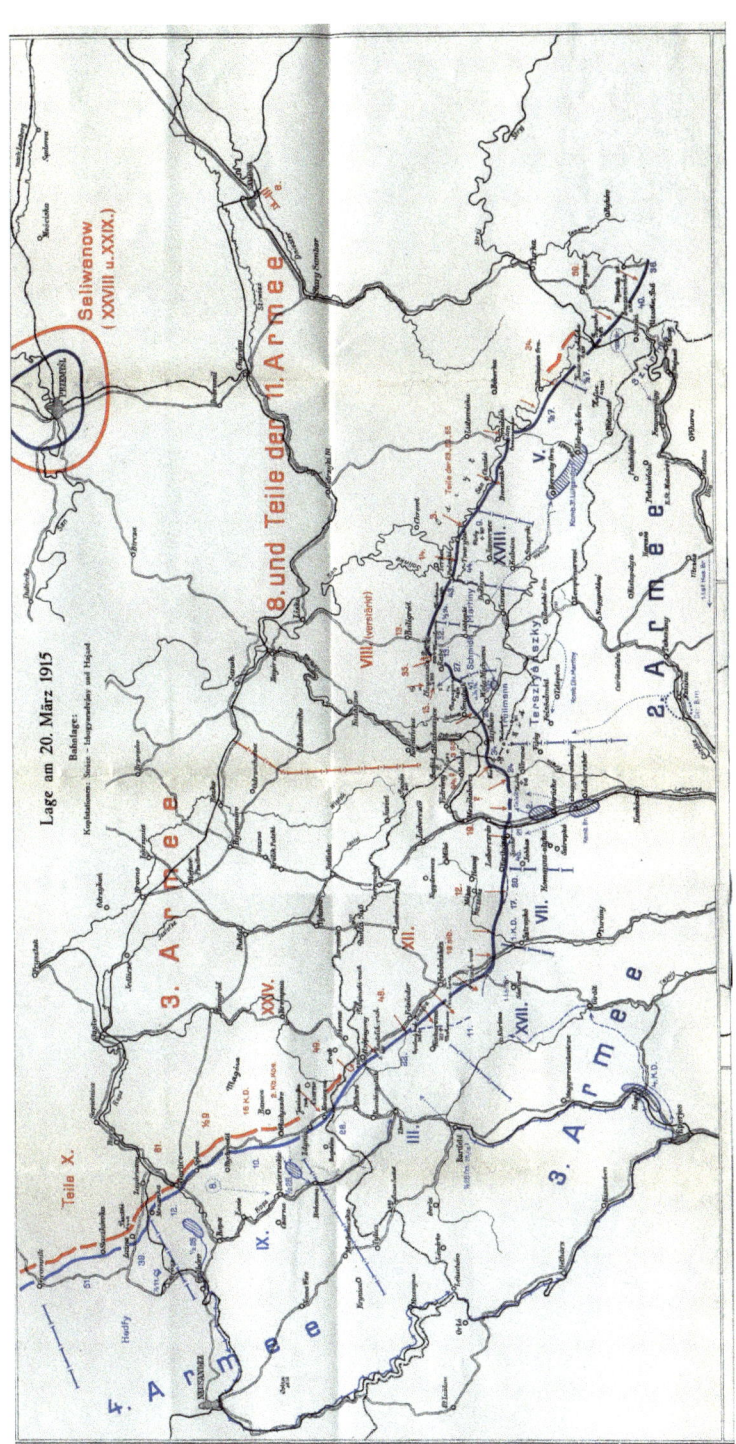

Carpathians in March 1915

Österreich-Ungarns letzter Krieg II

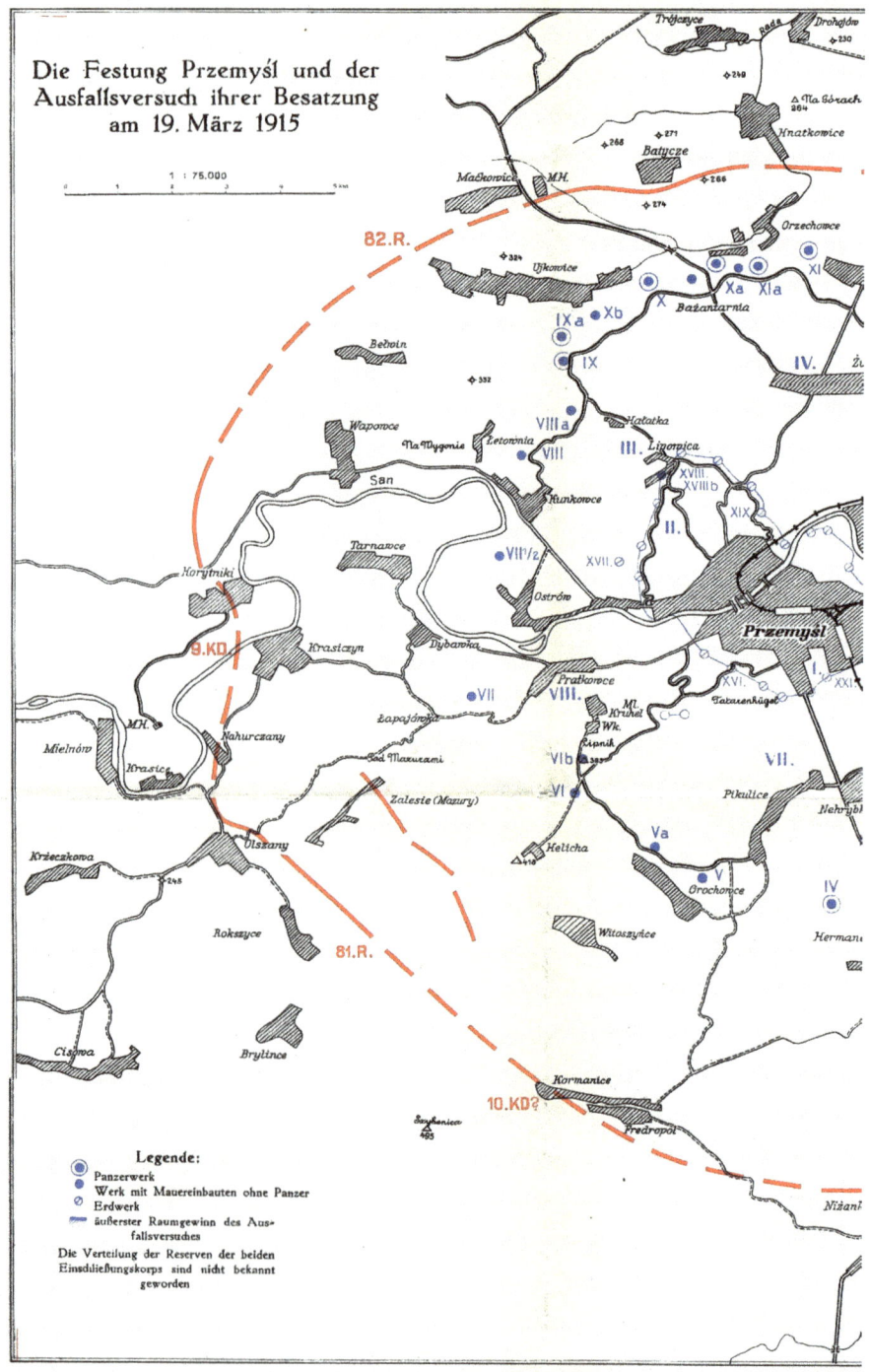

The Przemysl Fortress and its garrison's

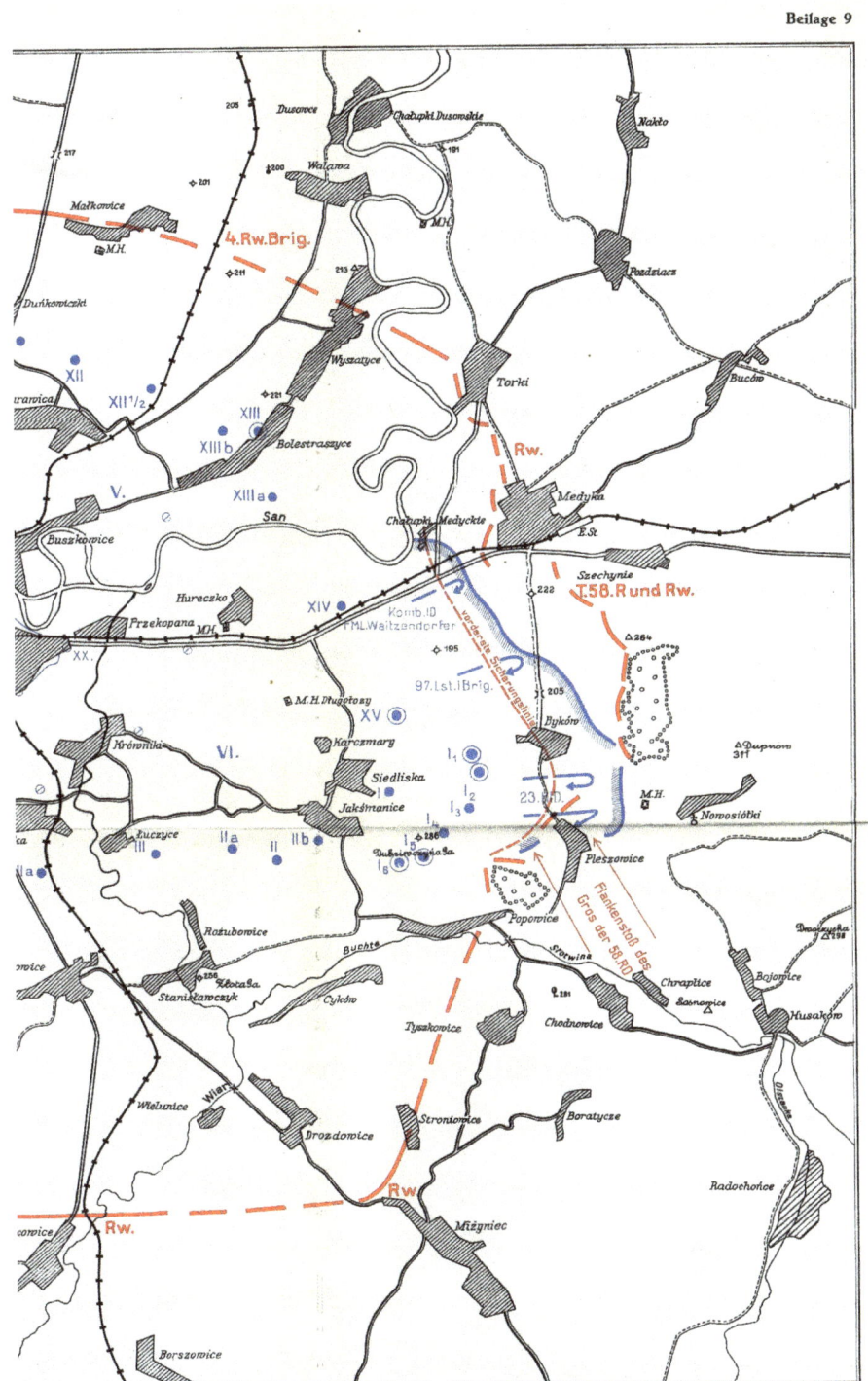

sally attempt on March 19 1915

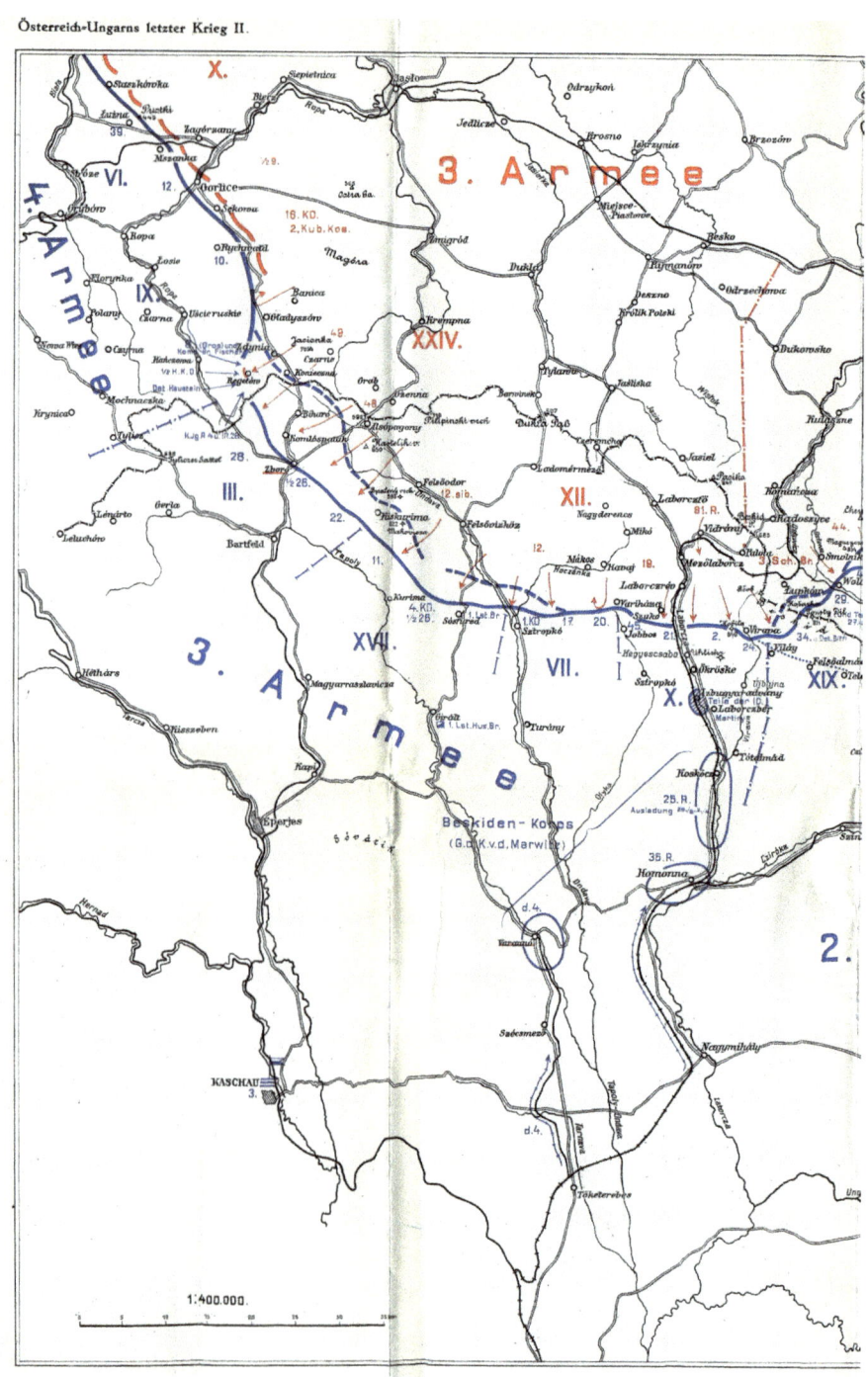

2nd and 3rd Armies

2. und 3. Armee am 31. März 1915

Legende:
- - - - Front am 25. März
———— Front am 31. März
.... Geplante neue Widerstands-
linie der 2. Armee

Bahnlage:
Kopfstationen: Izbugyaradvány und Hajasd

on March 31, 1915

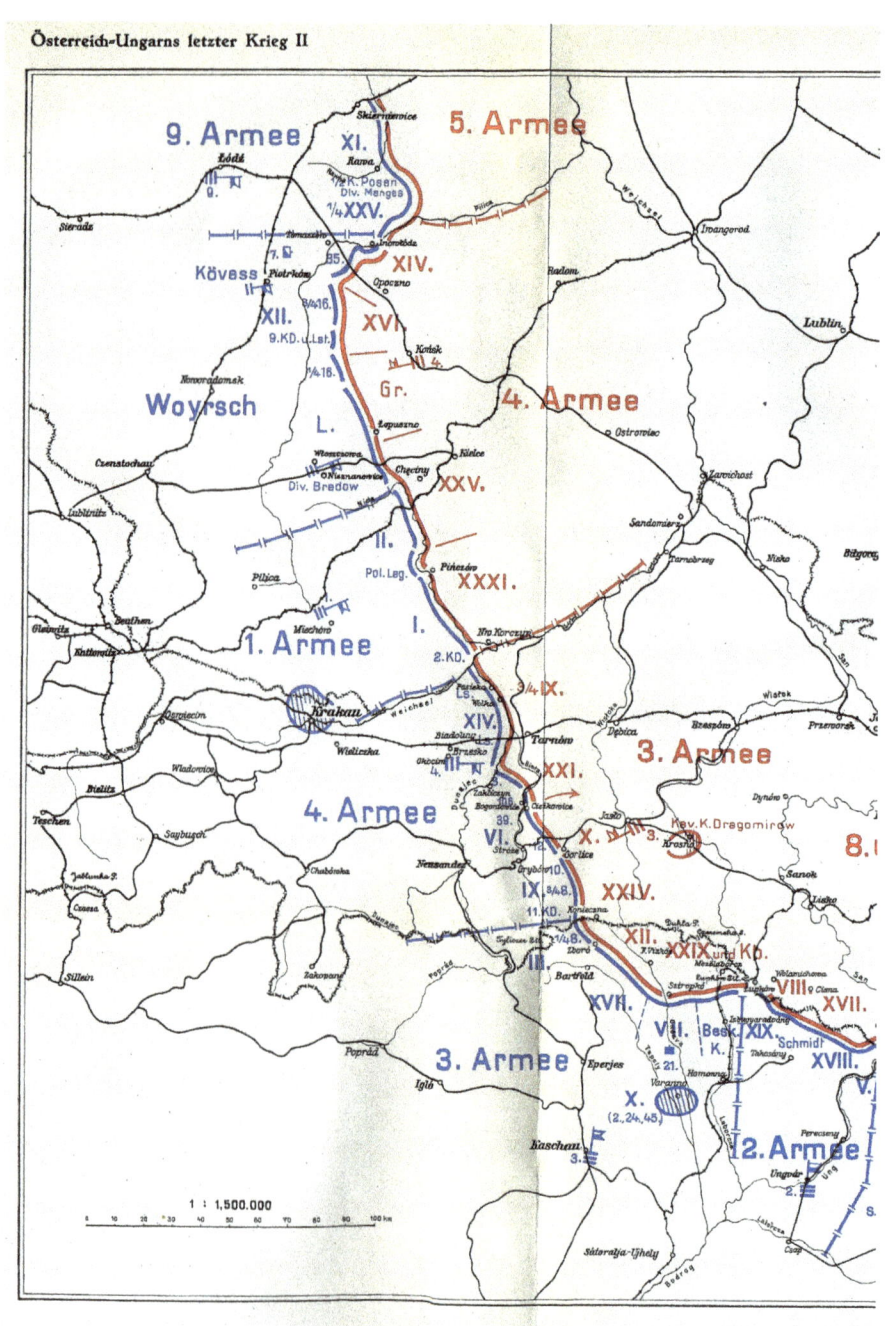

East: Hungarian Eastern

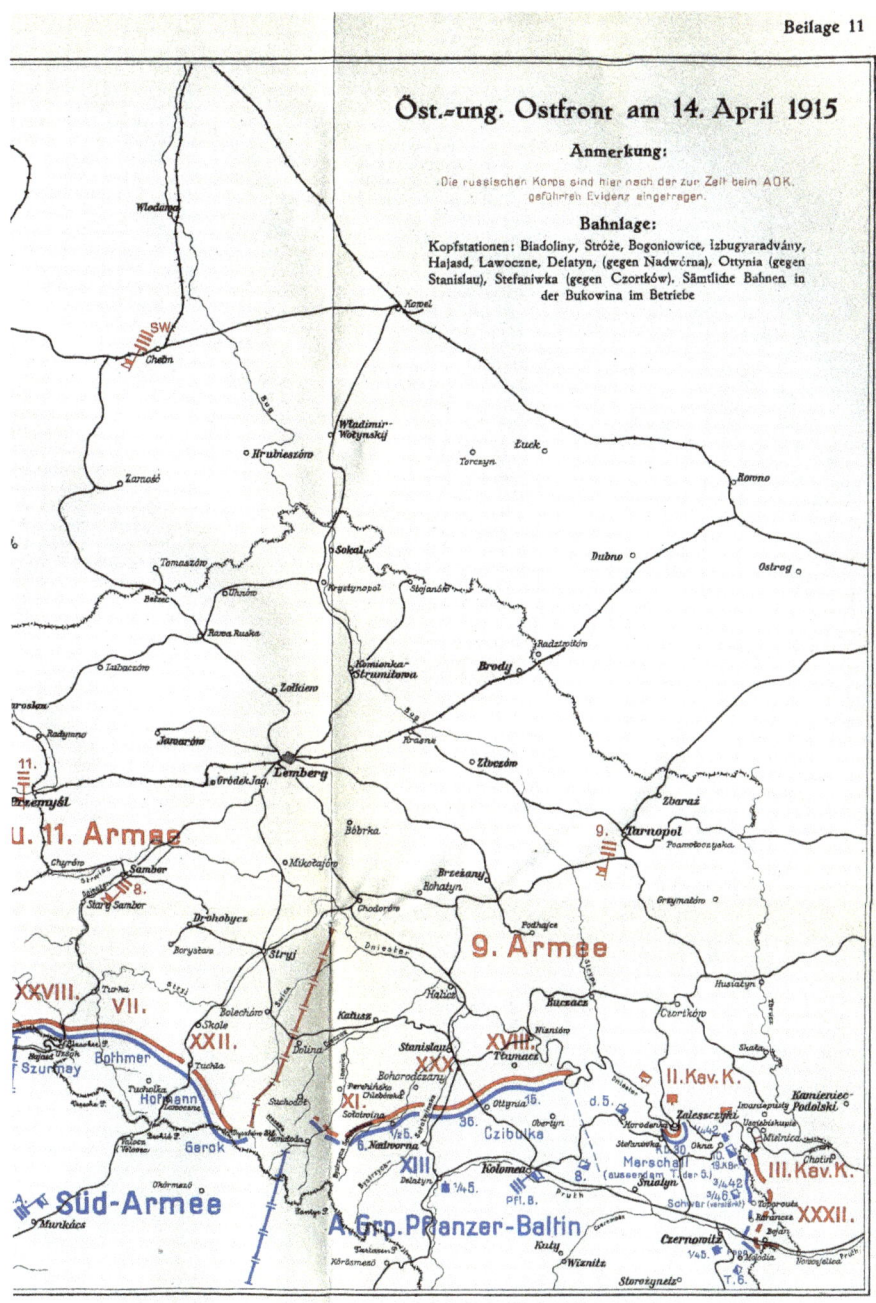

Front on April 14, 1915

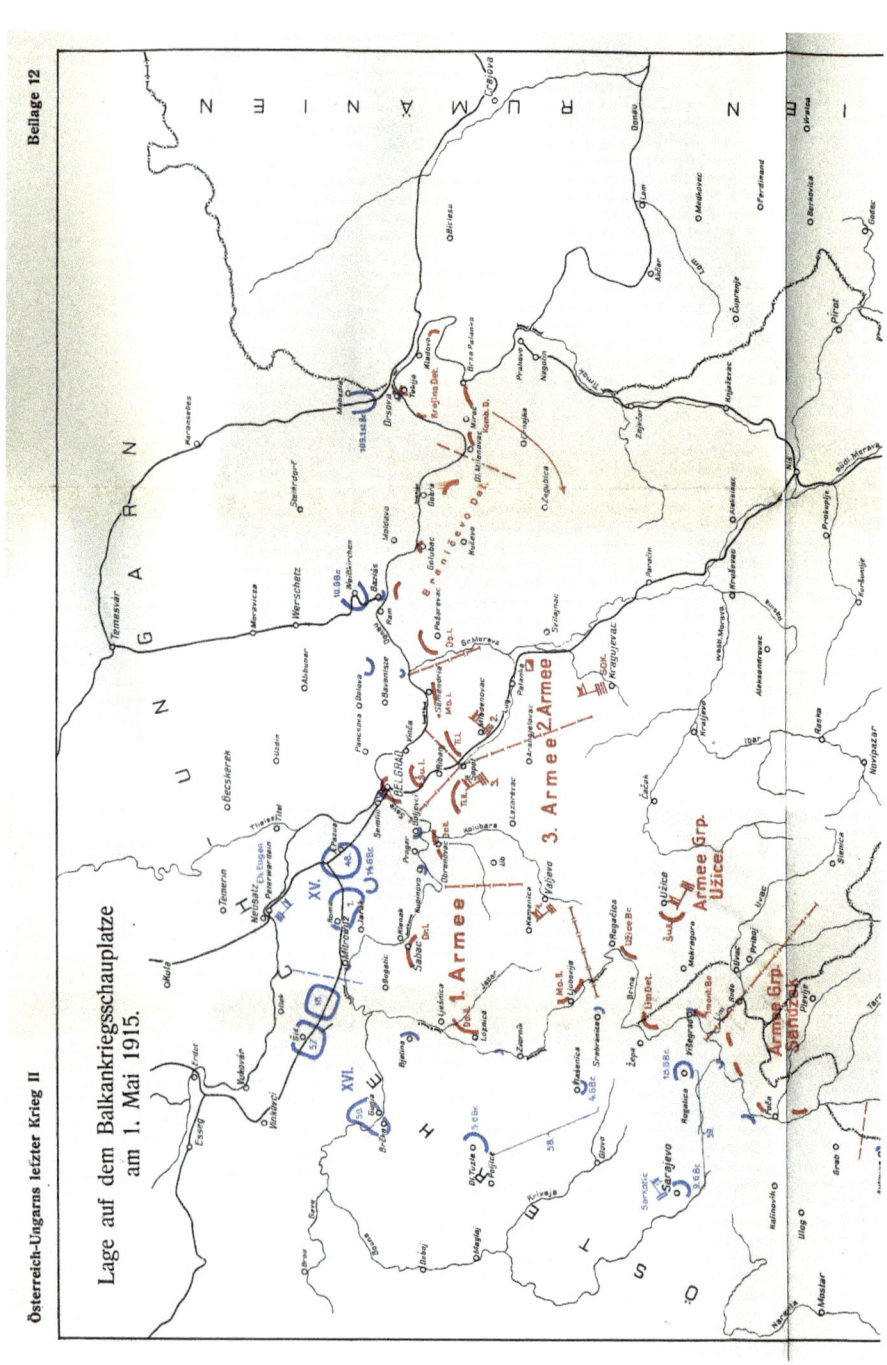

Situation in the Balkan theatre

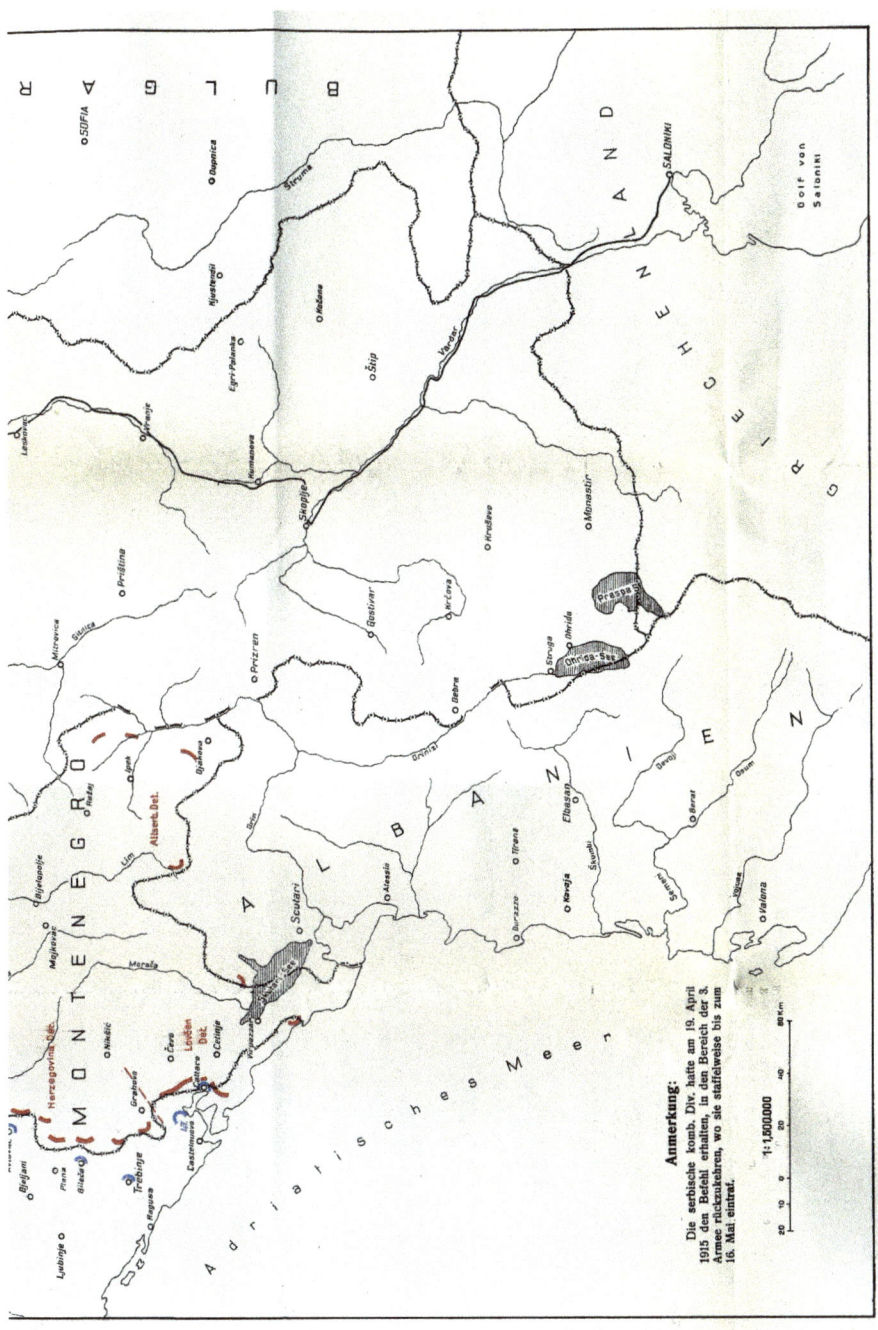

of war on May 1, 1915

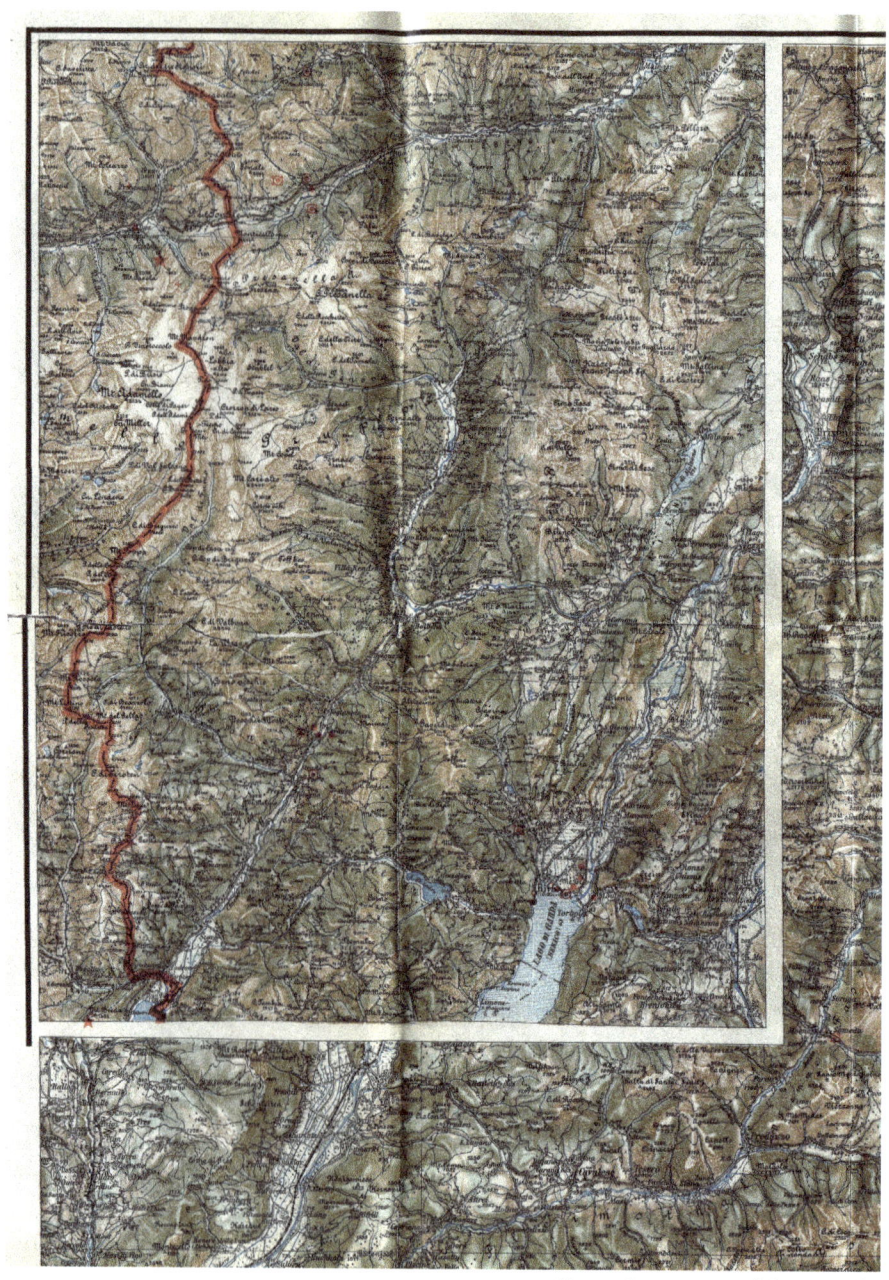

Overview map of the south-

western theater of war

Overview map of the south-

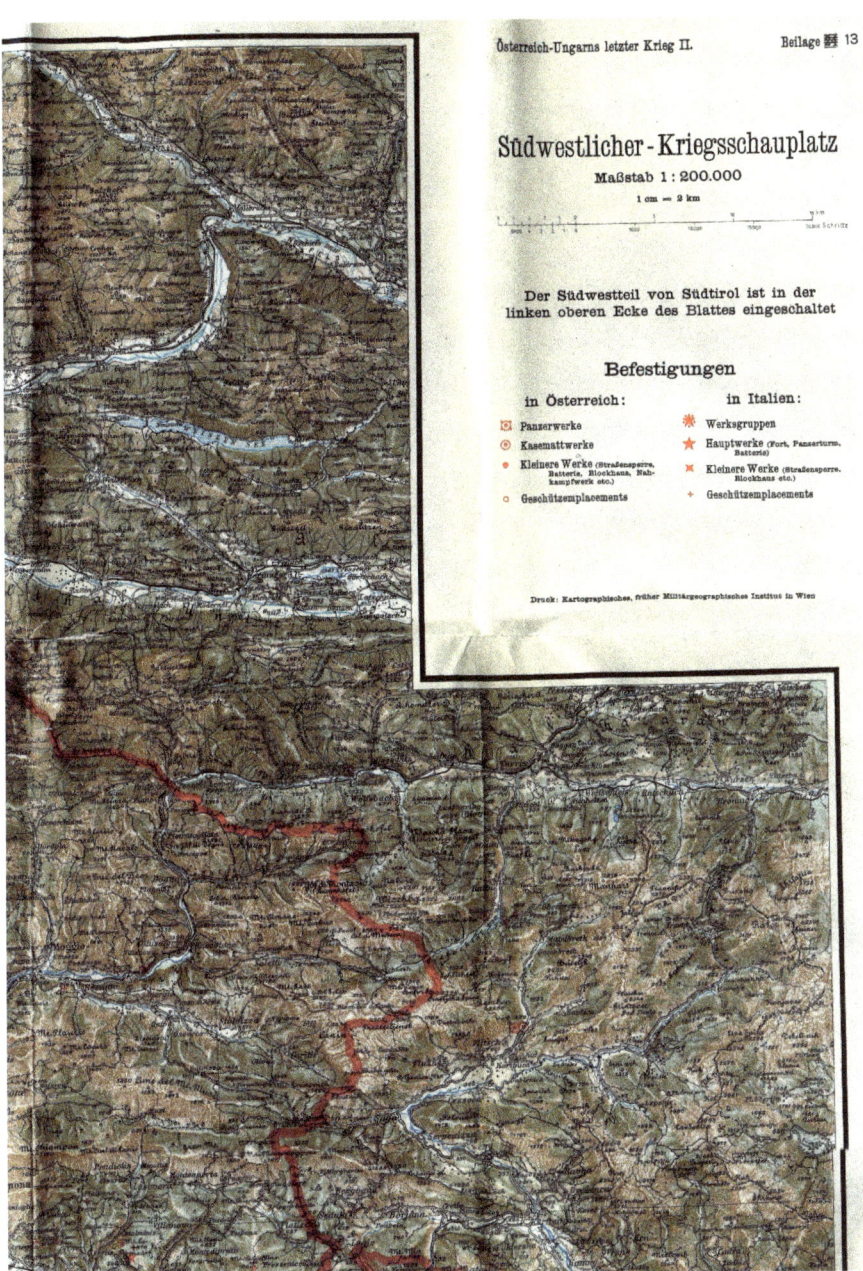

Österreich-Ungarns letzter Krieg II.   Beilage 13

Südwestlicher-Kriegsschauplatz

Maßstab 1 : 200.000

1 cm = 2 km

Der Südwestteil von Südtirol ist in der linken oberen Ecke des Blattes eingeschaltet

Befestigungen

in Österreich:

- Panzerwerke
- Kasemattwerke
- Kleinere Werke (Straßensperre, Batterie, Blockhaus, Nahkampfwerk etc.)
- Geschützemplacements

in Italien:

- Werksgruppen
- Hauptwerke (Fort, Panzerturm, Batterie)
- Kleinere Werke (Straßensperre, Blockhaus etc.)
- Geschützemplacements

Druck: Kartographisches, früher Militärgeographisches Institut in Wien

western theater of war

Overview map of the south-

western theater of war

Overview map of the south-

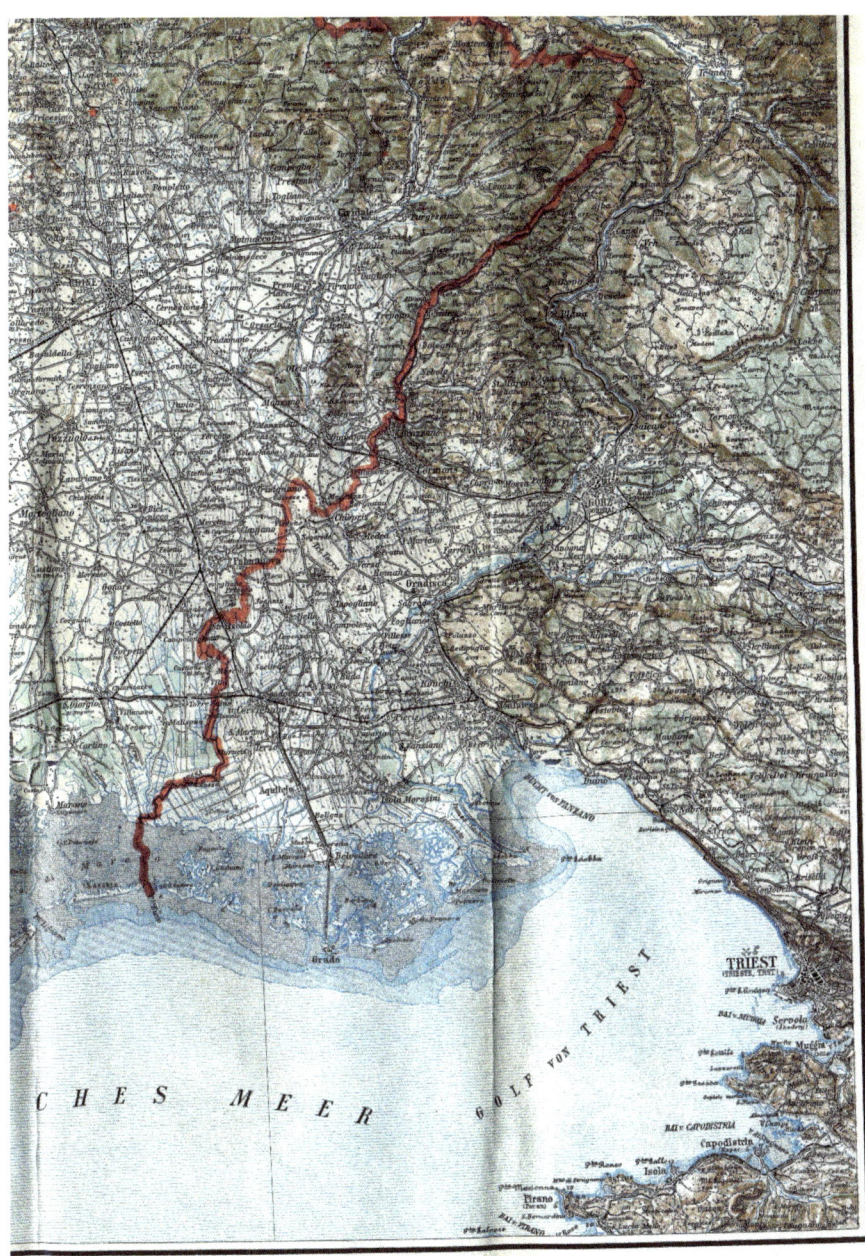

western theater of war

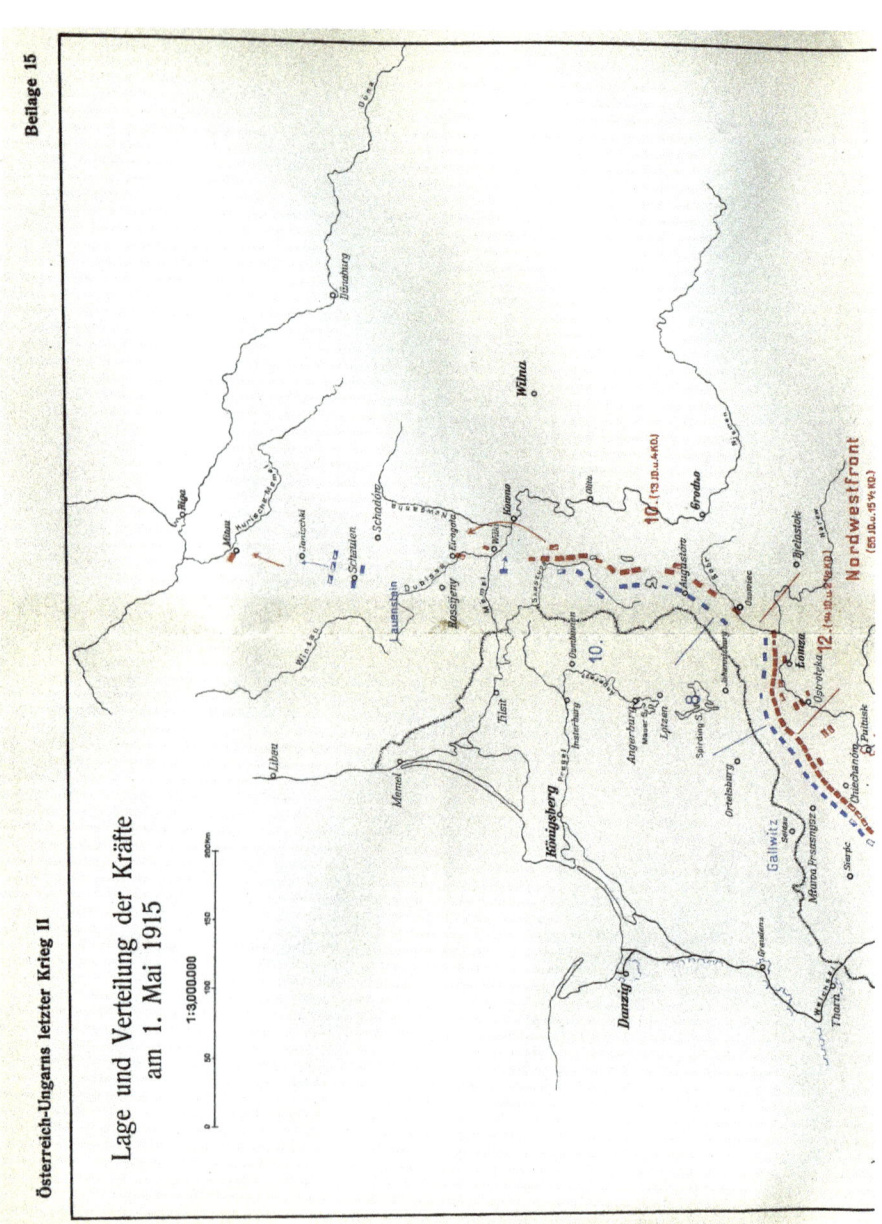

Position and distribution of forces

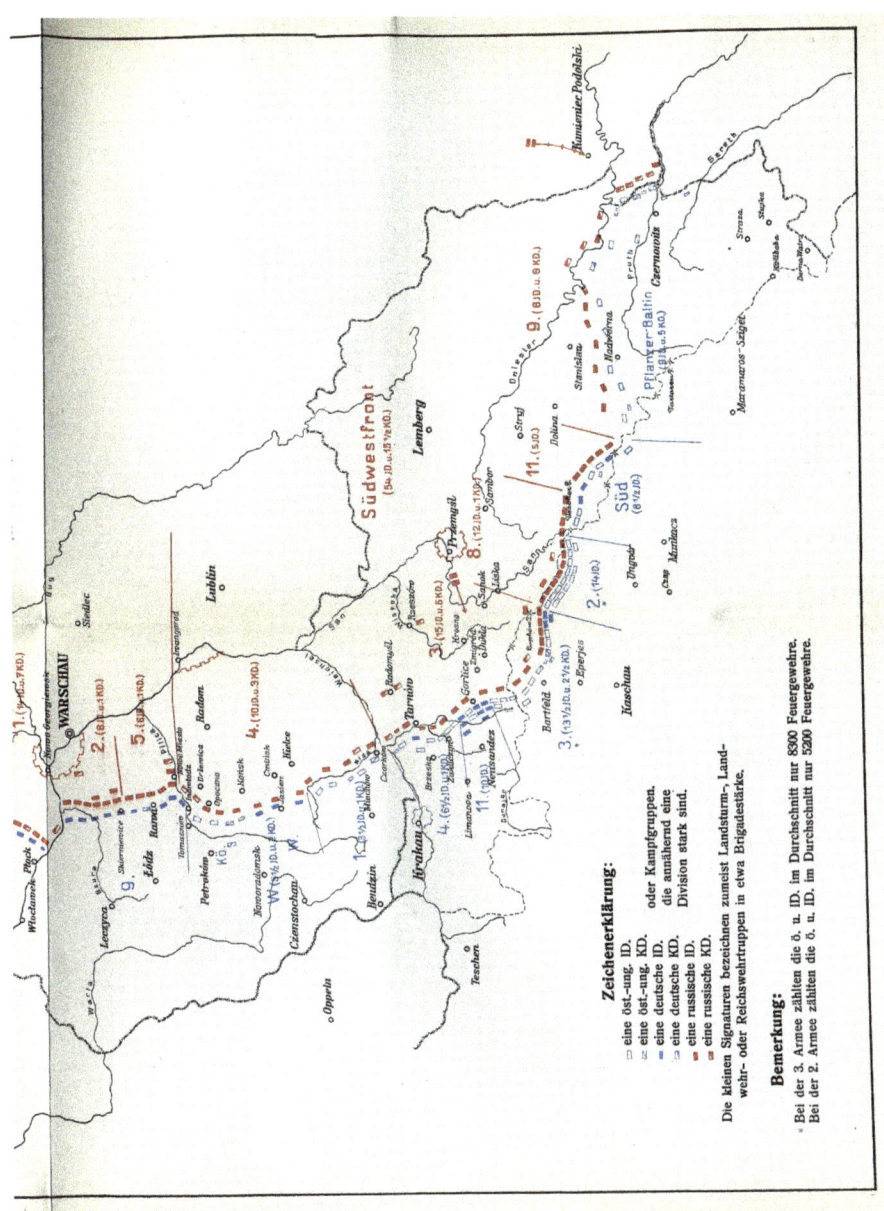

on May 1, 1915 (northeast)

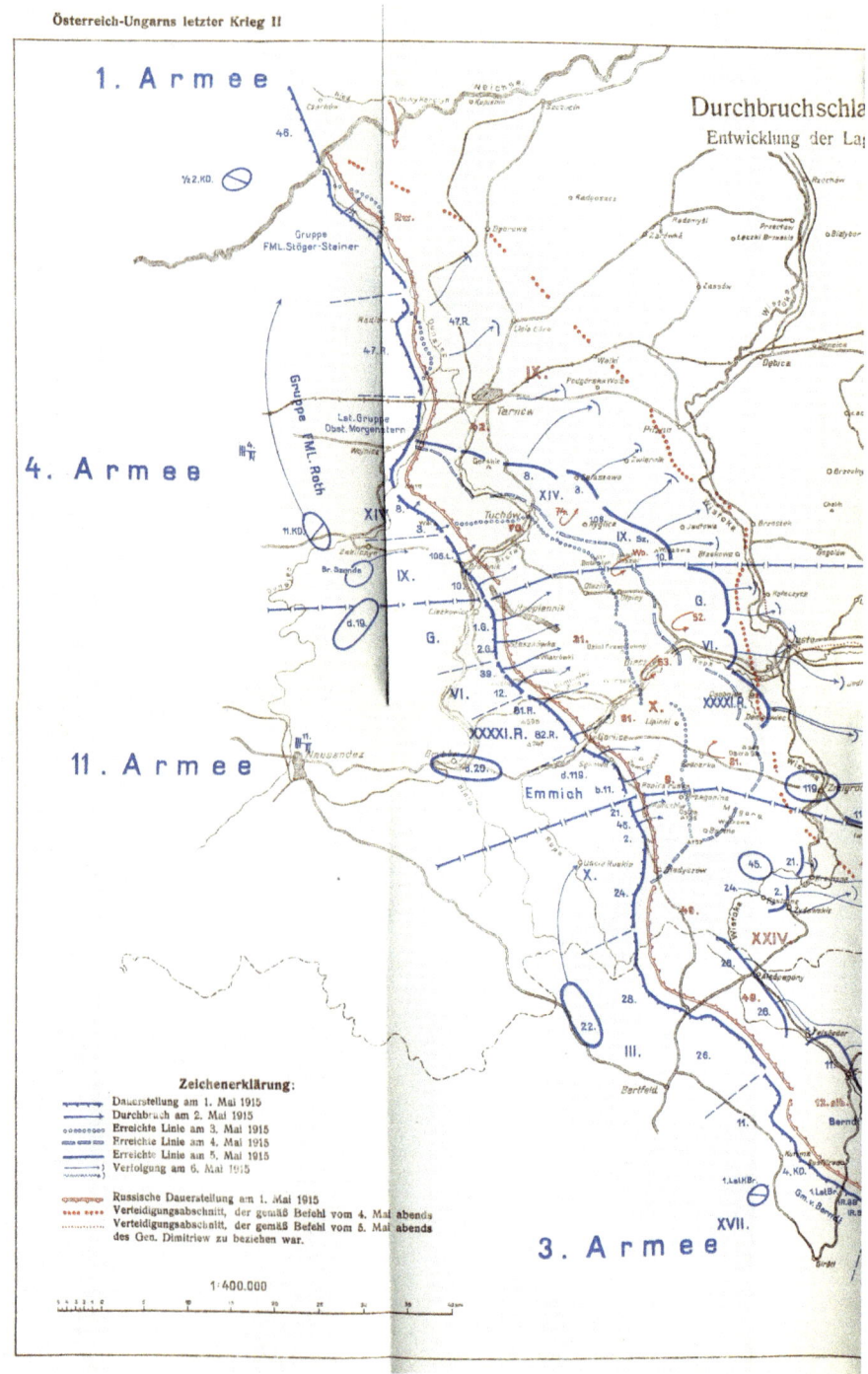

Breakthrough battle near Gorlice; Development of

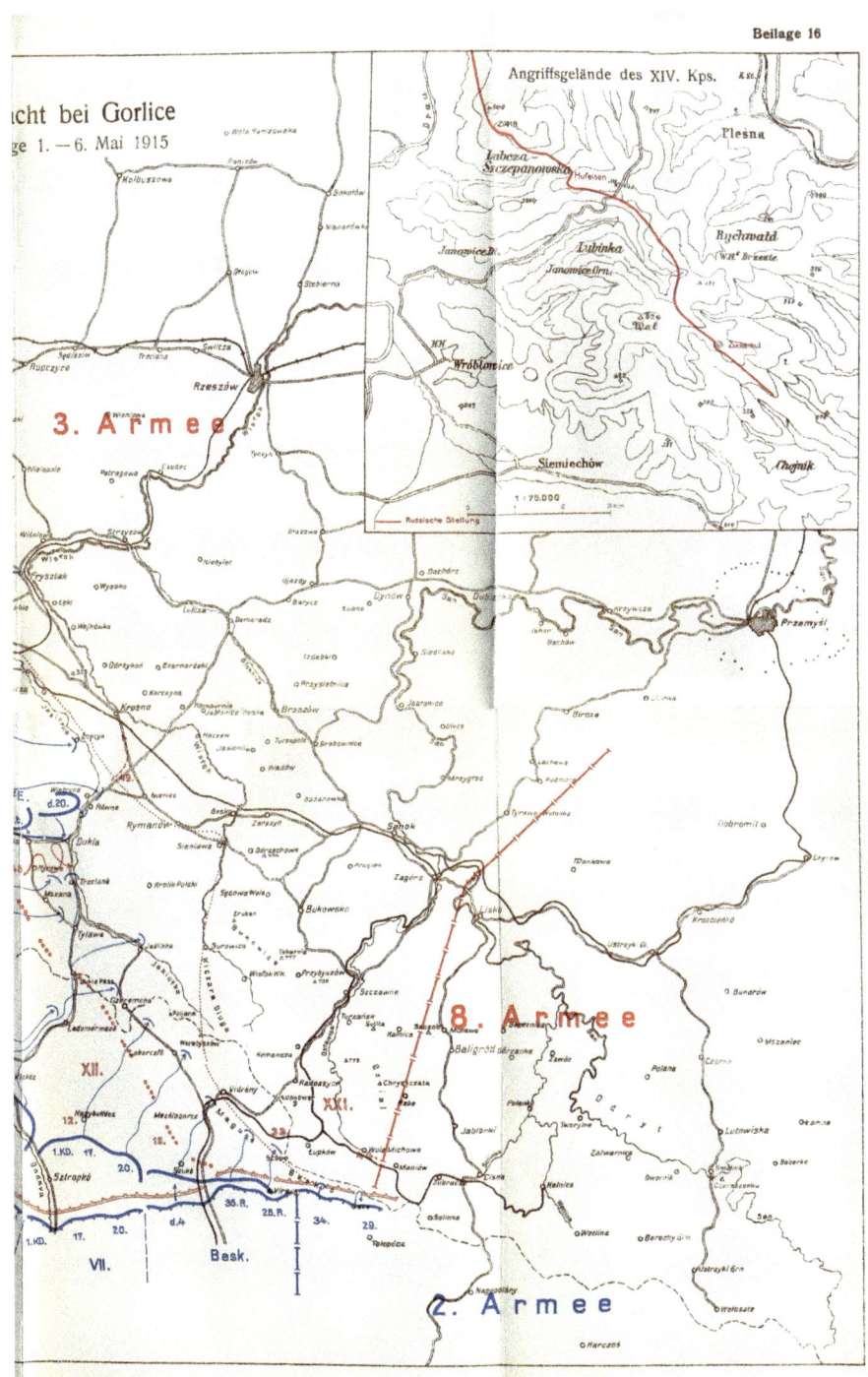

the situation from May 1 to May 6, 1915

Österreich-Ungarns letzter Krieg II

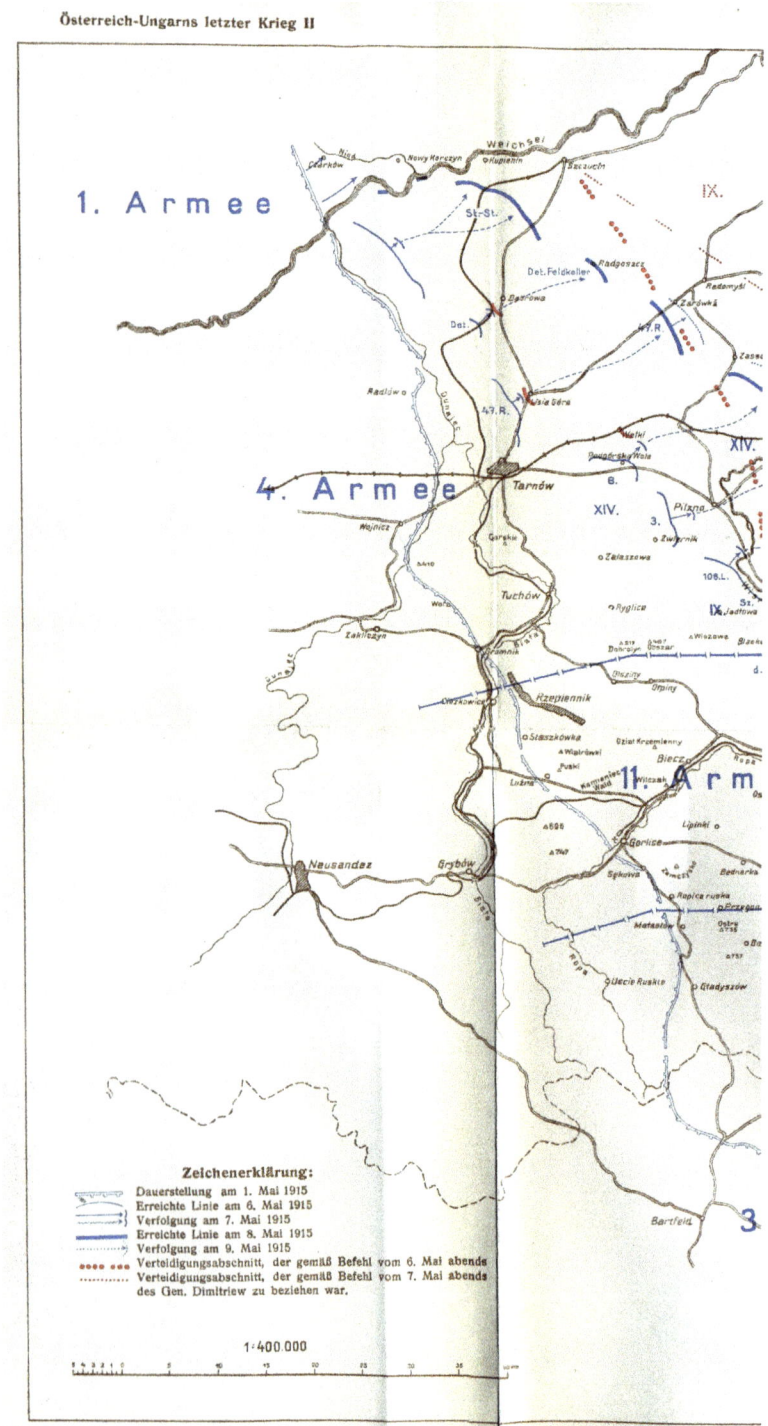

Breakthrough battle at Gorlice; continuation

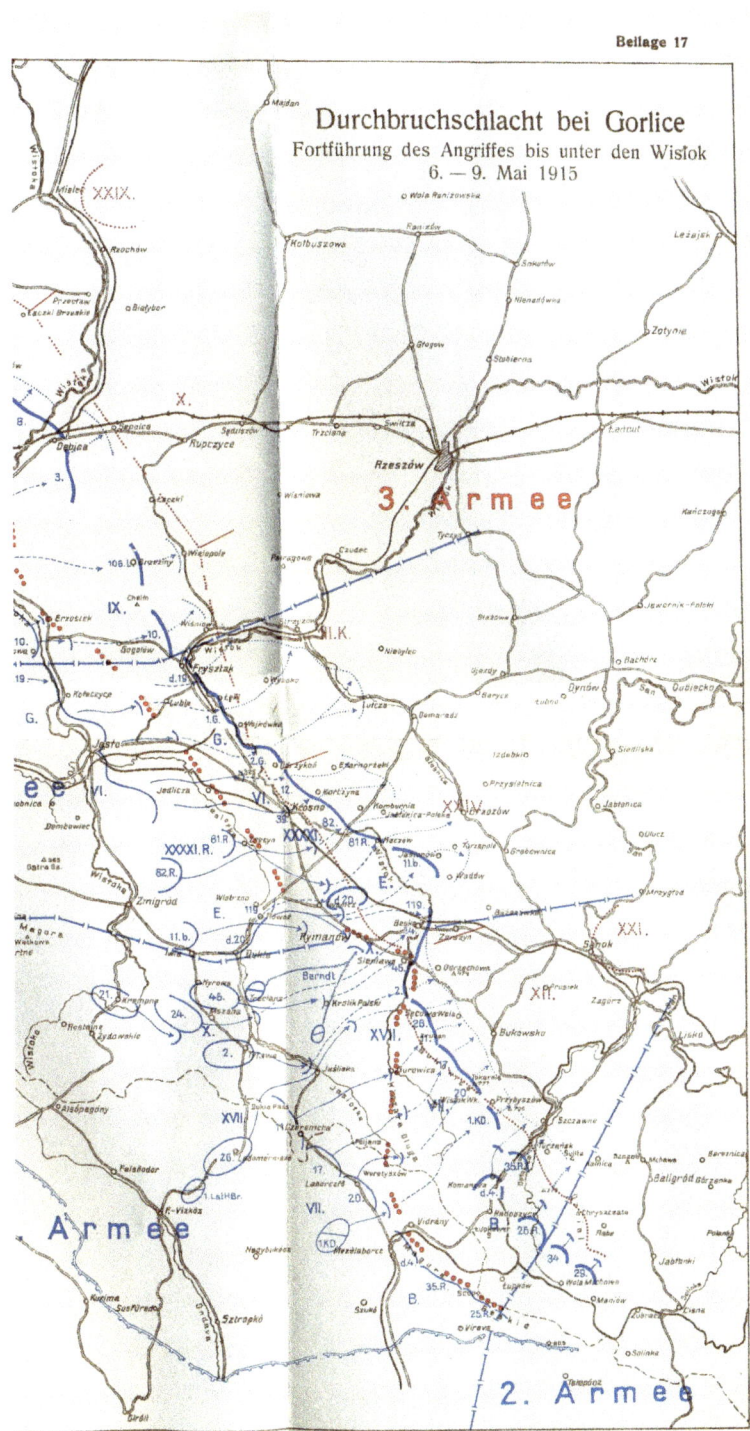

Beilage 17

Durchbruchschlacht bei Gorlice
Fortführung des Angriffes bis unter den Wislok
6. — 9. Mai 1915

of Wislok May 6-9, 1915

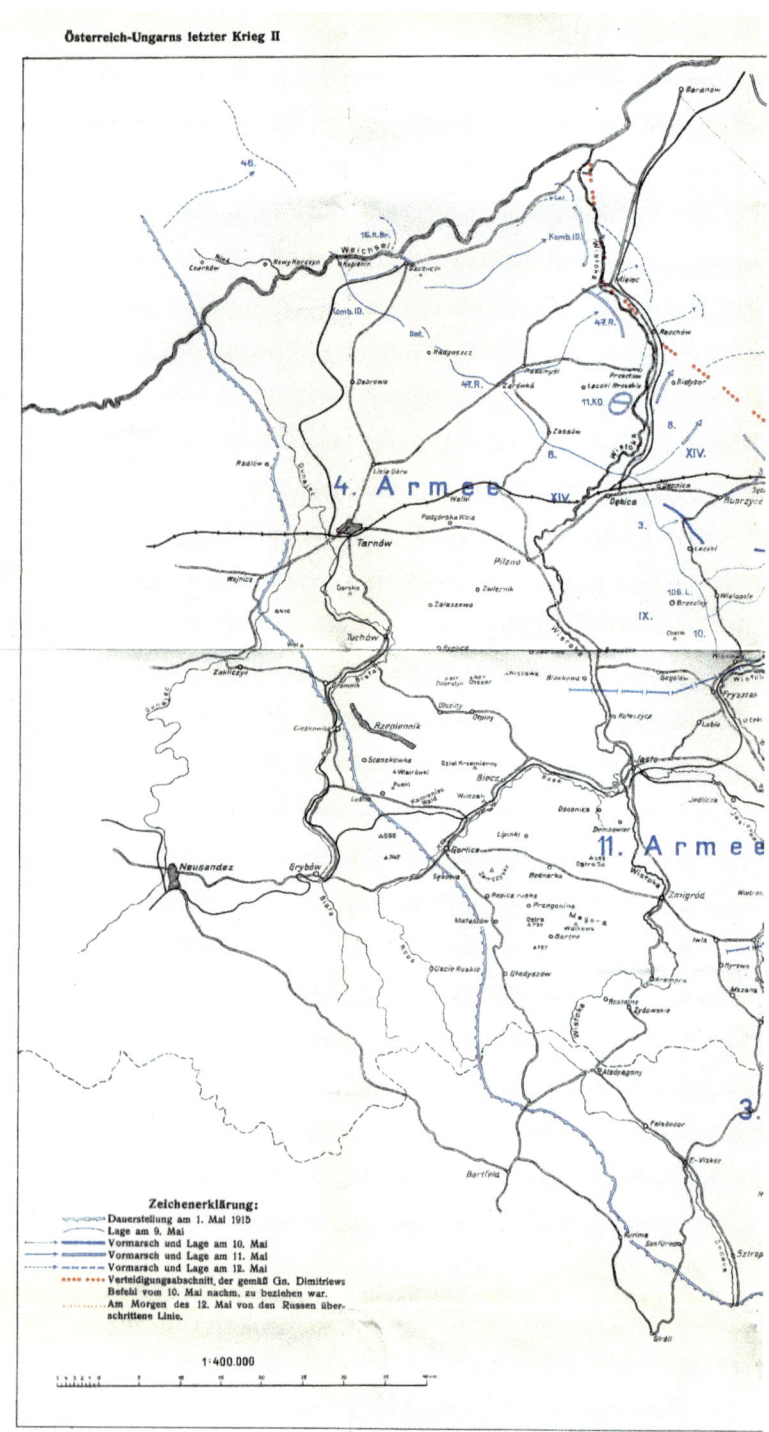

Breakthrough battle near Gorlice; Development of

the situation May 9 to 12, 1915

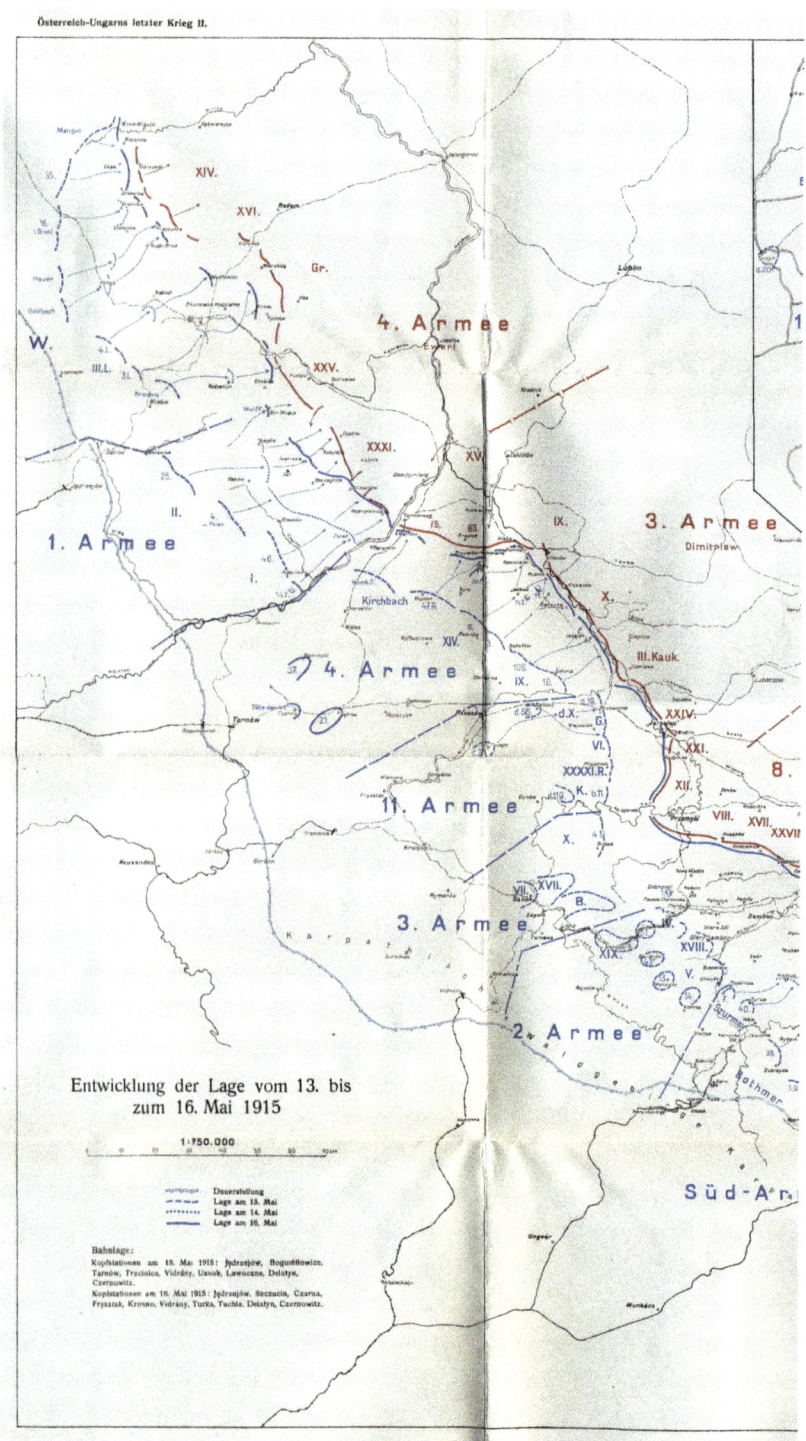

Österreich-Ungarns letzter Krieg II.

Entwicklung der Lage vom 13. bis
zum 16. Mai 1915

1:750.000

Bahnlagen:
Kopfstationen am 13. Mai 1915: Jędrzejów, Bogucicowice,
Tarnów, Frncisica, Vidrány, Uznok, Lawoczne, Delatyn,
Czernowitz.
Kopfstationen am 16. Mai 1915: Jędrzejów, Szczucin, Czarna,
Fryszrak, Krosno, Vidrány, Turka, Tuchla, Delatyn, Czernowitz.

Beginning of the Battle of Jaroslau and departure

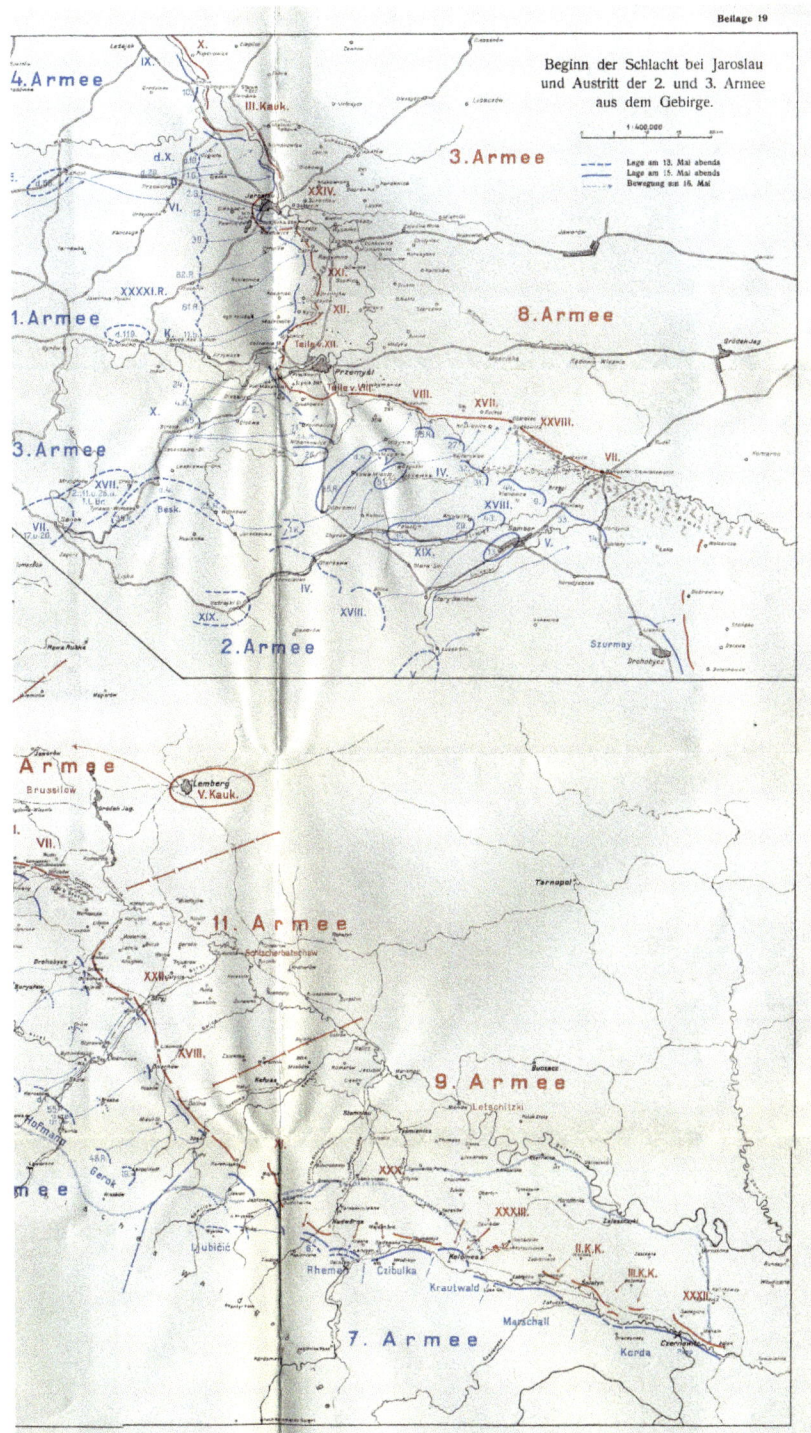

of the 2nd and 3rd Armies from the mountains

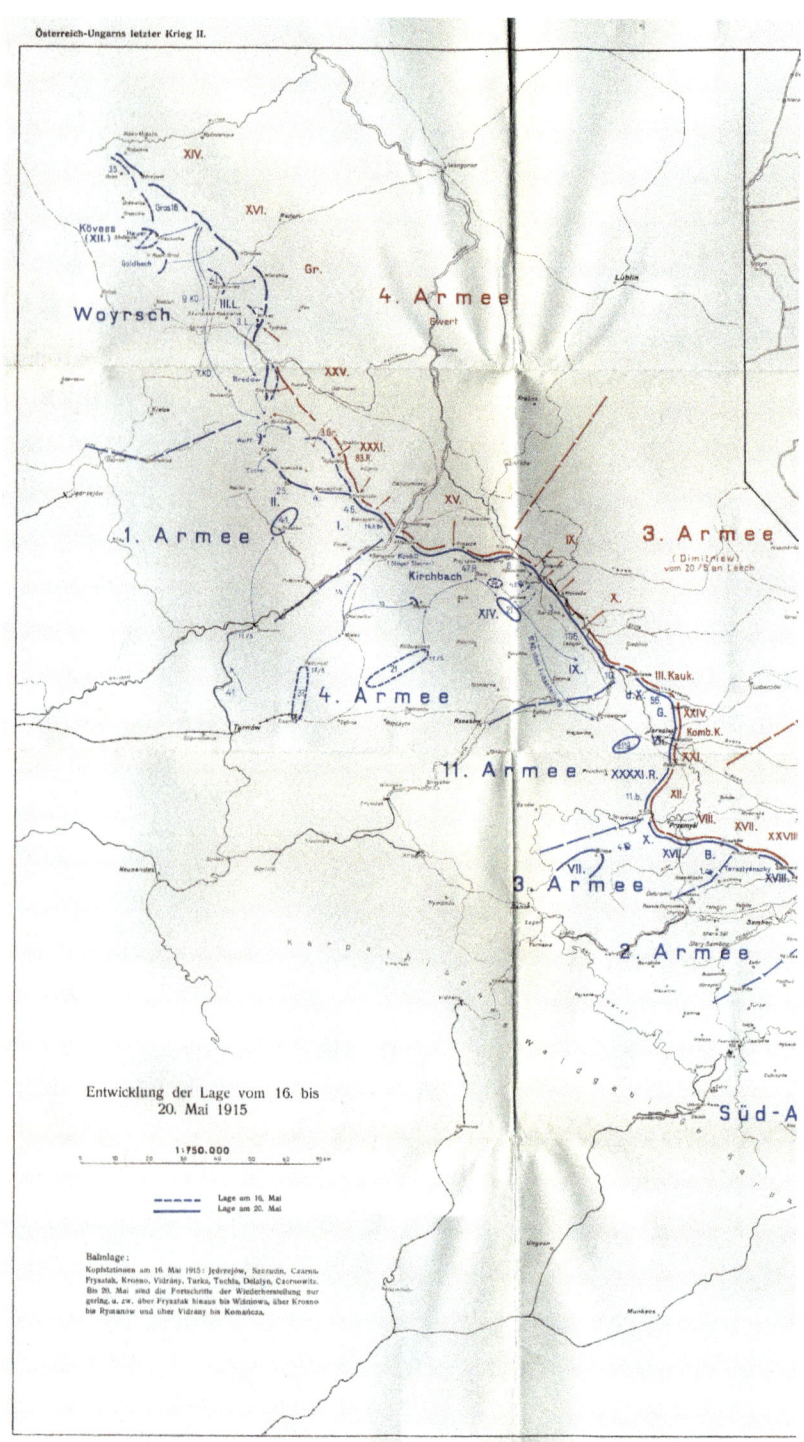

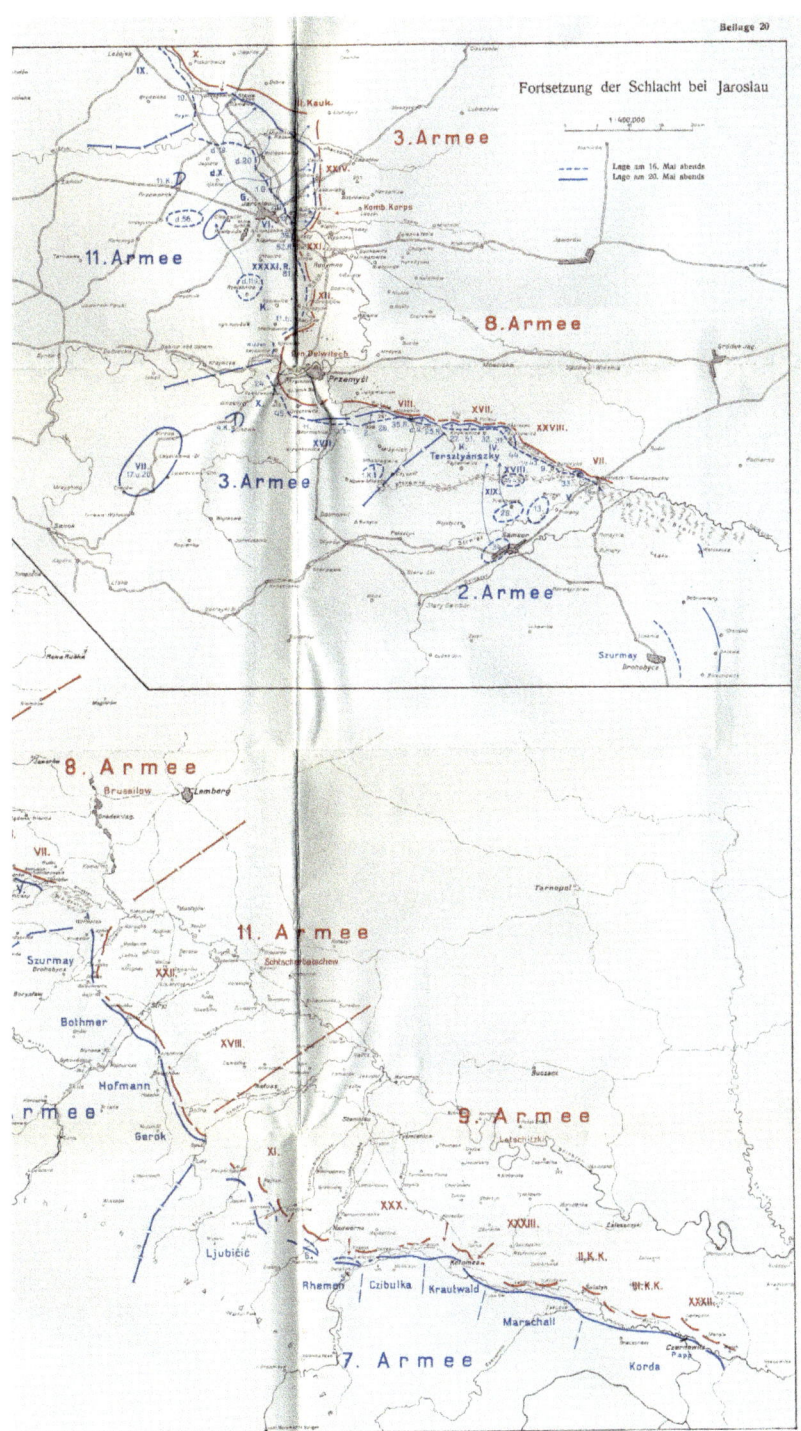

Battle of Jaroslan

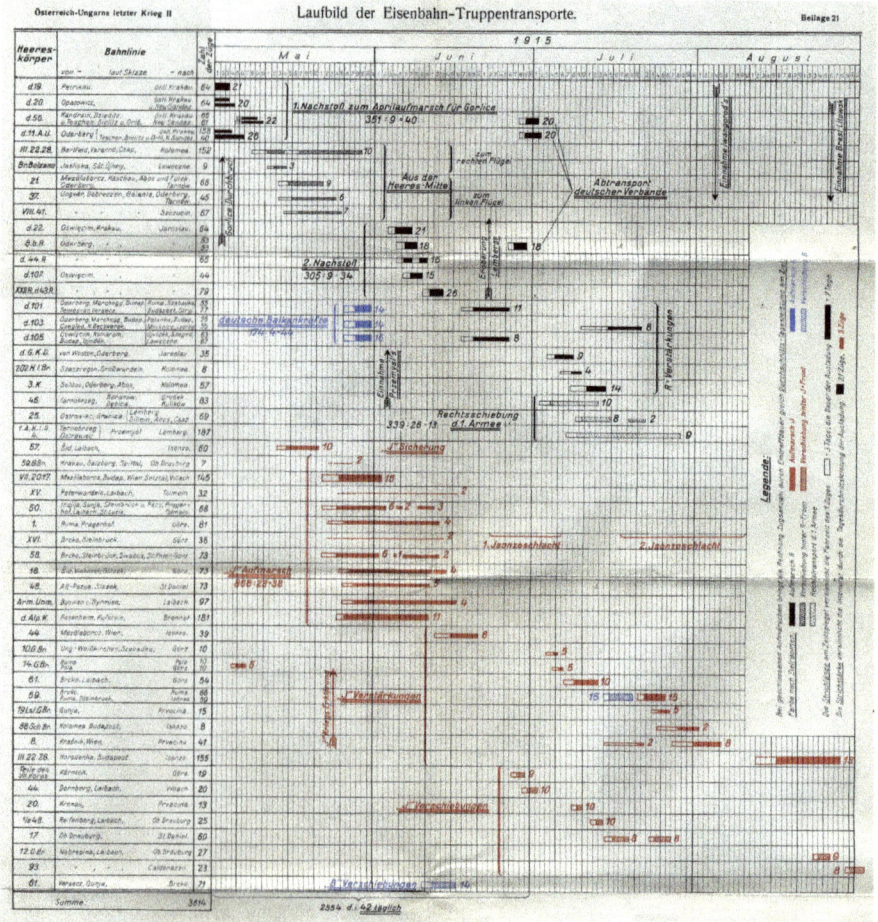

Troop transport routes May to August 1915

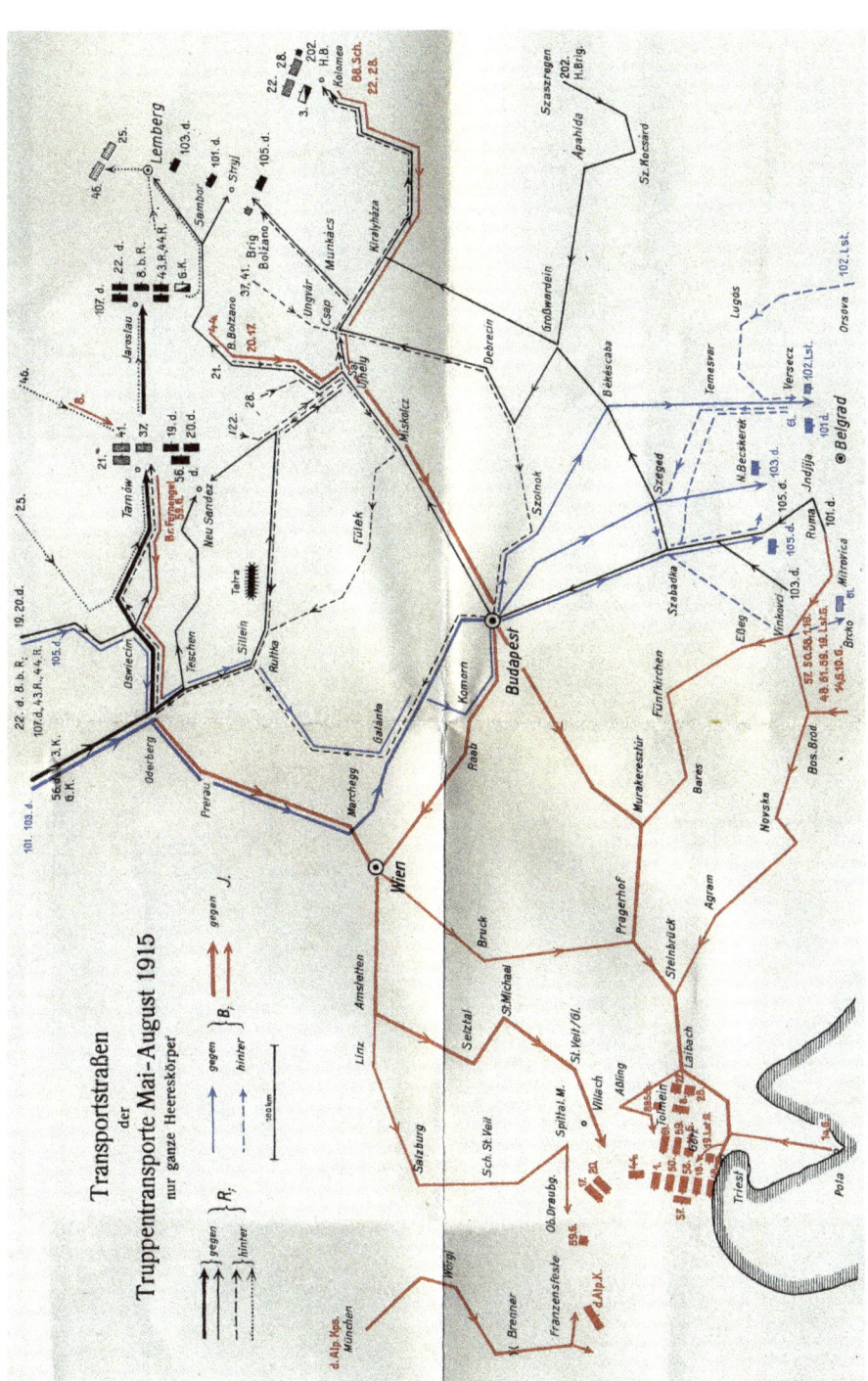

Troop transport routes May to August 1915

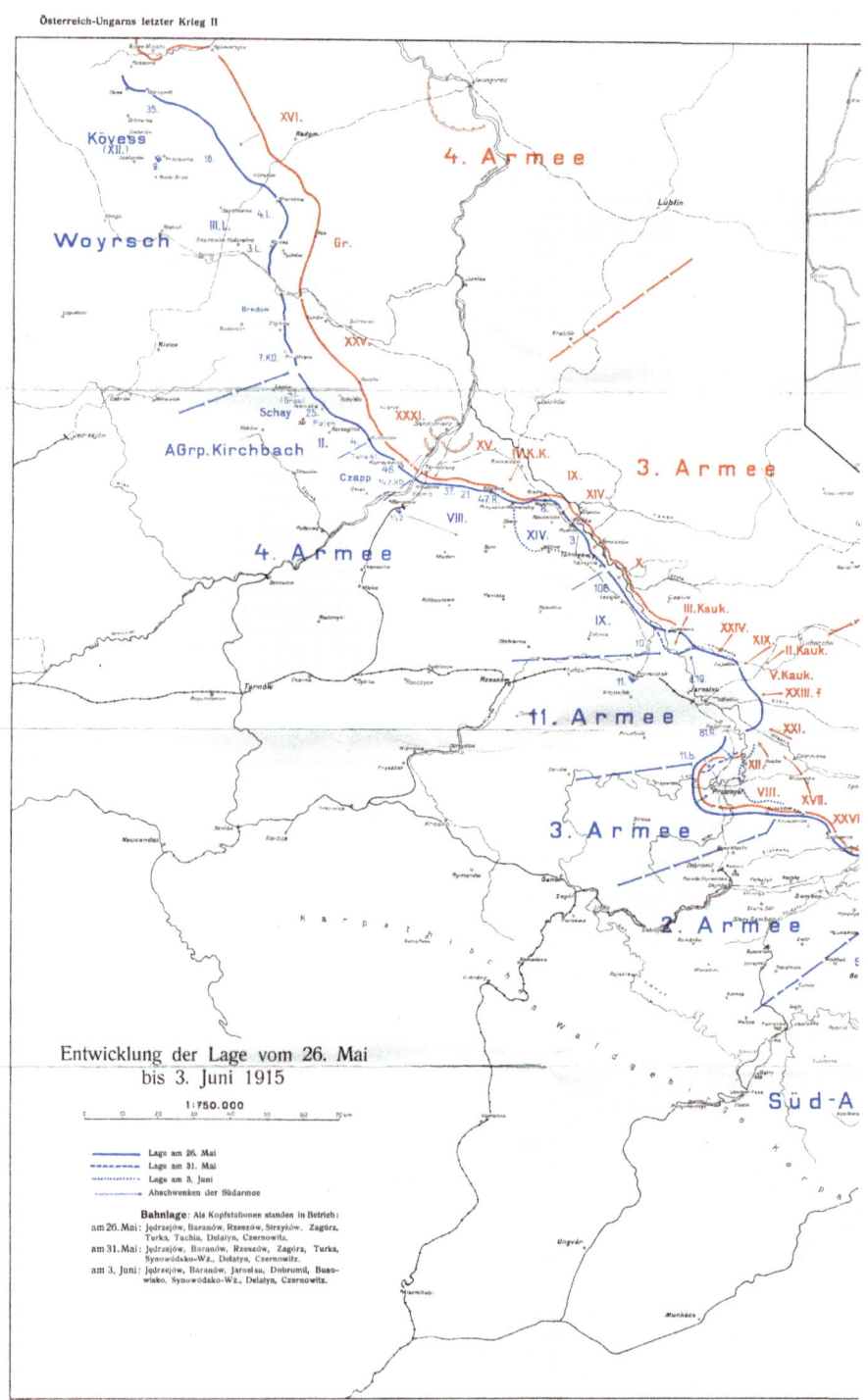

Österreich-Ungarns letzter Krieg II

Entwicklung der Lage vom 26. Mai
bis 3. Juni 1915

1:750.000

Lage am 26. Mai
Lage am 31. Mai
Lage am 3. Juni
Abschwenken der Südarmee

Bahnlage: Als Kopfstationen standen in Betrieb:
am 26. Mai: Jędrzejów, Baranów, Rzeszów, Strzyżów, Zagórz,
   Turka, Tuchla, Delatyn, Czernowitz.
am 31. Mai: Jędrzejów, Baranów, Rzeszów, Zagórz, Turka,
   Synowódsko-Wż., Delatyn, Czernowitz.
am 3. Juni: Jędrzejów, Baranów, Jarosław, Dobromil, Buso-
   wisko, Synowódsko-Wż., Delatyn, Czernowitz.

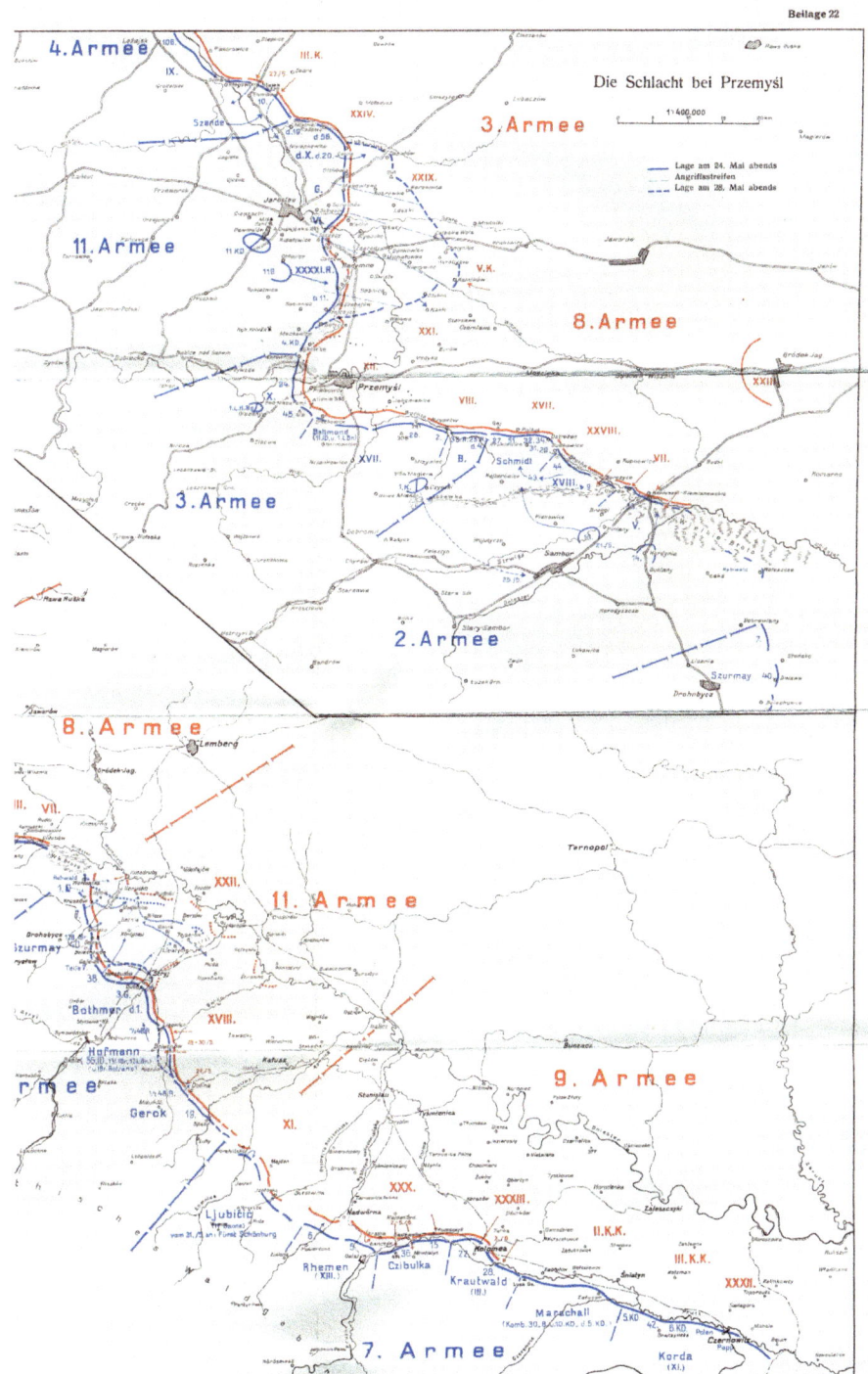

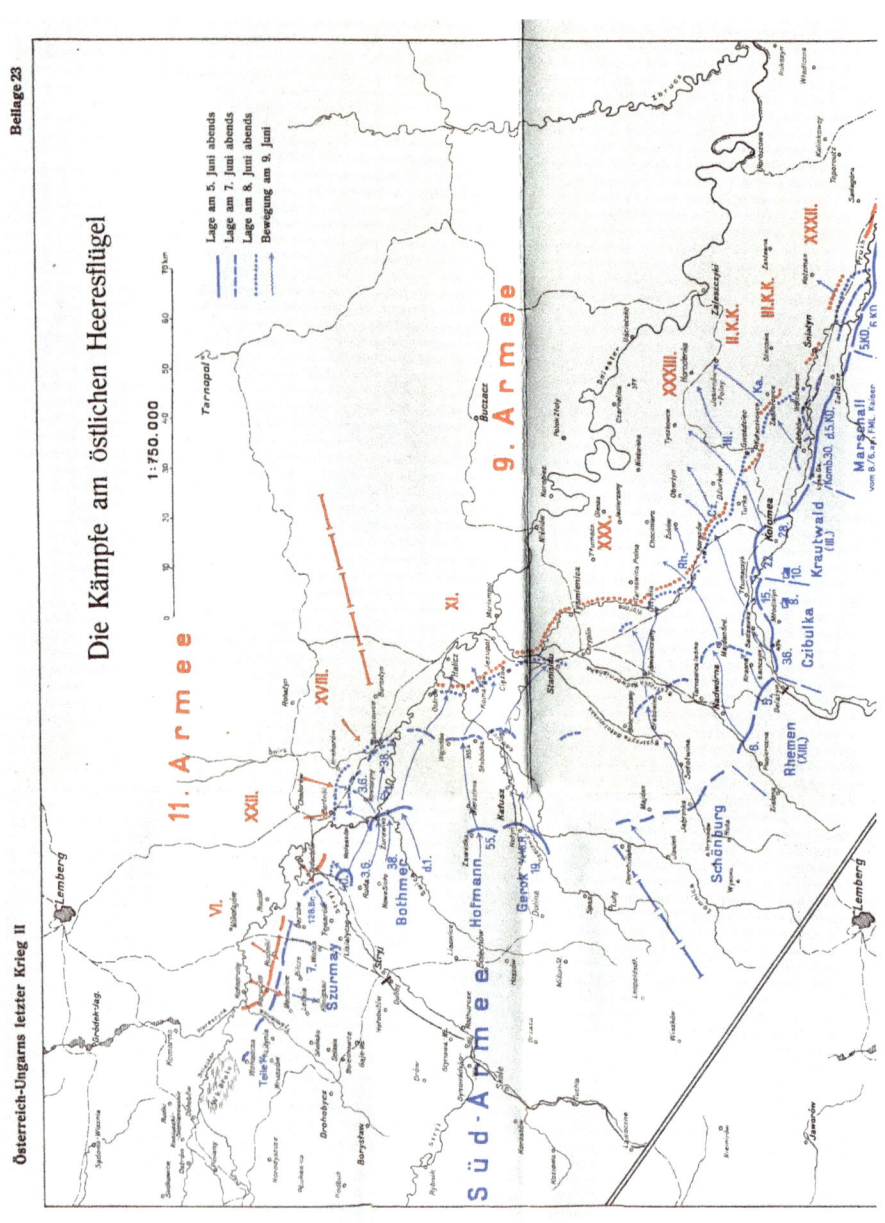

Die Kämpfe am östlichen Heeresflügel

1:750.000

Beilage 23

Österreich-Ungarns letzter Krieg II

The Battles of the Army's

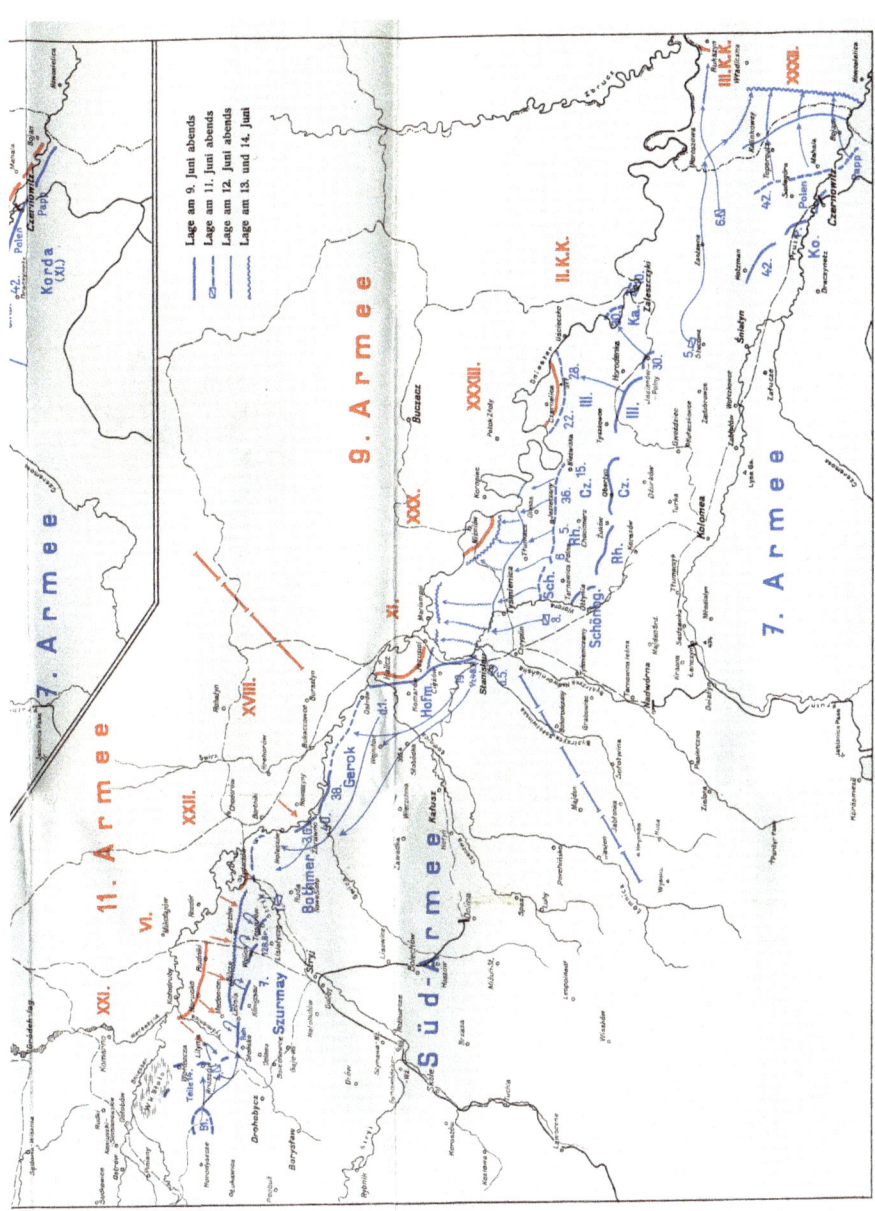

Eastern Wing (7th Army)

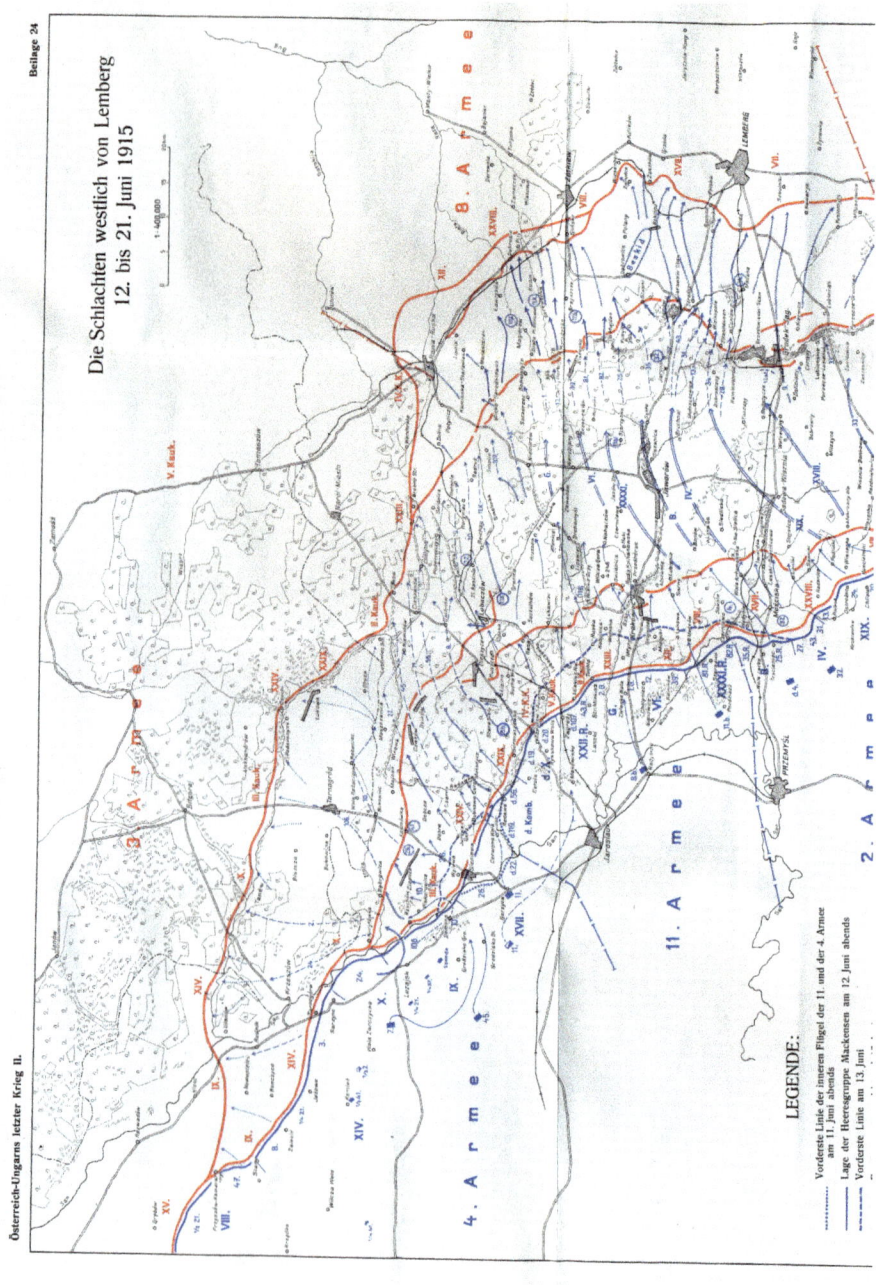

The Battles West of Lemberg

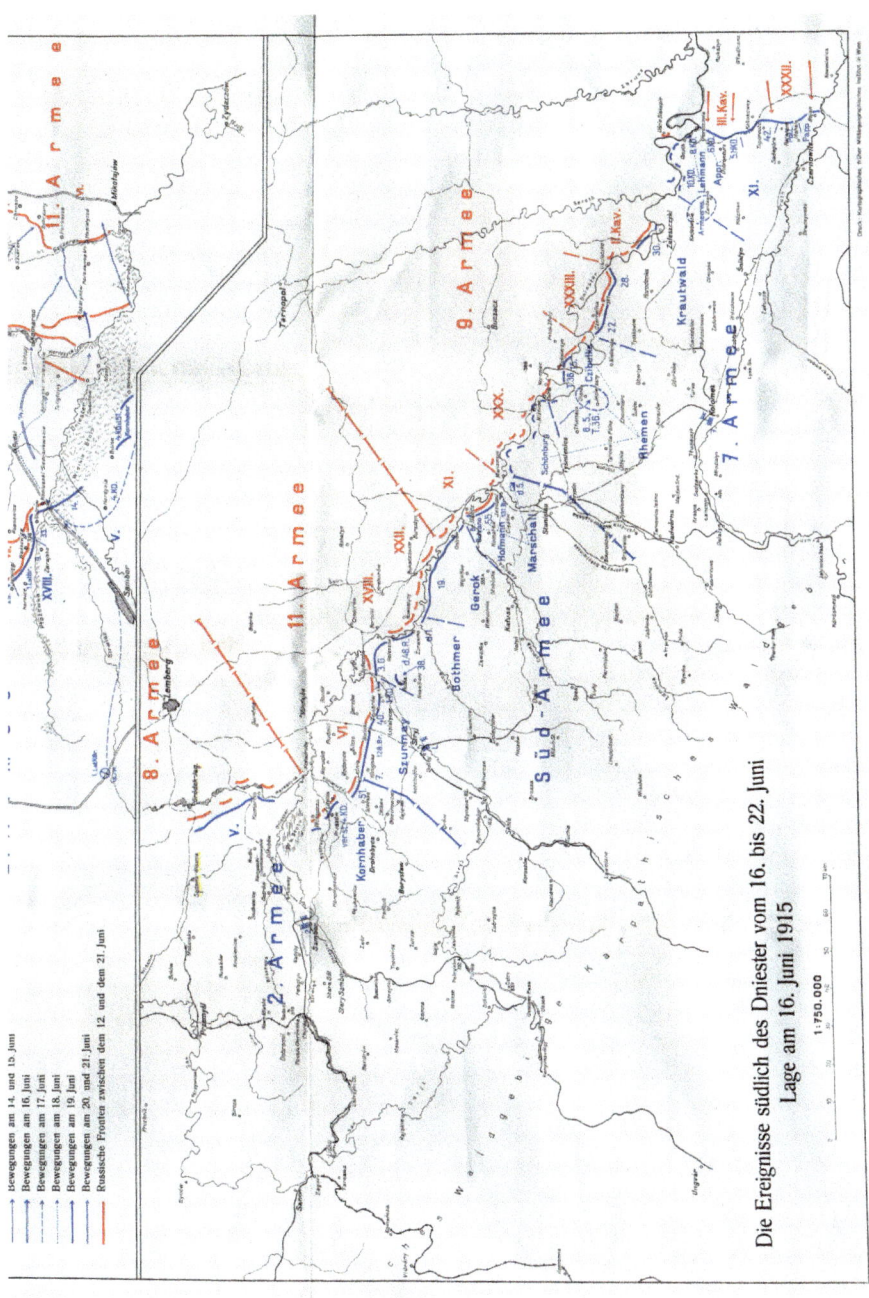

Die Ereignisse südlich des Dniester vom 16. bis 22. Juni
Lage am 16. Juni 1915

1 : 750.000

June 12-21, 1915

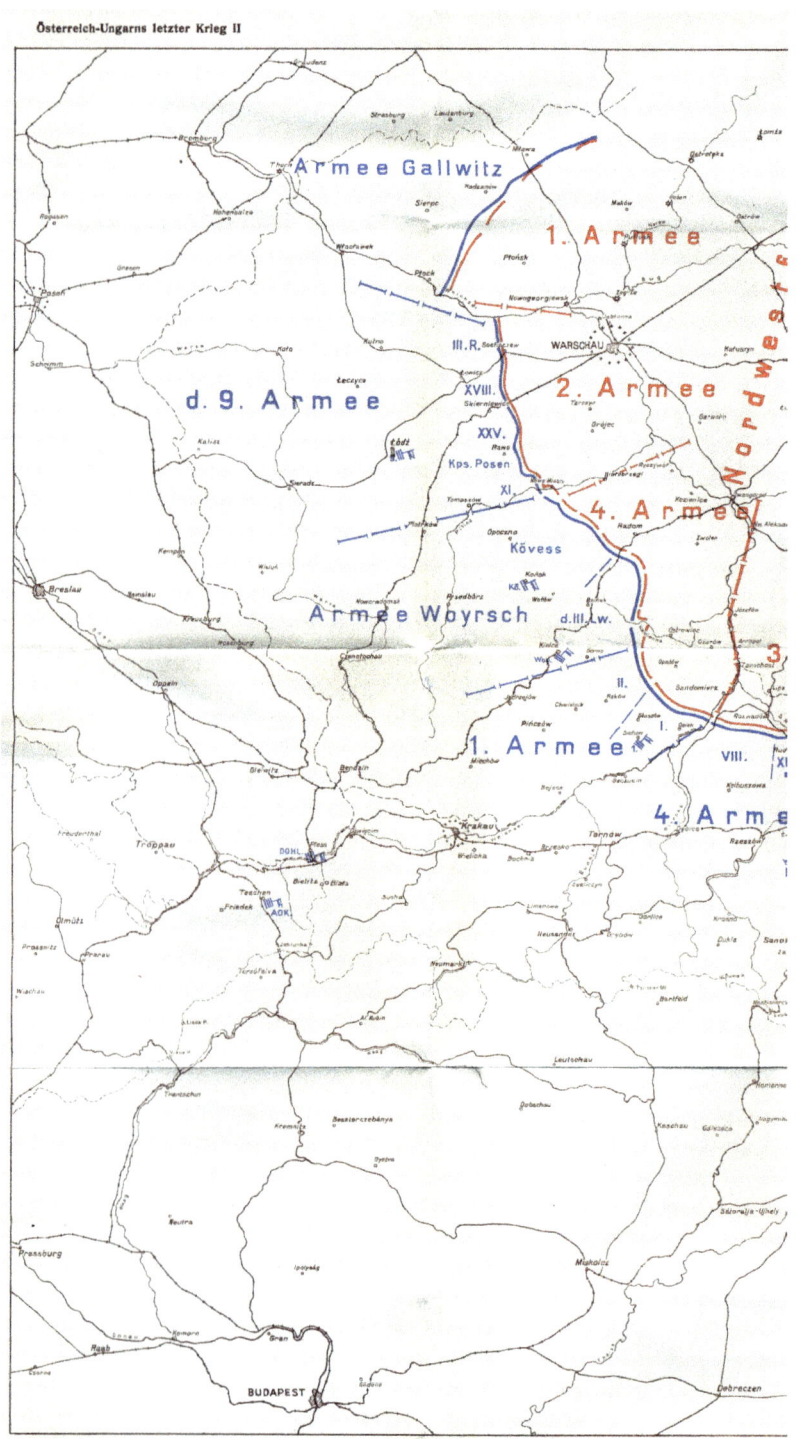

Position on June 22

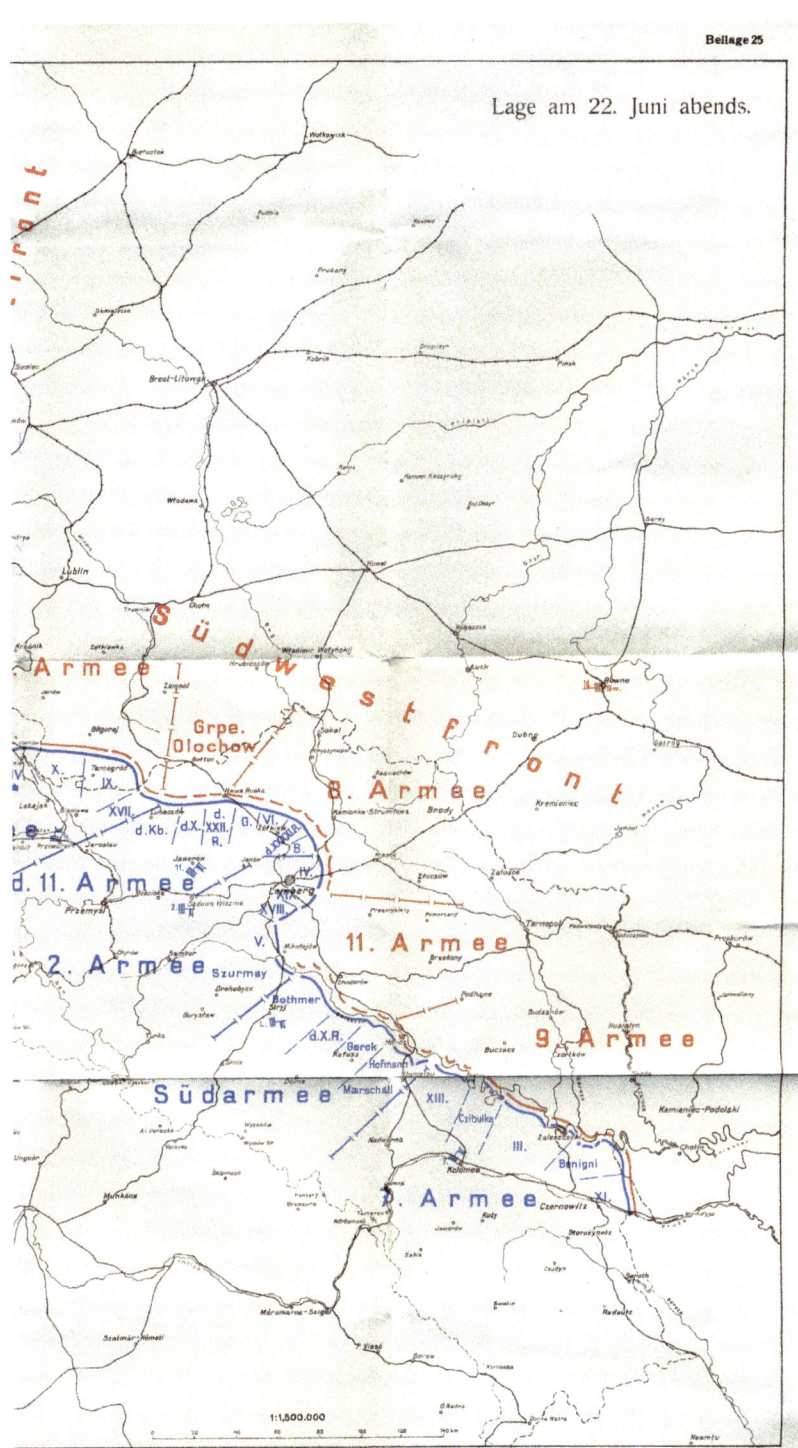

Bellage 25

Lage am 22. Juni abends.

evening (Northeast)

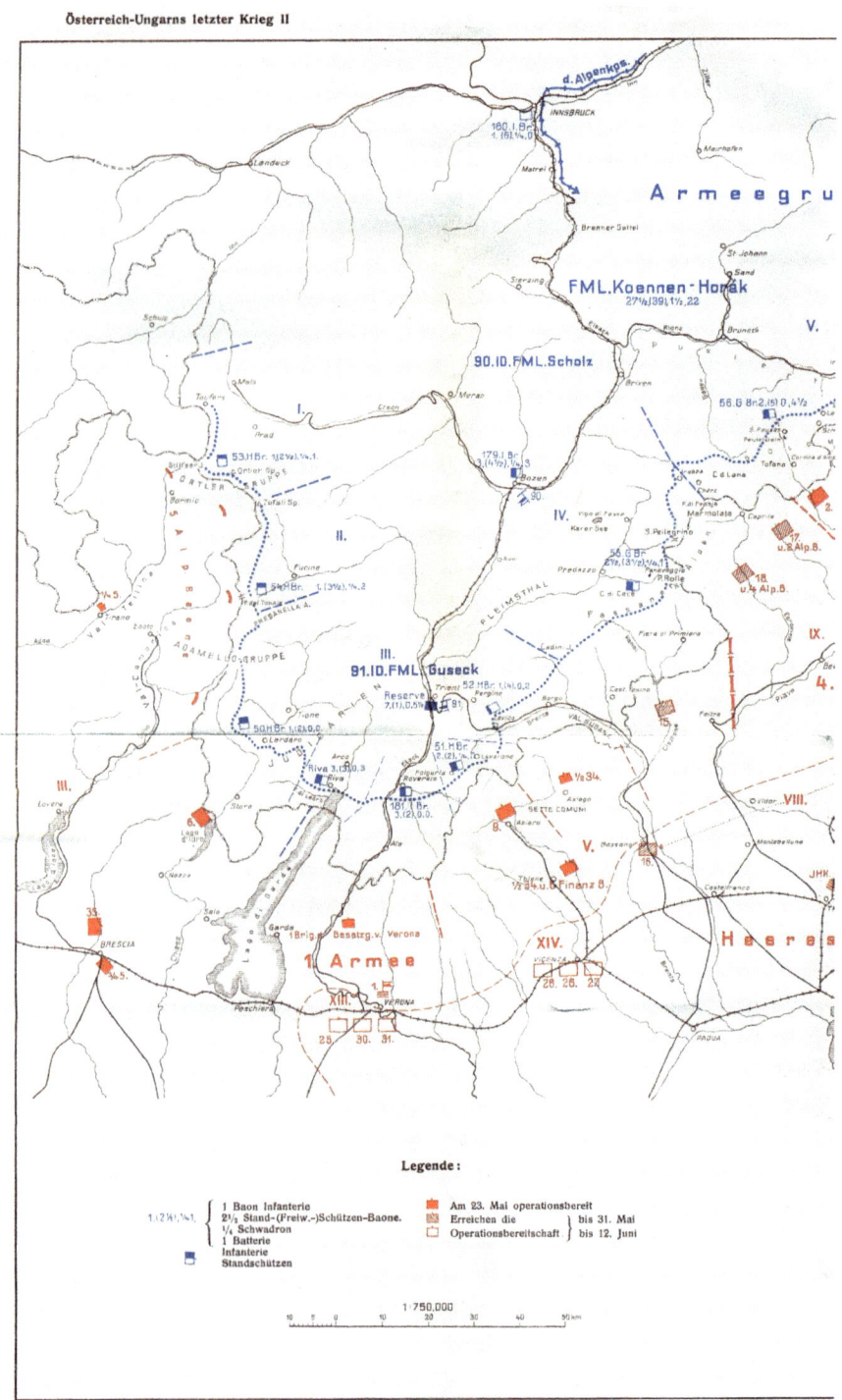

Situation of the Mutual Armed Forces at

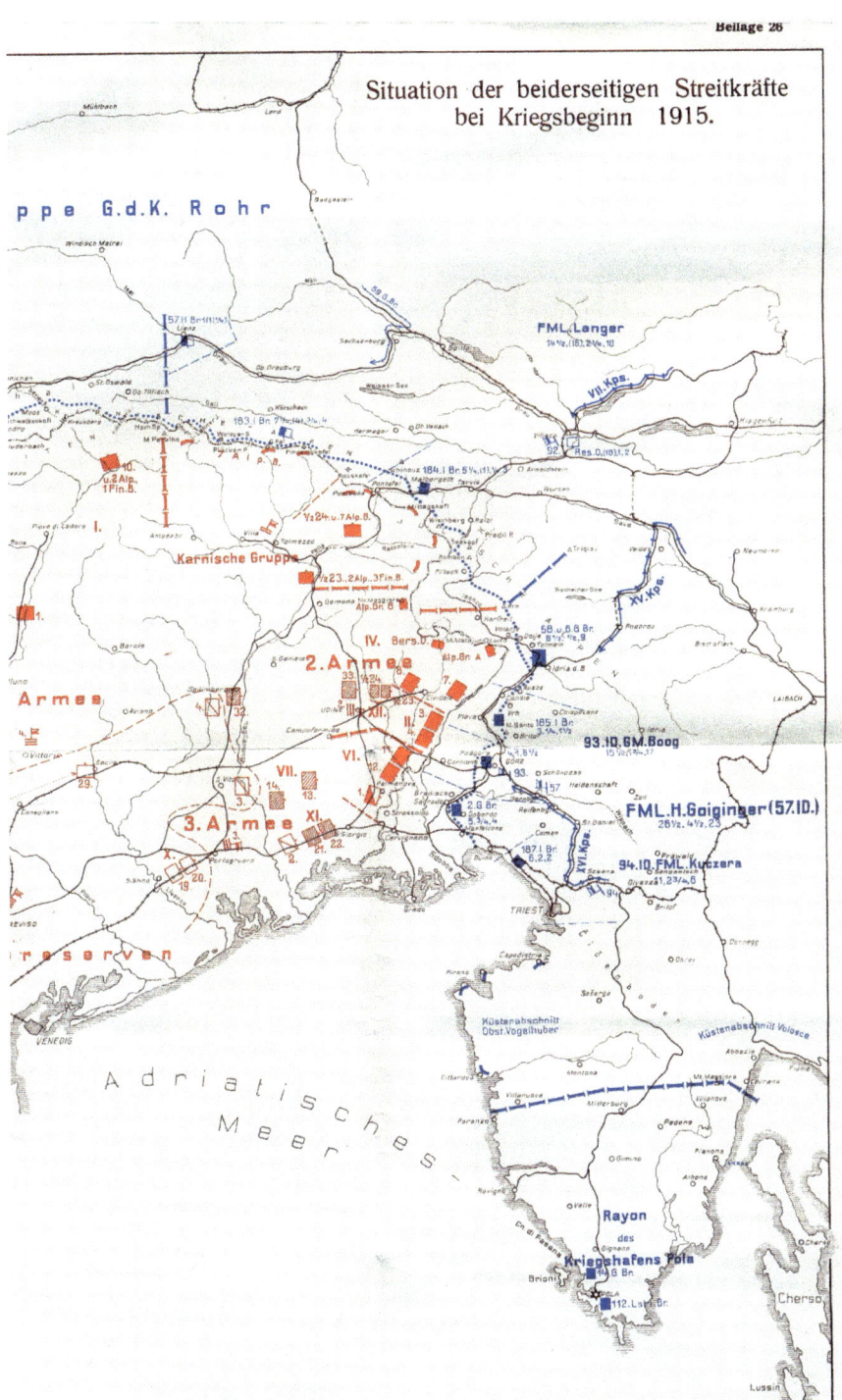

the Start of the War in 1915 (Southwest)

The battles in Tyrol in May and June 1915. The battles

Die Kämpfe in Tirol im

in the Dolomites in July and August 1915

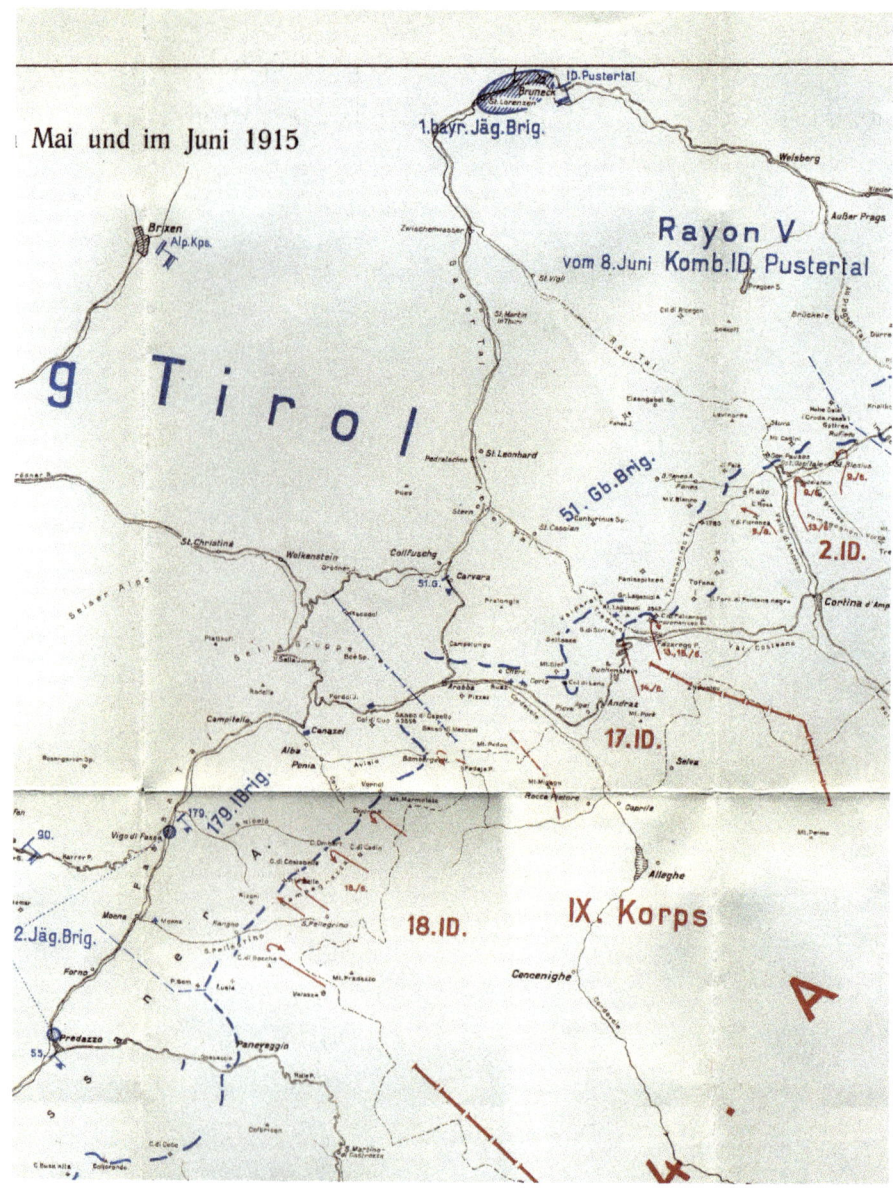

The battles in Tyrol in May and June 1915. The battles

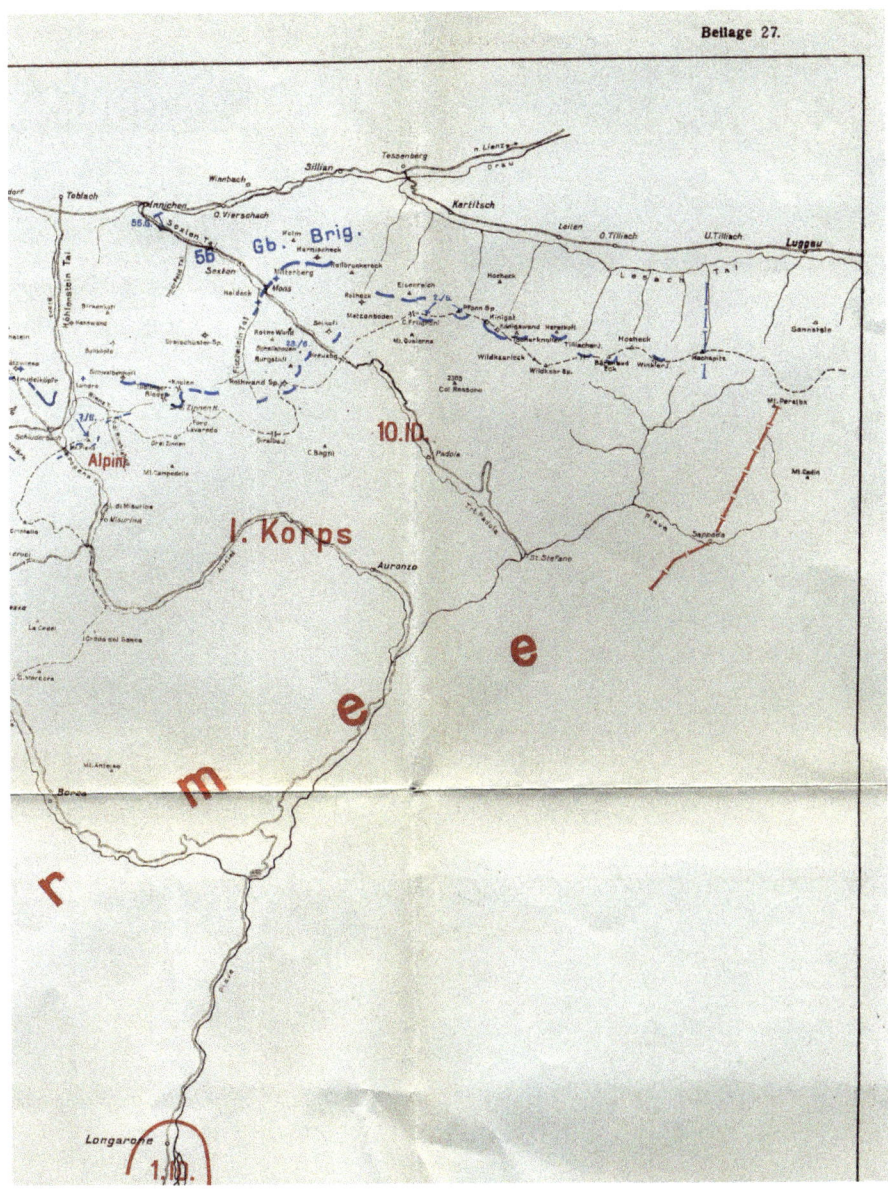

in the Dolomites in July and August 1915

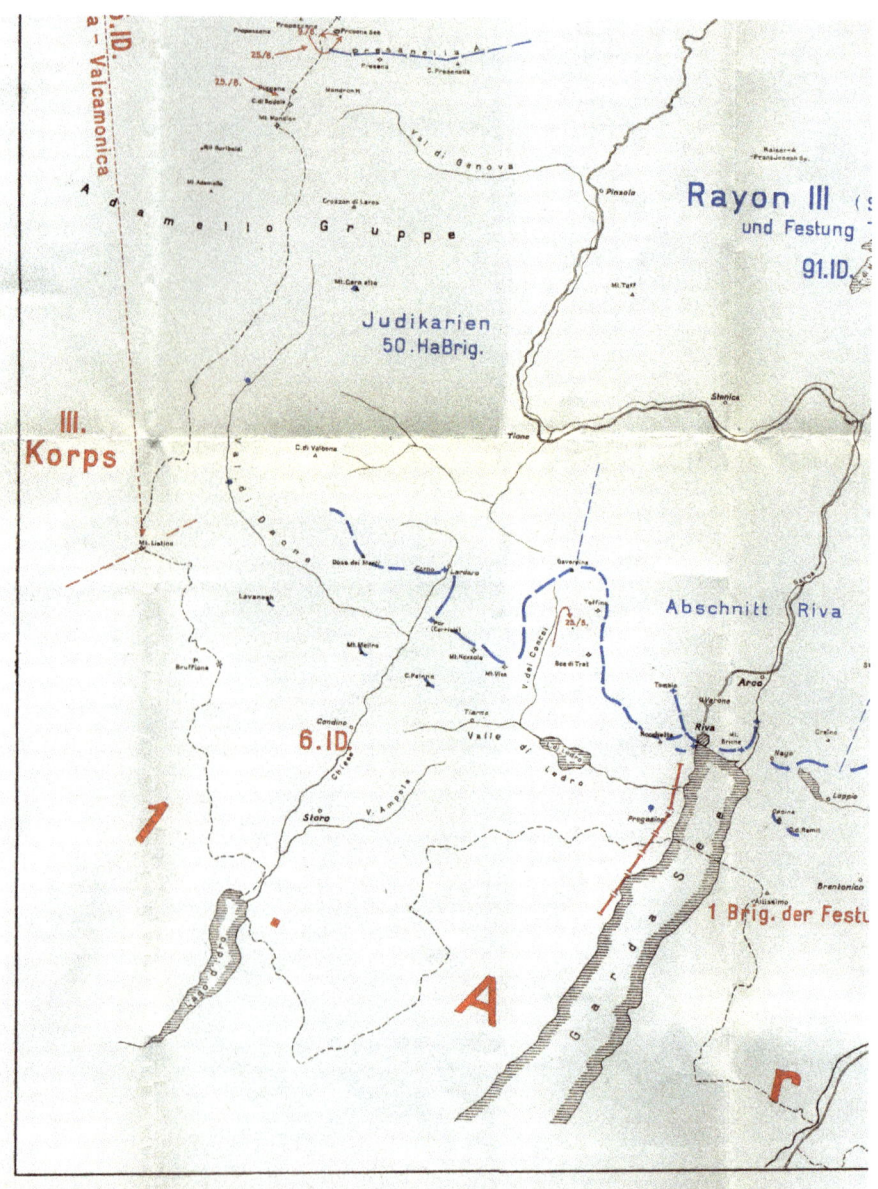

The battles in Tyrol in May and June 1915. The battles

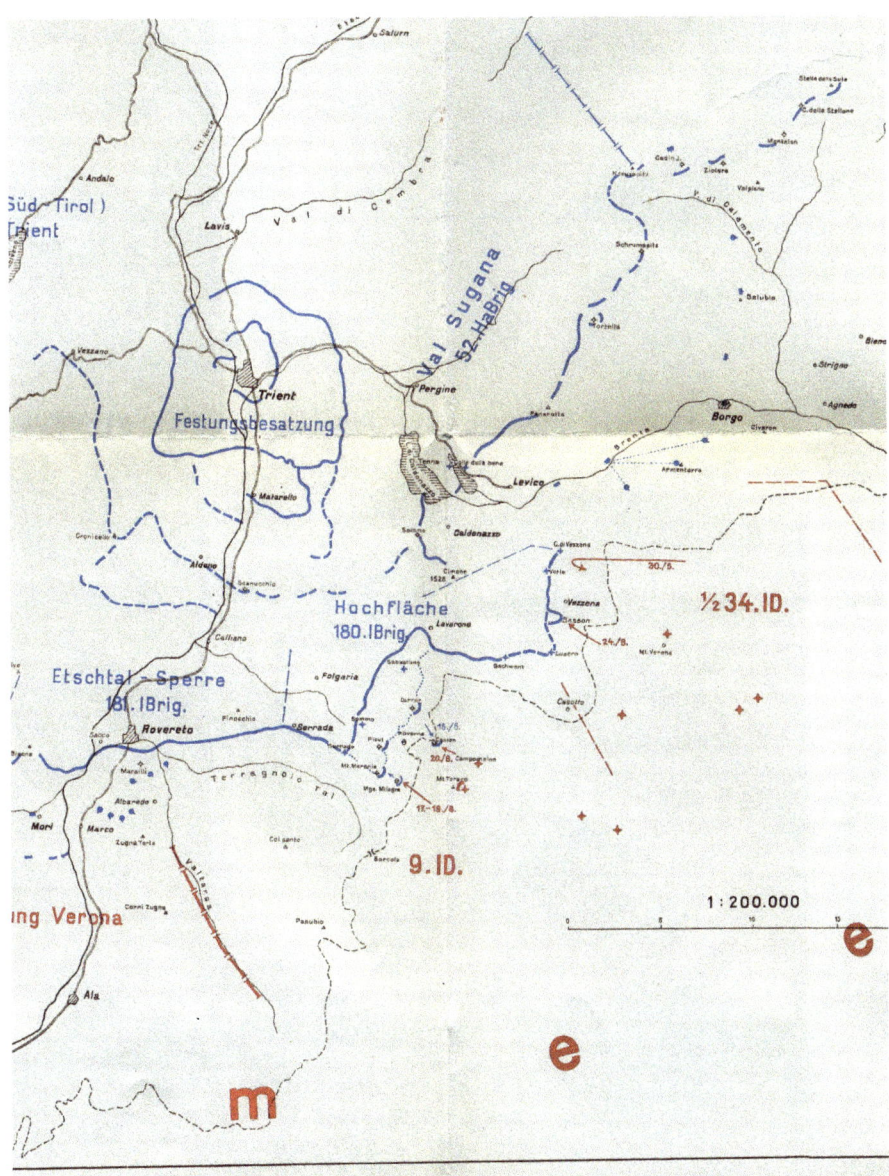

in the Dolomites in July and August 1915

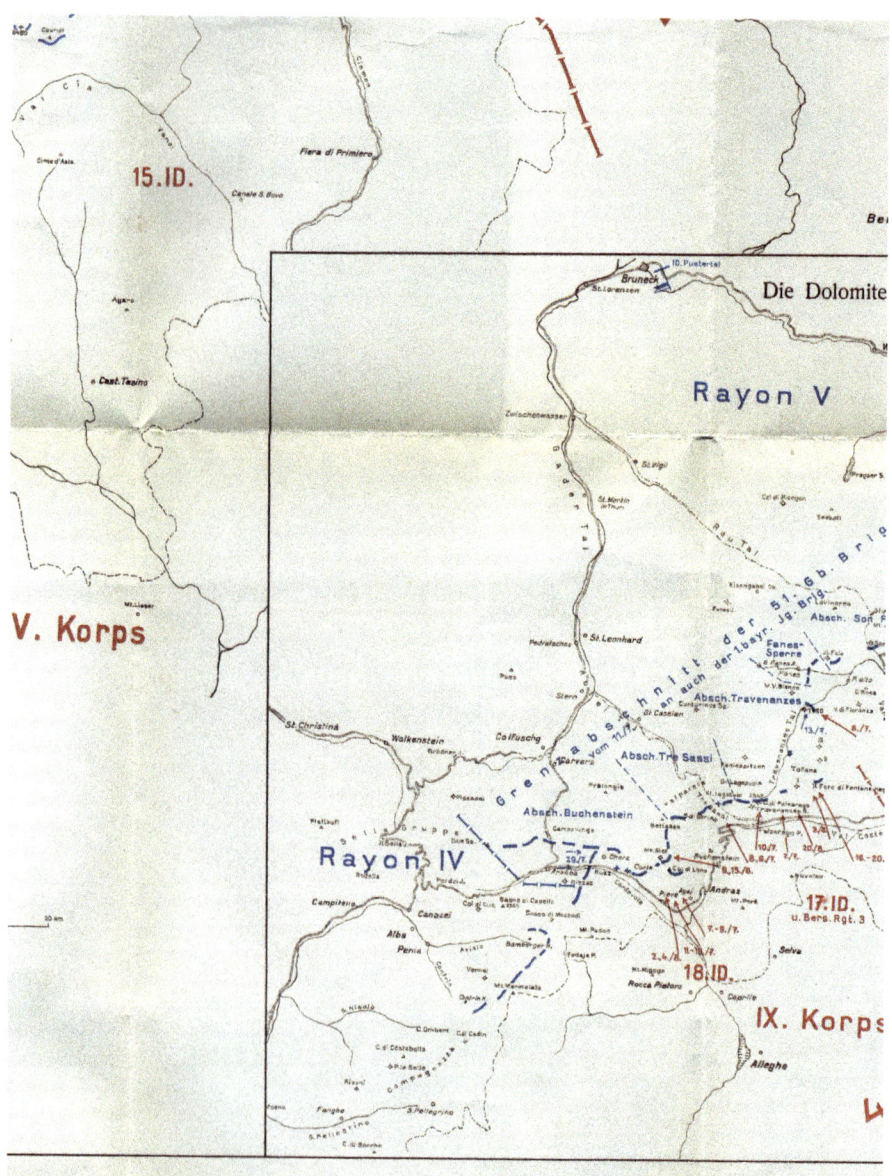

The battles in Tyrol in May and June 1915. The battles

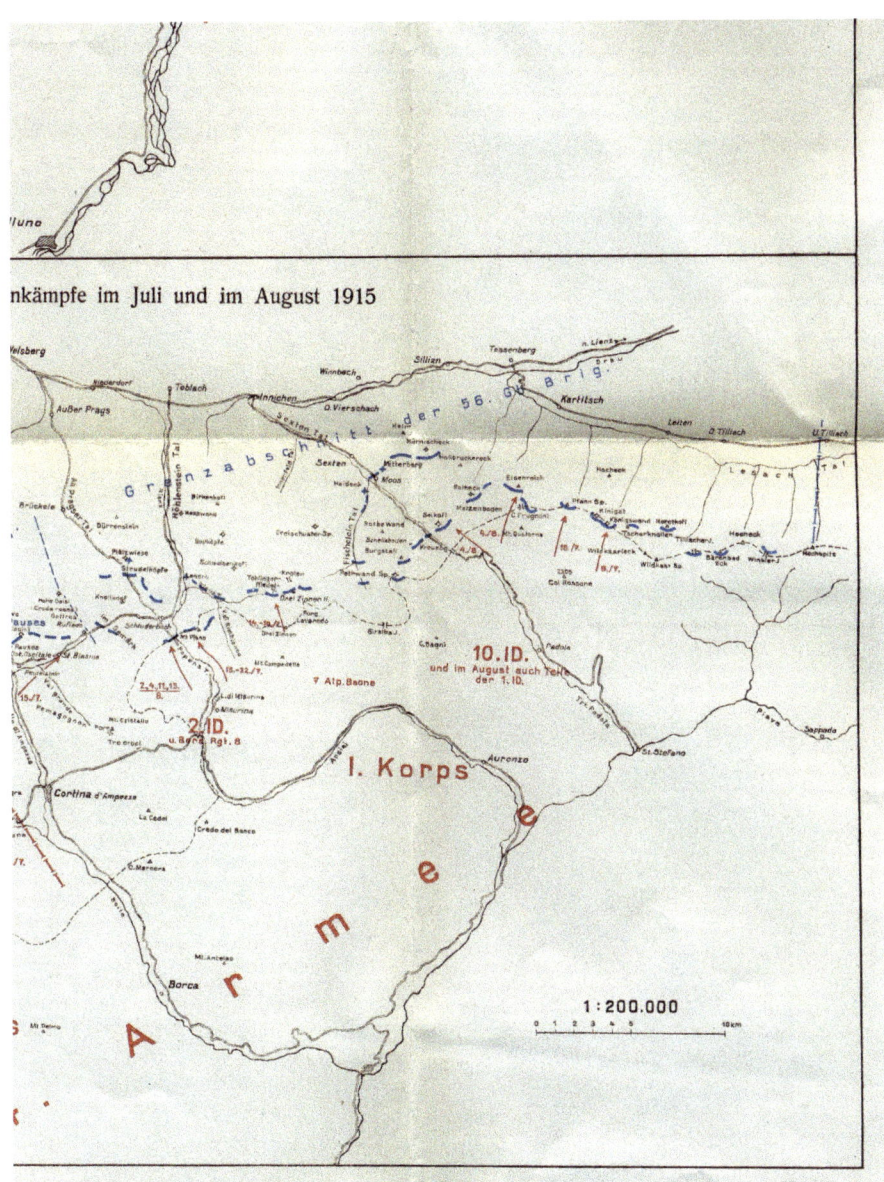

in the Dolomites in July and August 1915

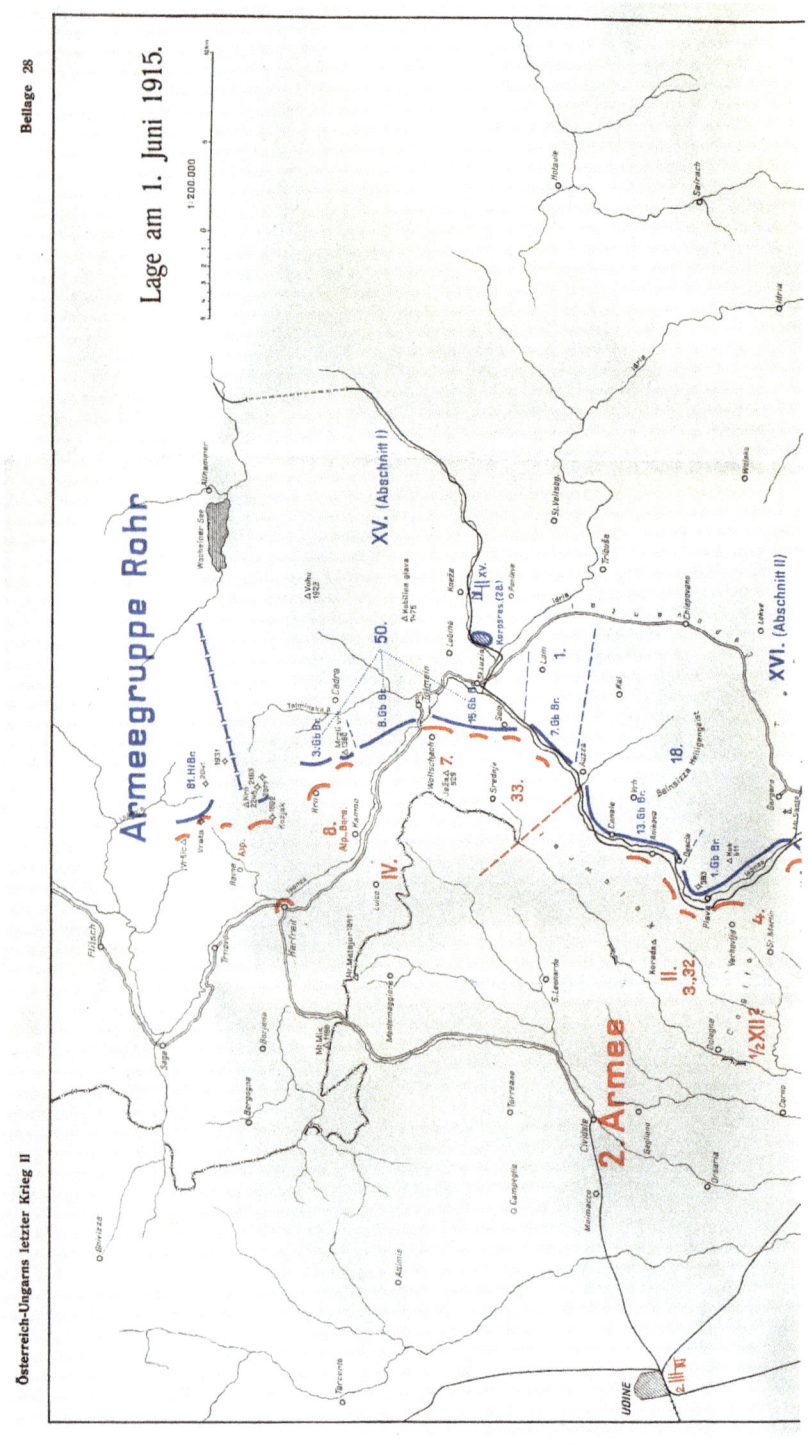

Situation on June 1,

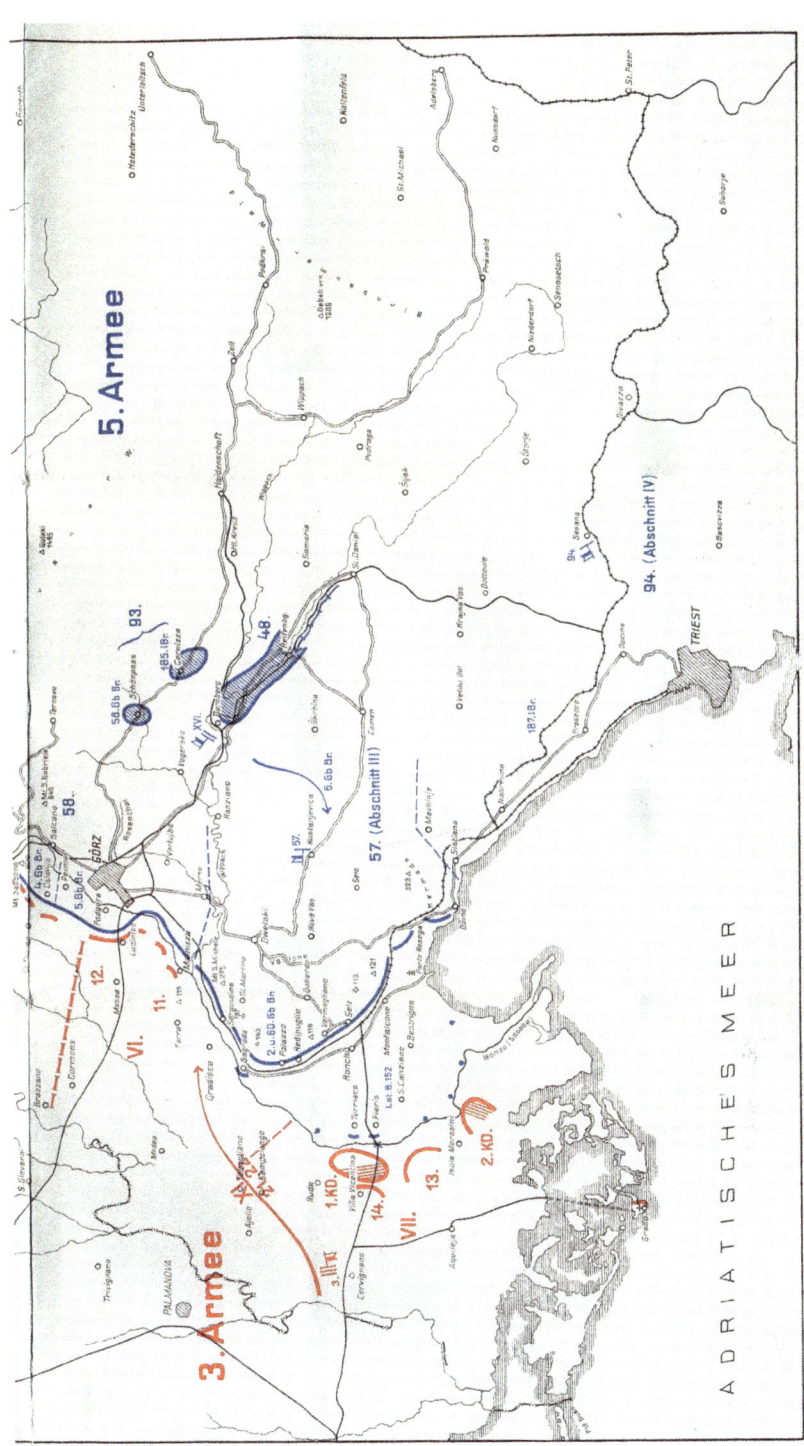

1915 (Isonzo Front)

Österreich-Ungarns letzter Krieg II

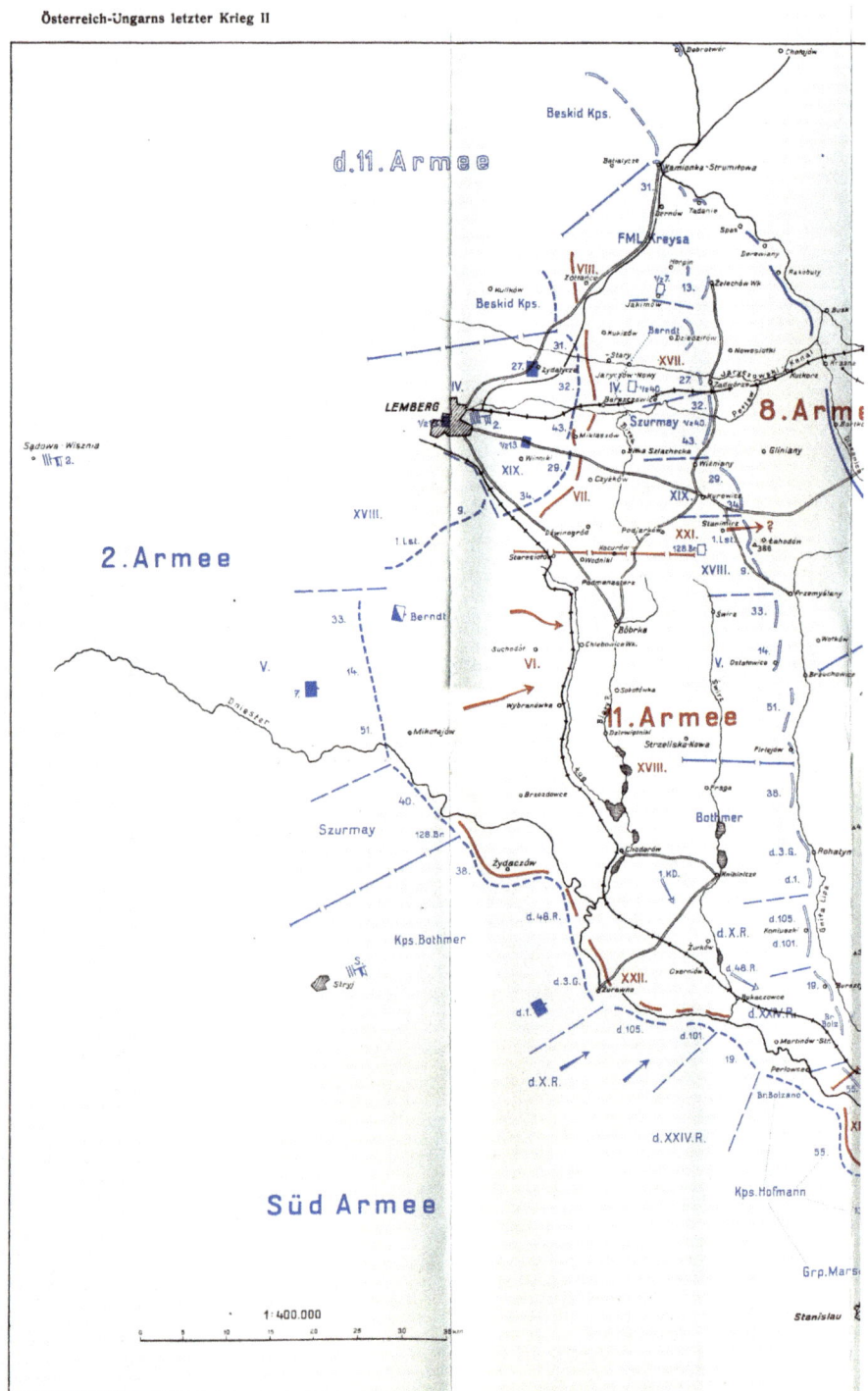

Fighting between Lemberg and the

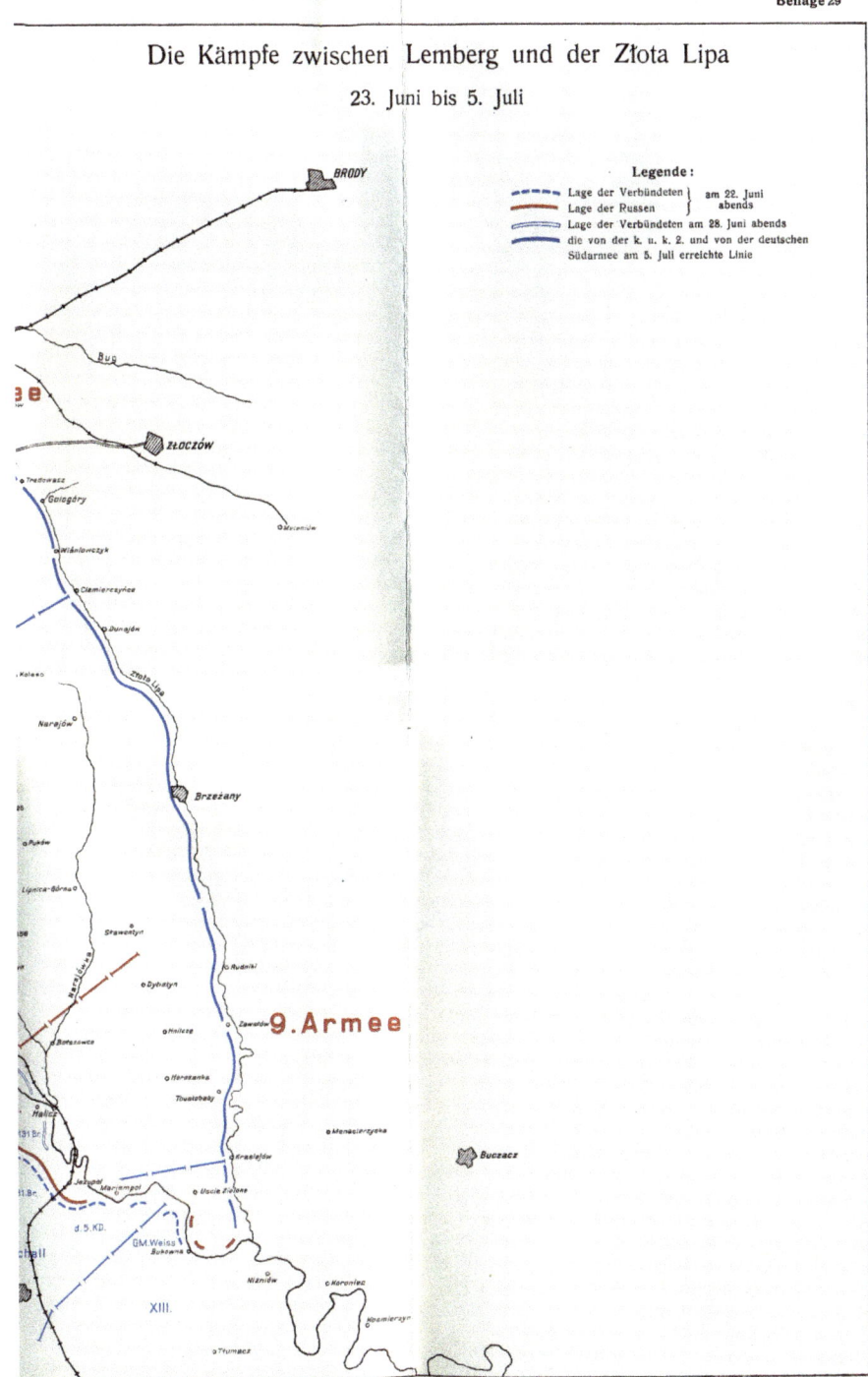

Zlota Lipa June 23 to July 5

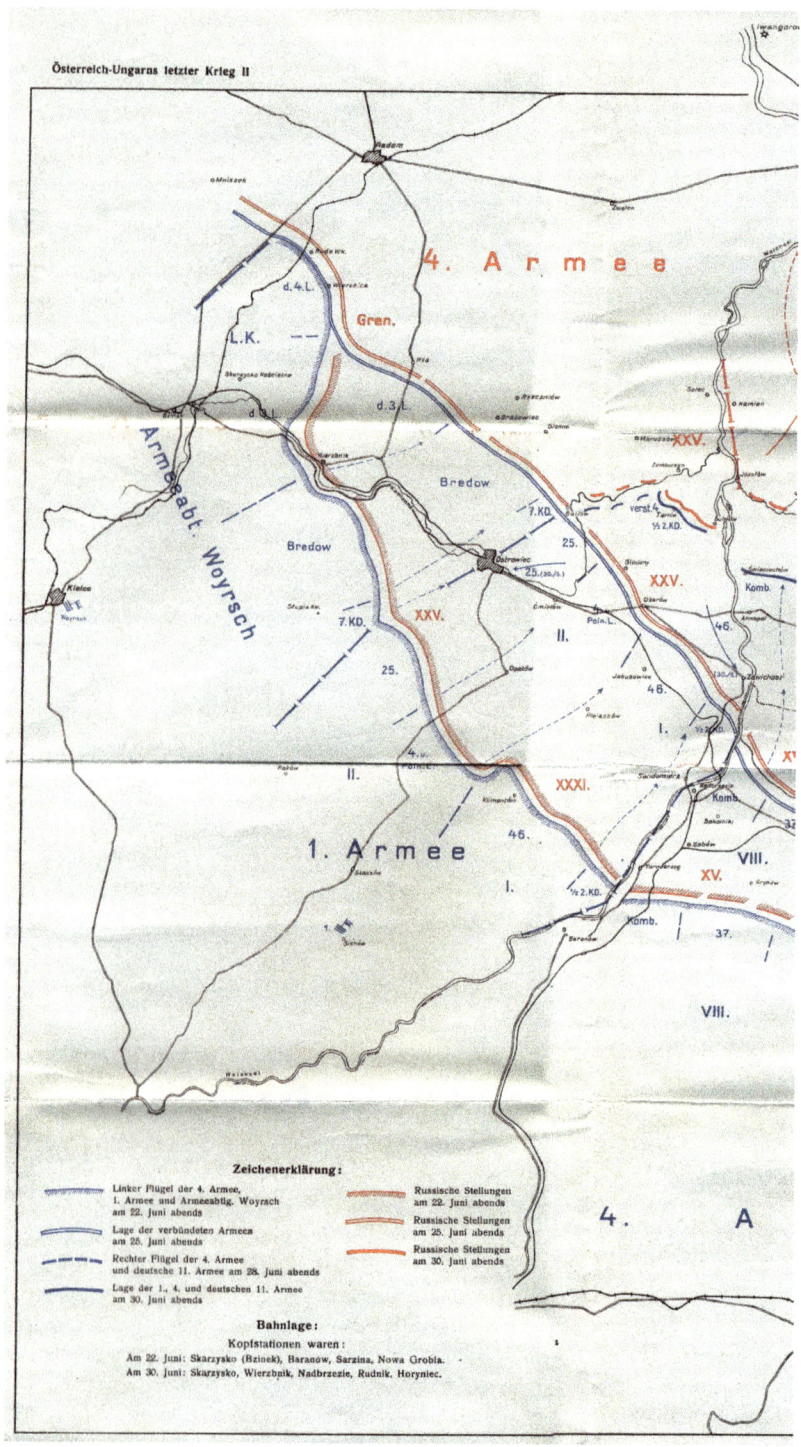

Allied advance on both sides of

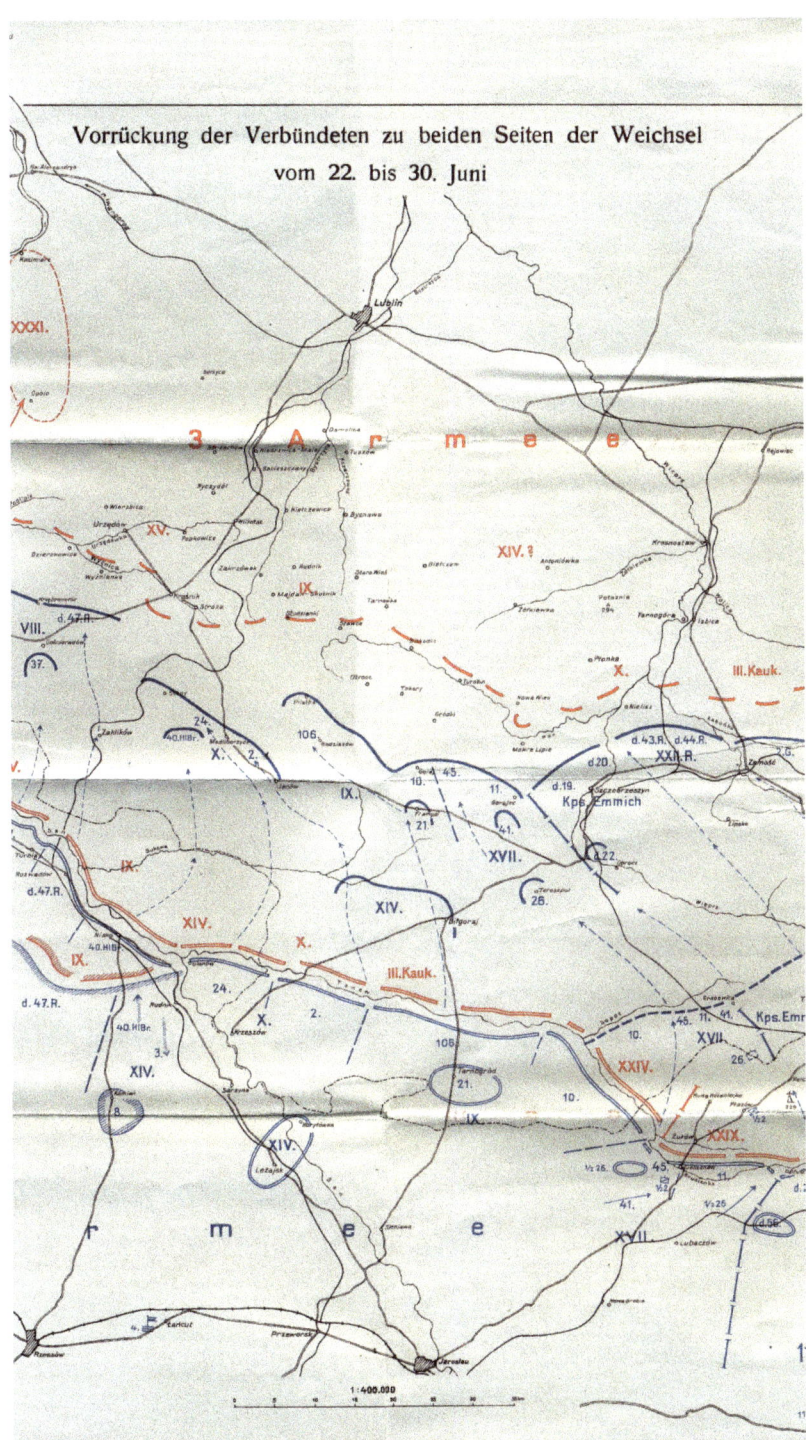

the Vistula from July 22 to 30

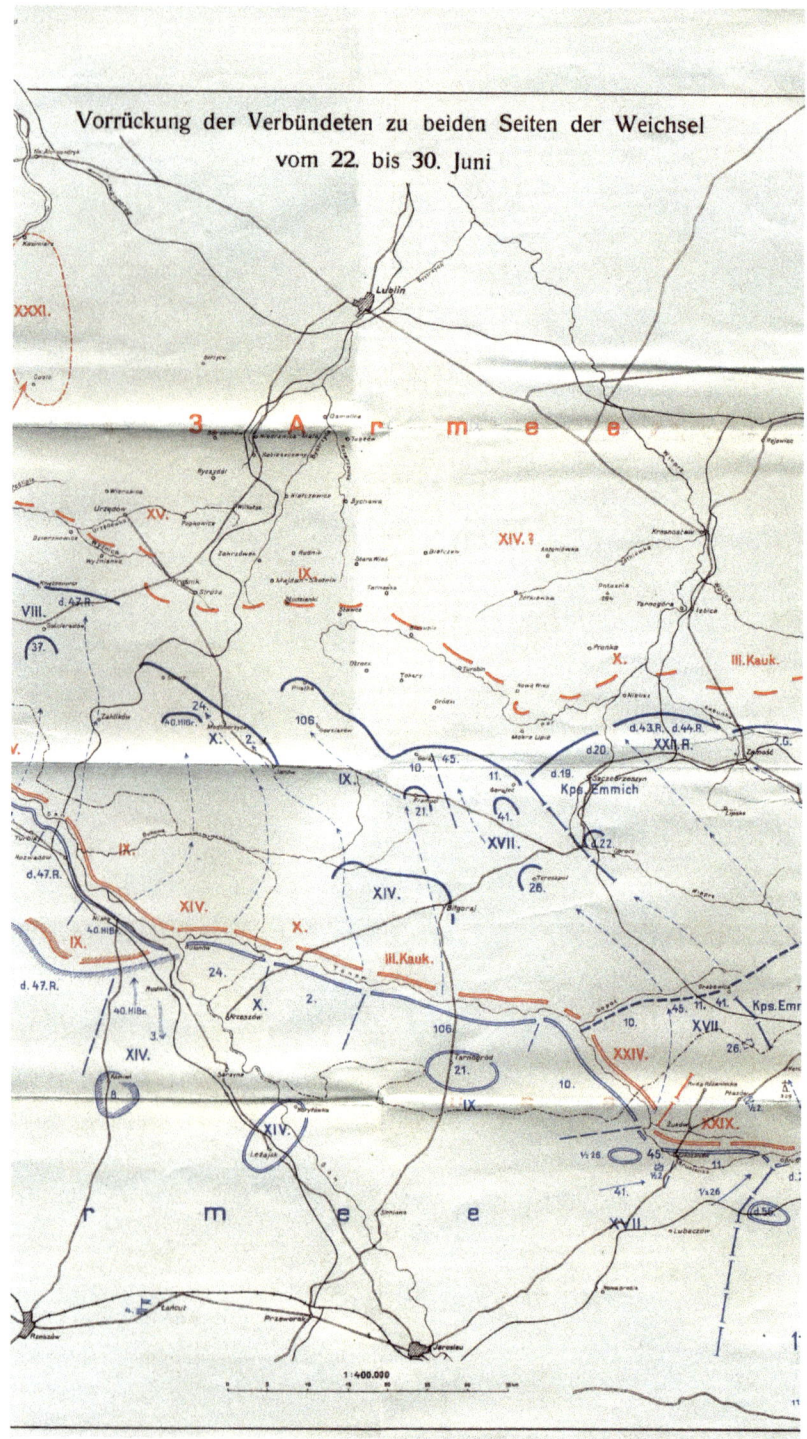

Allied advance on both sides of

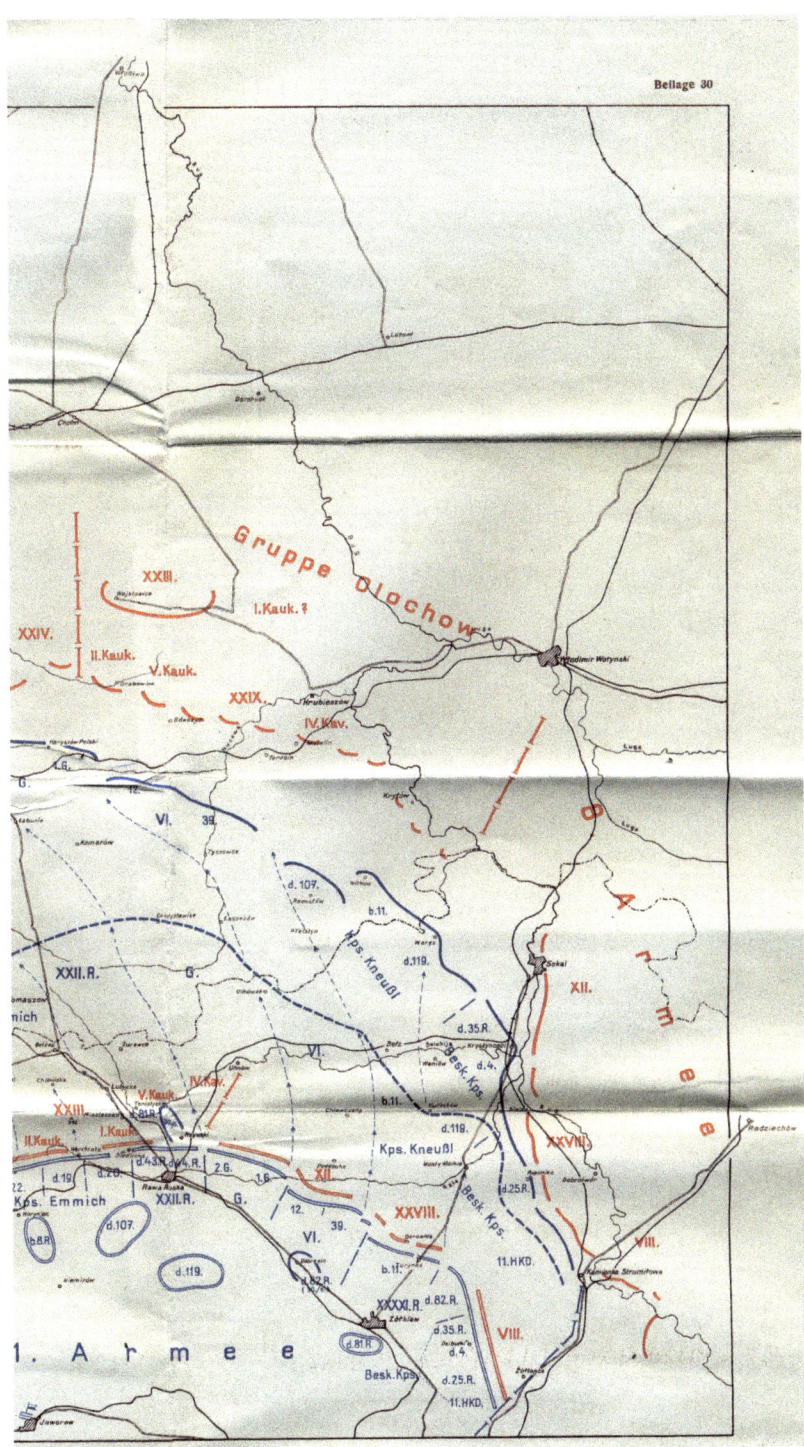

the Vistula from July 22 to 30

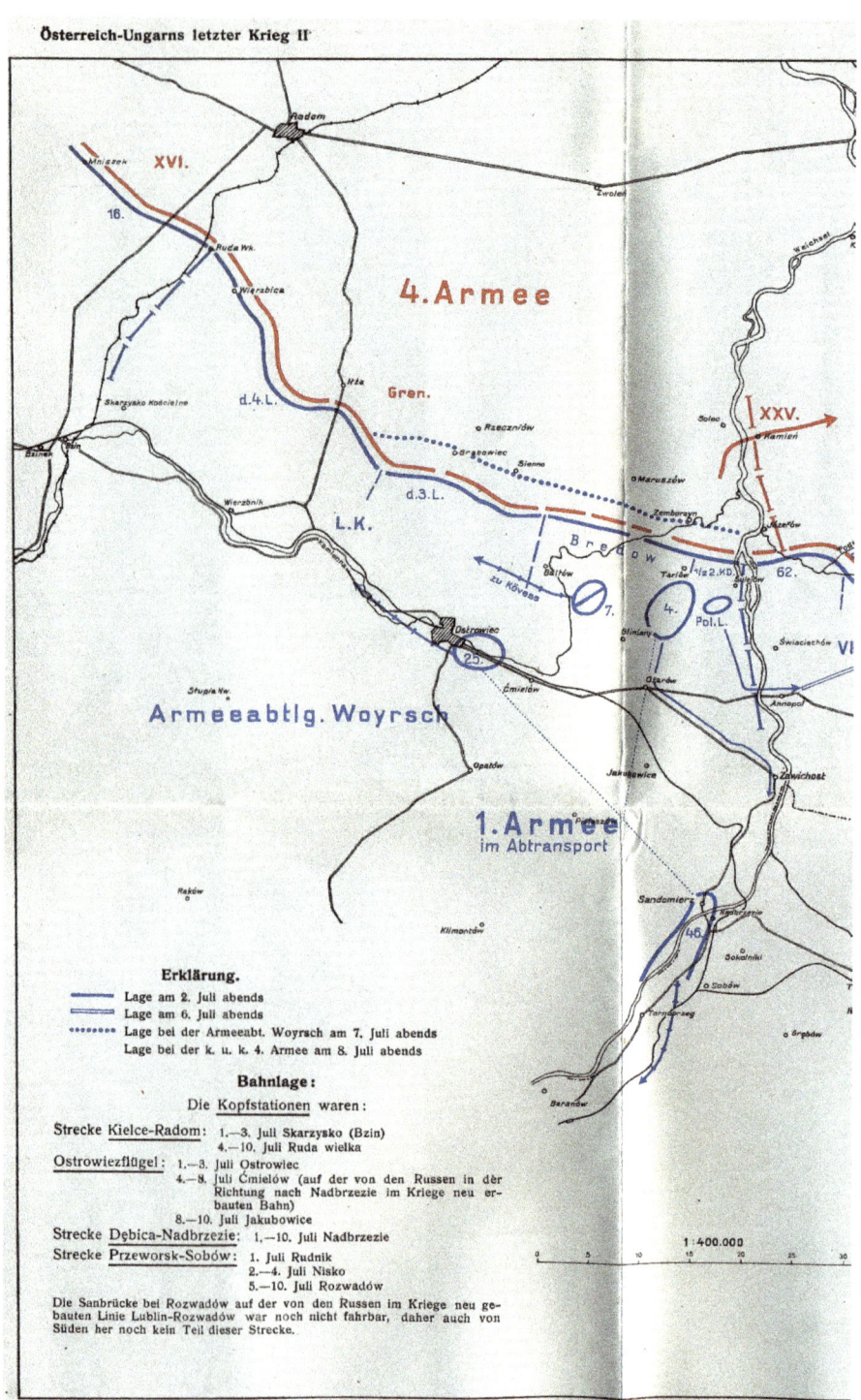

Österreich-Ungarns letzter Krieg II

Erklärung.

Lage am 2. Juli abends
Lage am 6. Juli abends
Lage bei der Armeeabt. Woyrsch am 7. Juli abends
Lage bei der k. u. k. 4. Armee am 8. Juli abends

Bahnlage:

Die Kopfstationen waren:

Strecke Kielce–Radom: 1.—3. Juli Skarzysko (Bzin)
4.—10. Juli Ruda wielka

Ostrowiezflügel: 1.—3. Juli Ostrowiec
4.—8. Juli Ćmielów (auf der von den Russen in der
Richtung nach Nadbrzezie im Kriege neu er-
bauten Bahn)
8.—10. Juli Jakubowice

Strecke Dębica–Nadbrzezie: 1.—10. Juli Nadbrzezie

Strecke Przeworsk–Sobów: 1. Juli Rudnik
2.—4. Juli Nisko
5.—10. Juli Rozwadów

Die Sanbrücke bei Rozwadów auf der von den Russen im Kriege neu ge-
bauten Linie Lublin–Rozwadów war noch nicht fahrbar, daher auch von
Süden her noch kein Teil dieser Strecke.

1 : 400.000

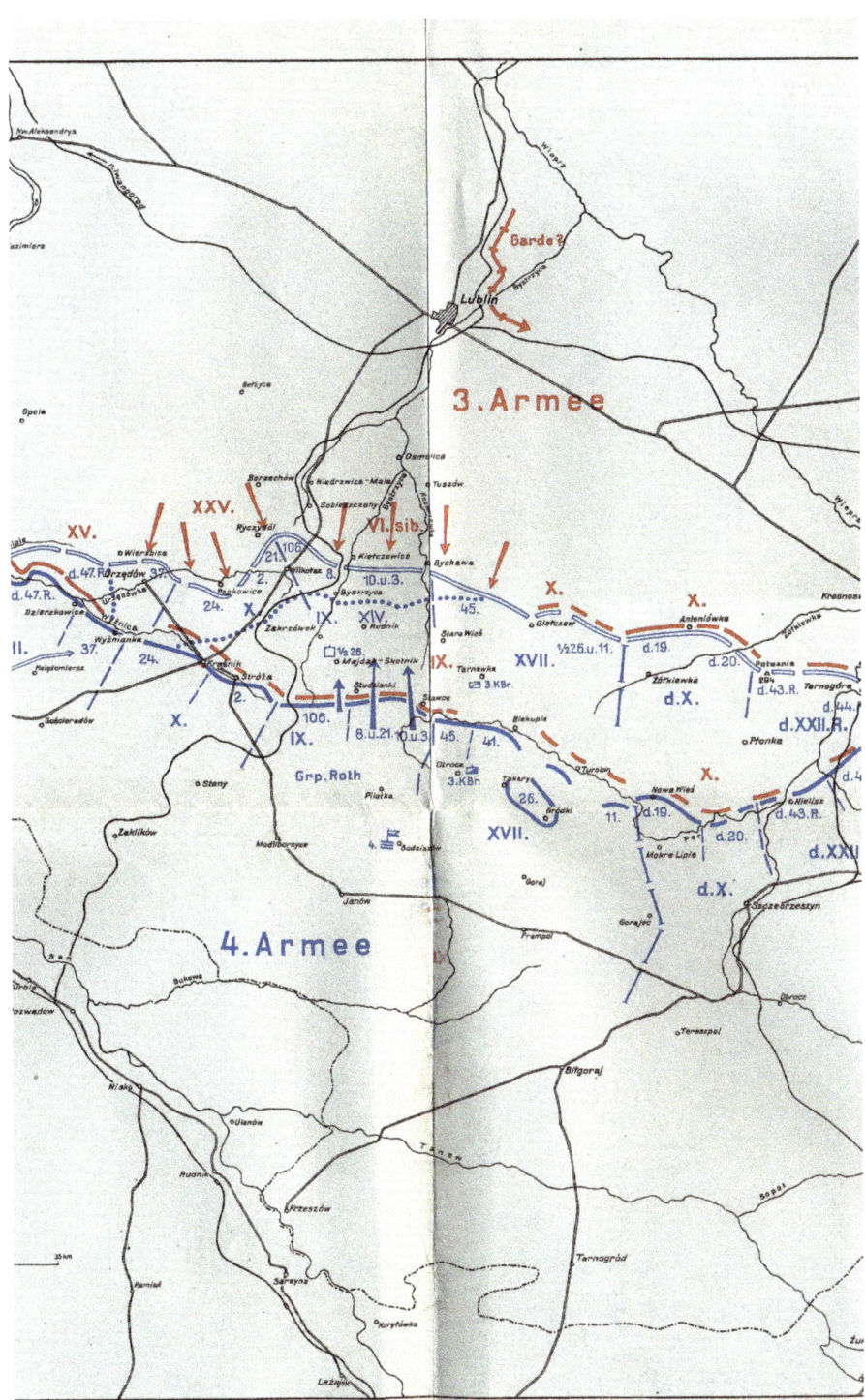

Krasnik (July 1-10)

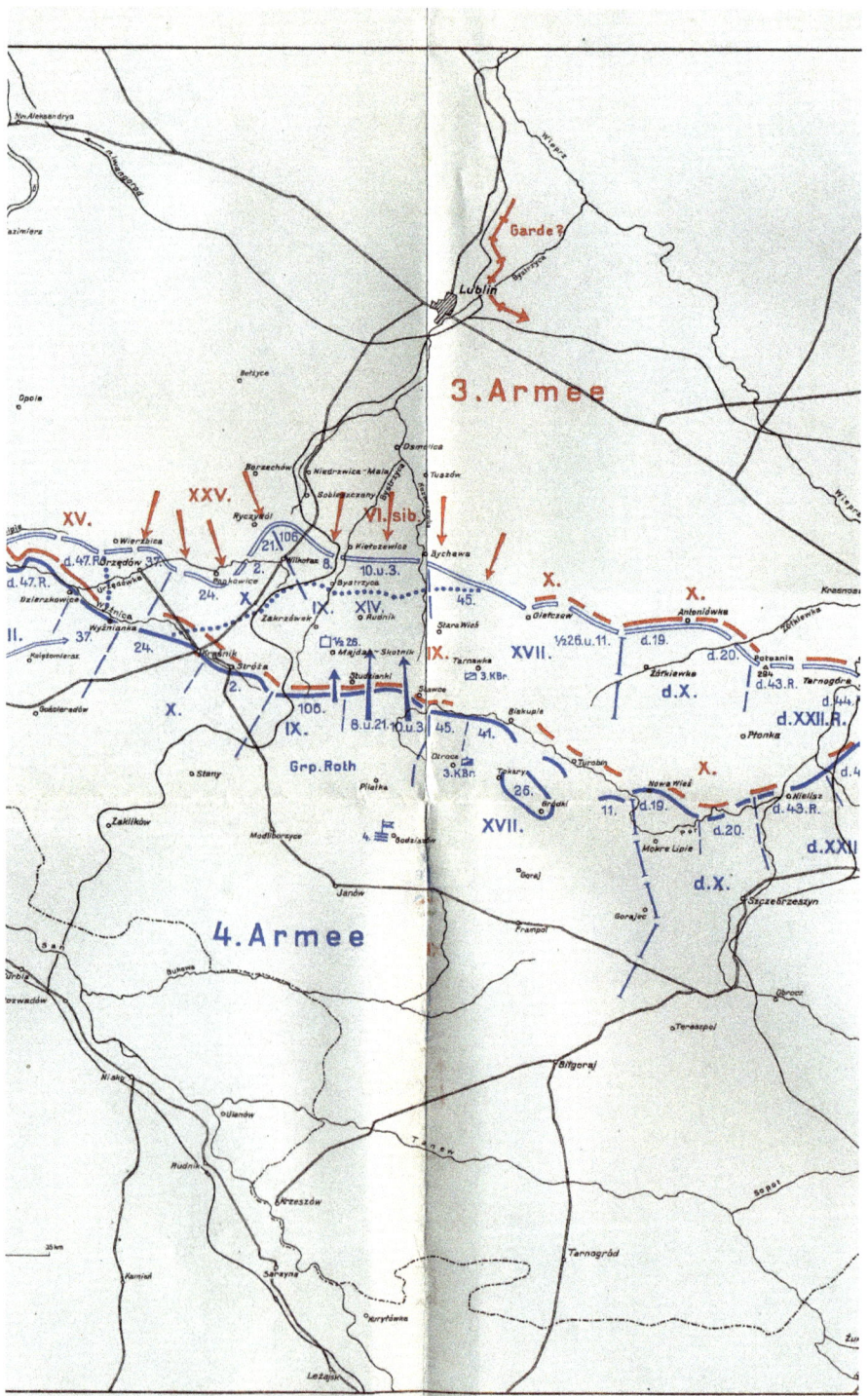

The Second Battle of

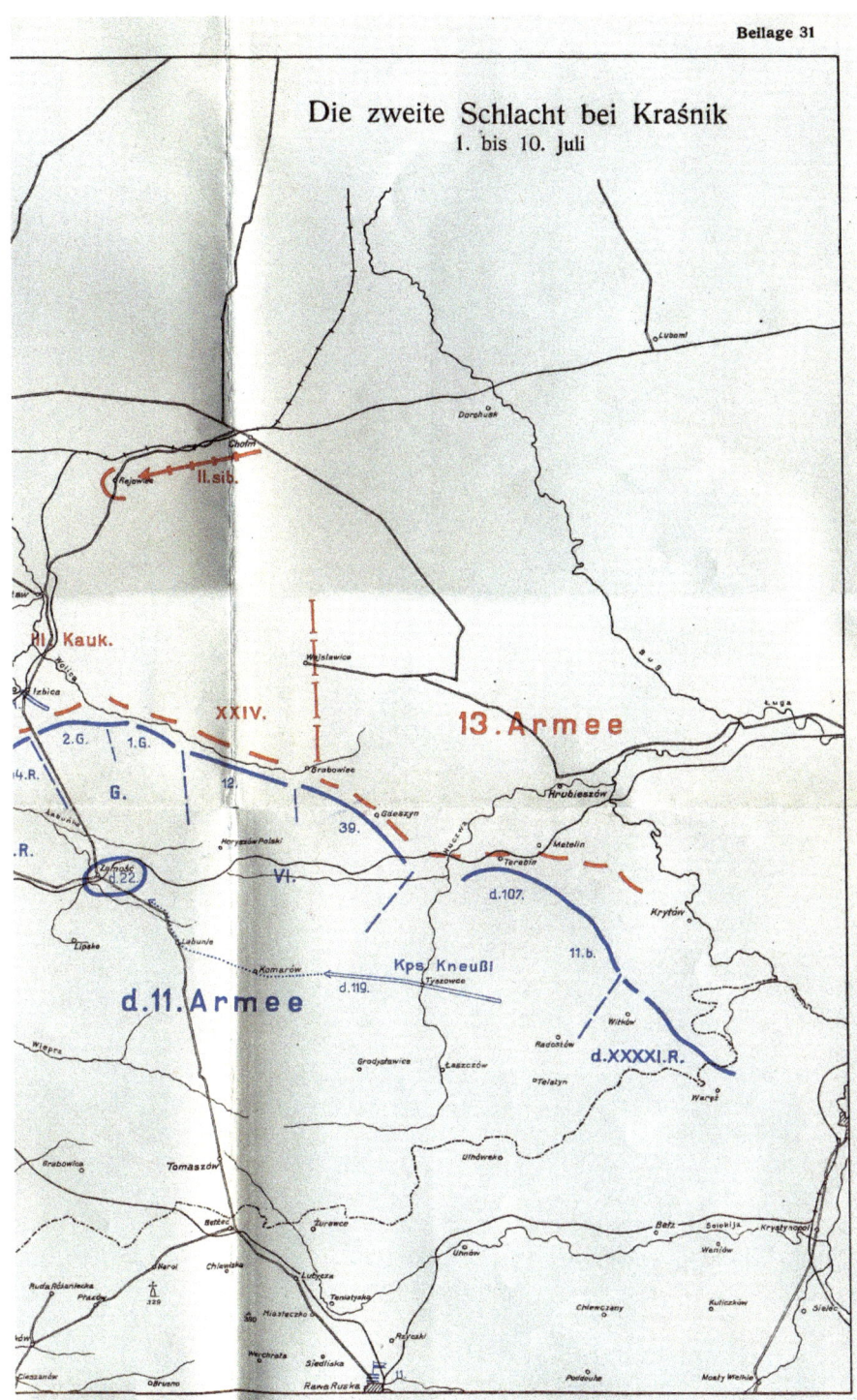

Krasnik (July 1-10)

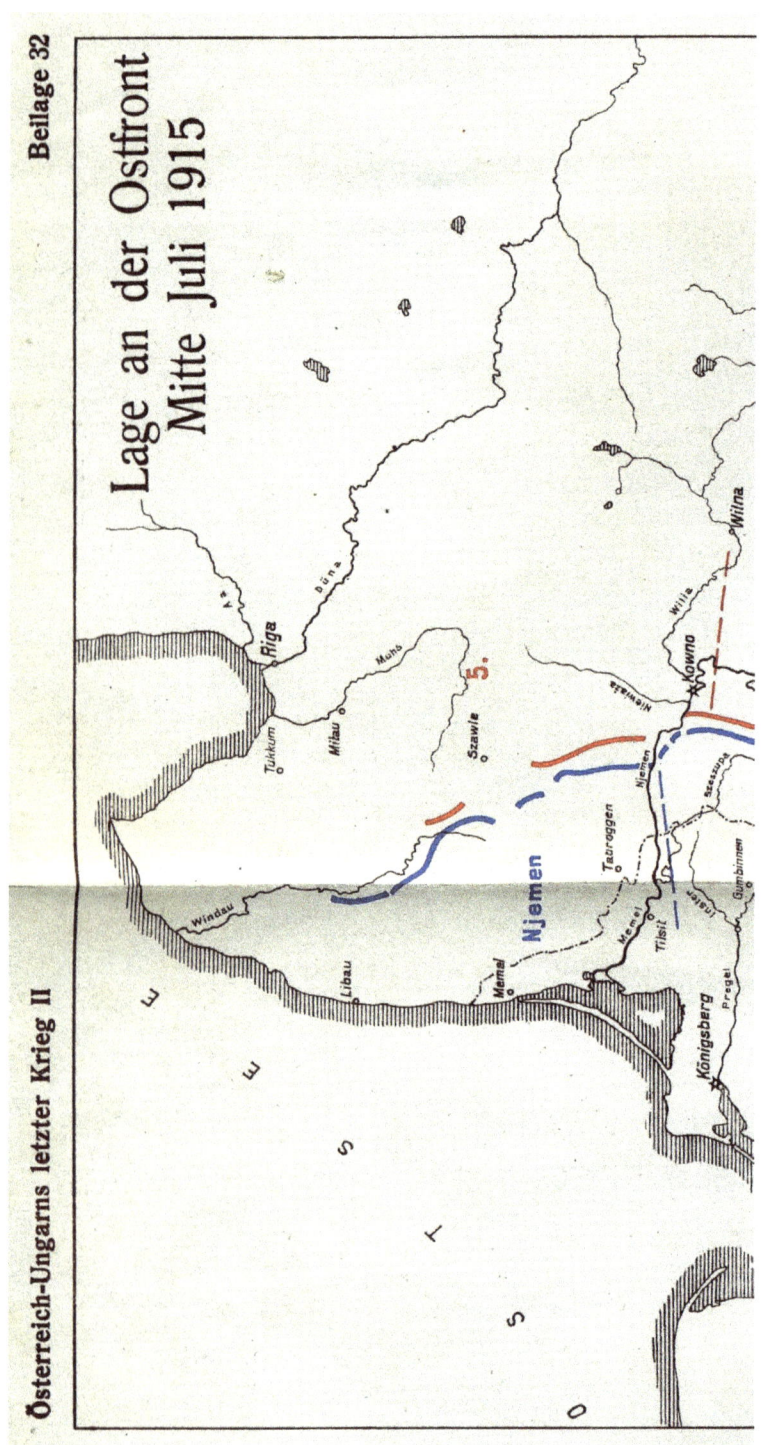

Situation in the Russian theater

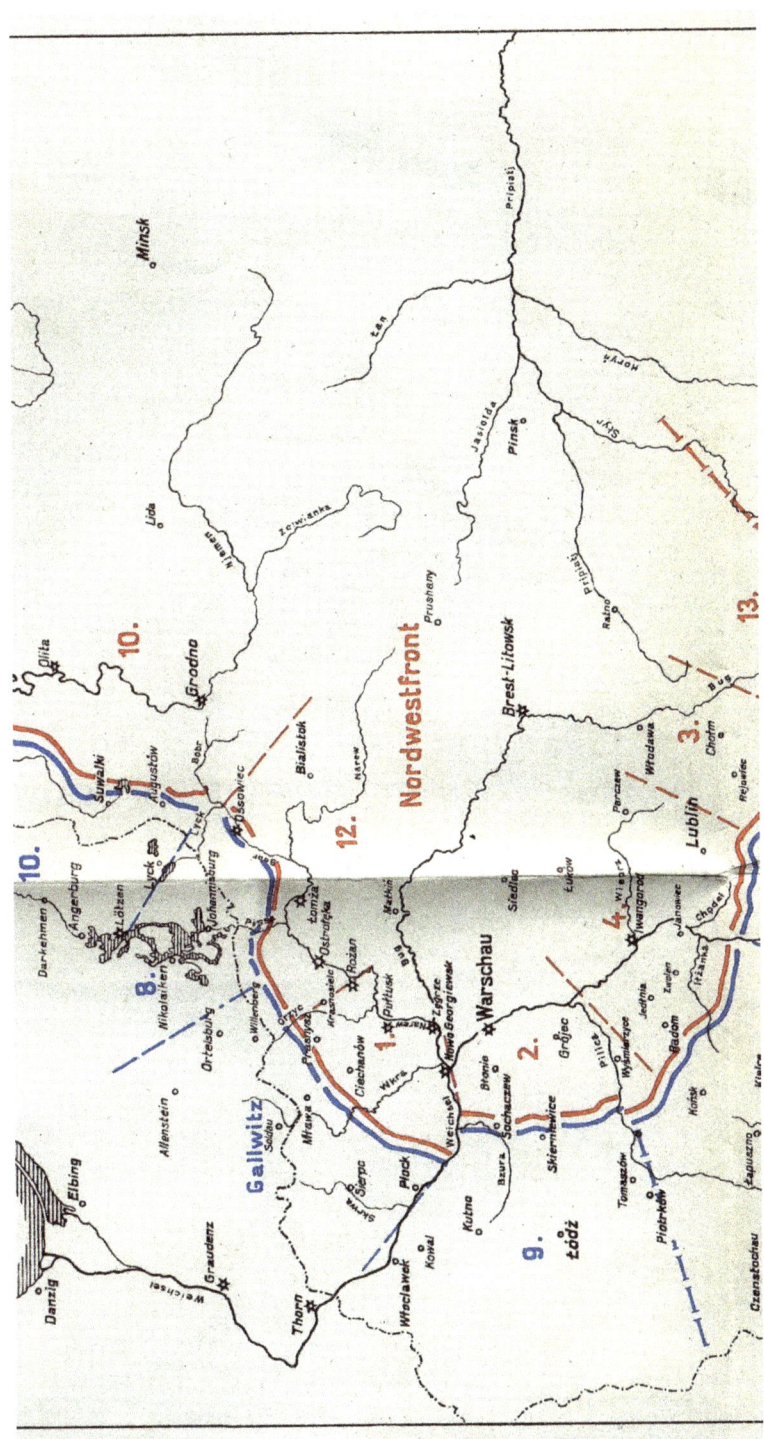

of war on July 5, 1915

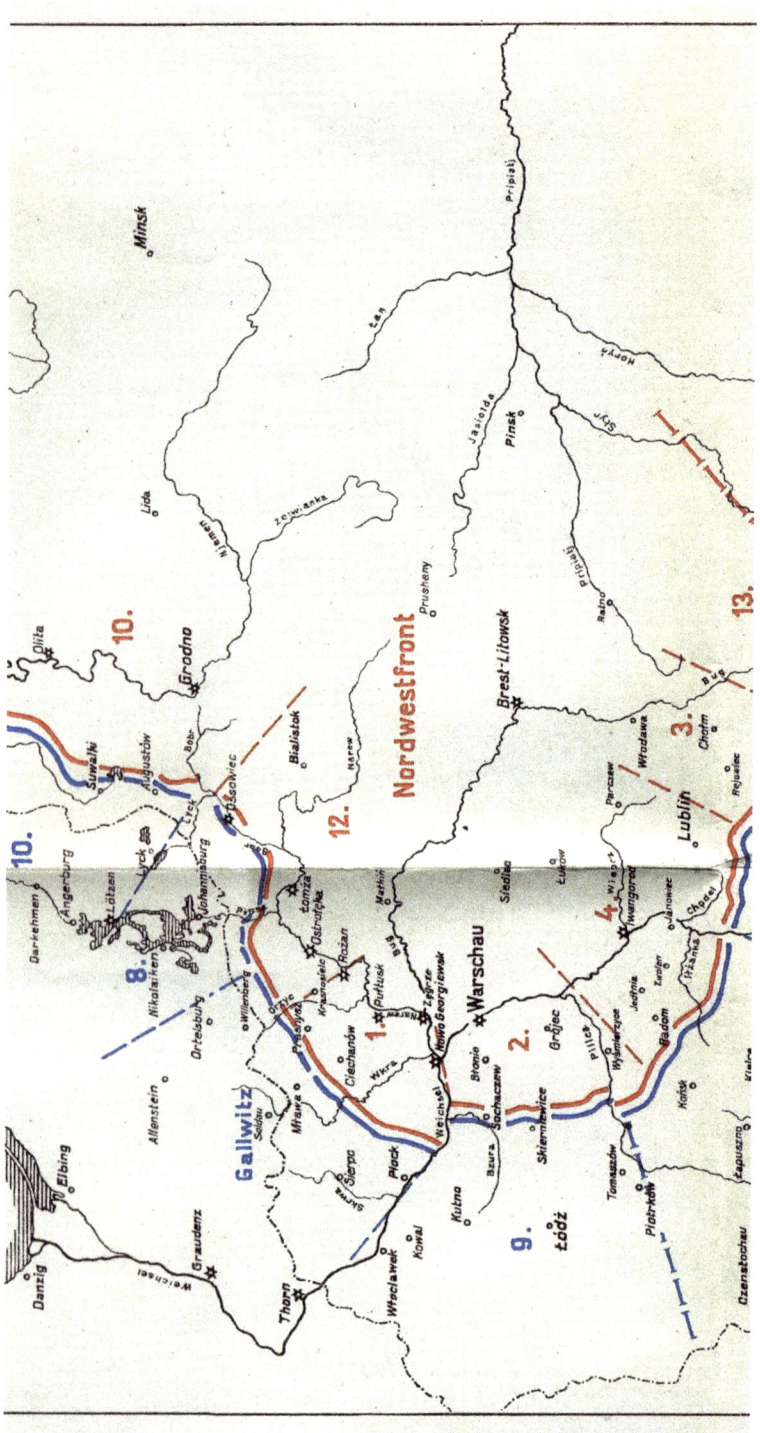

Situation in the Russian theater

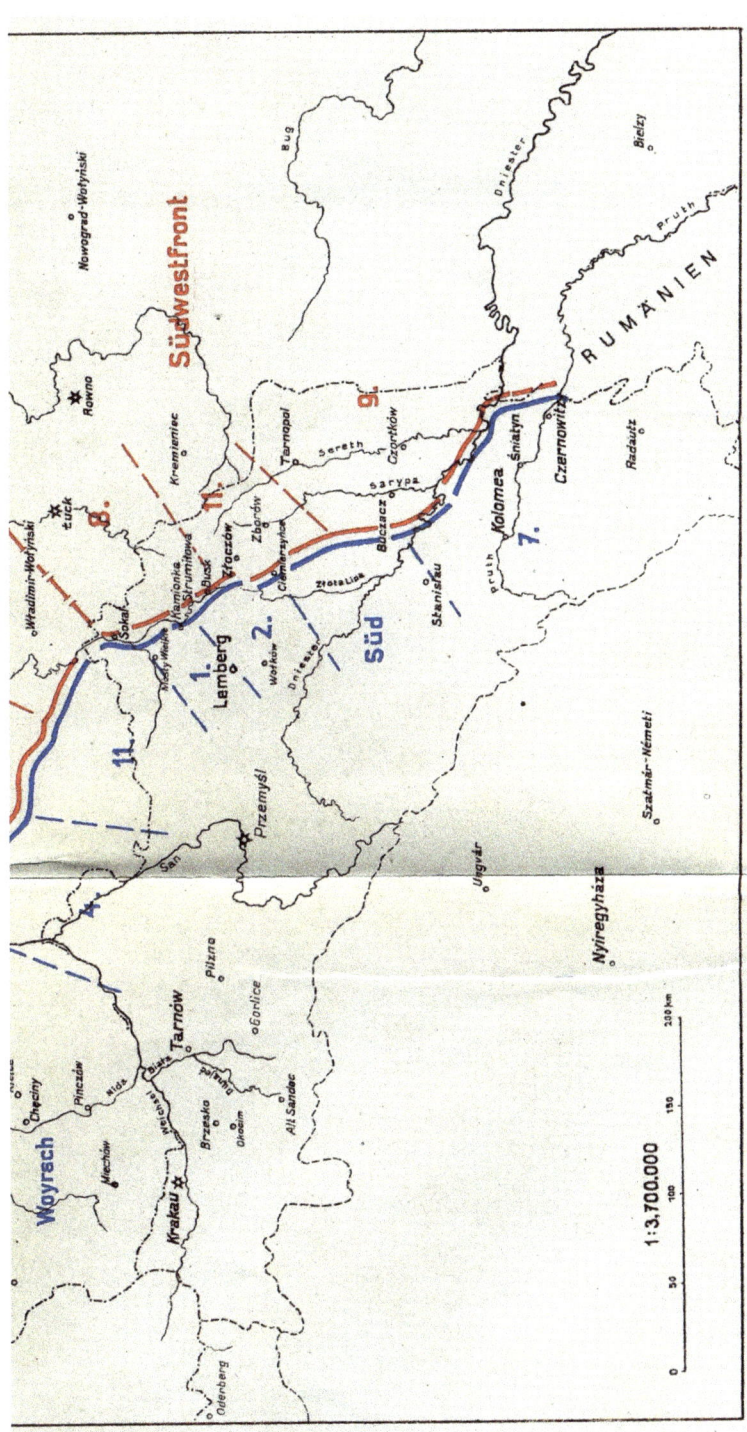

of war on July 5, 1915

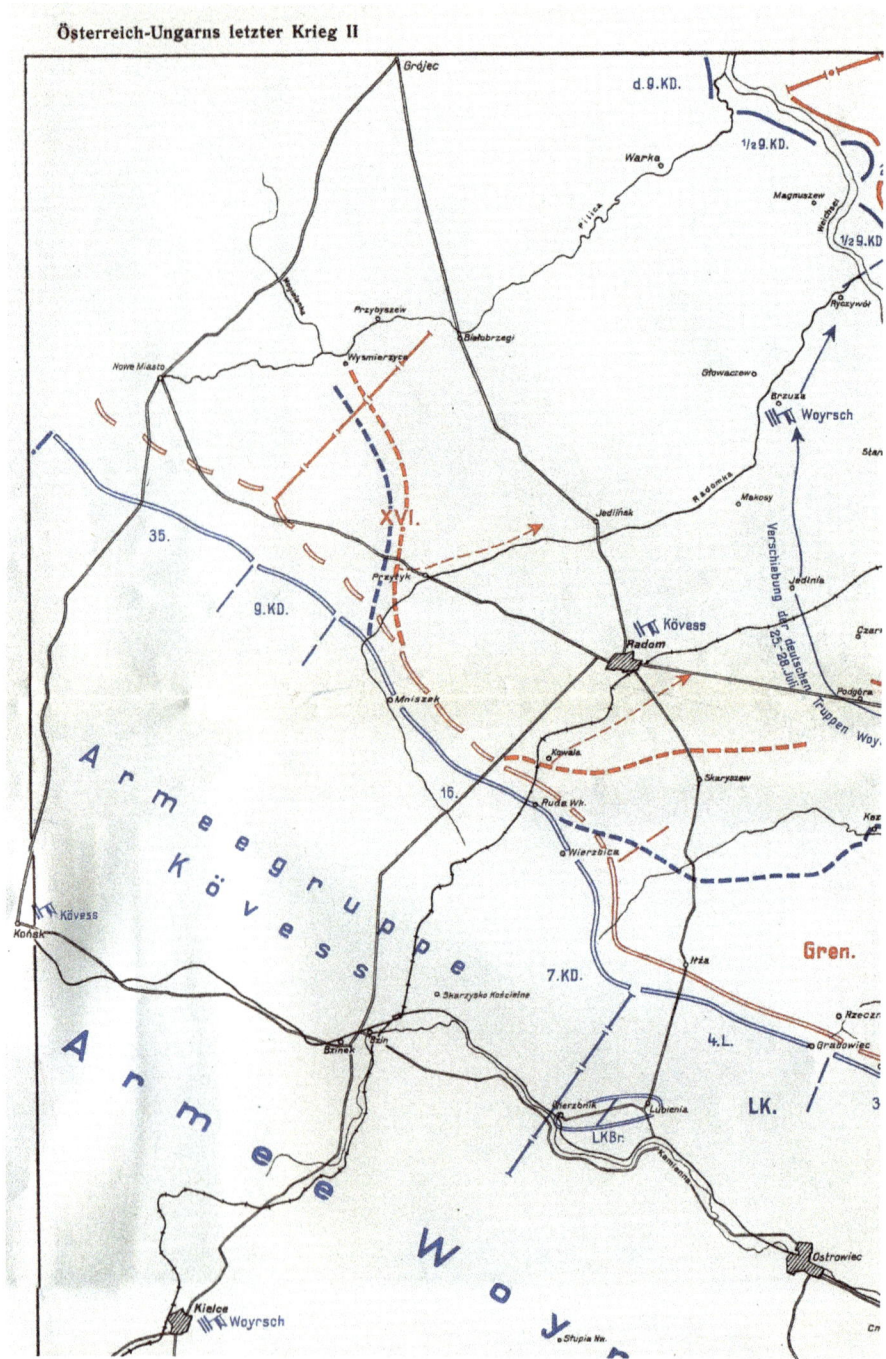

The Events on Both Sides of the Vistula, July 15-31.

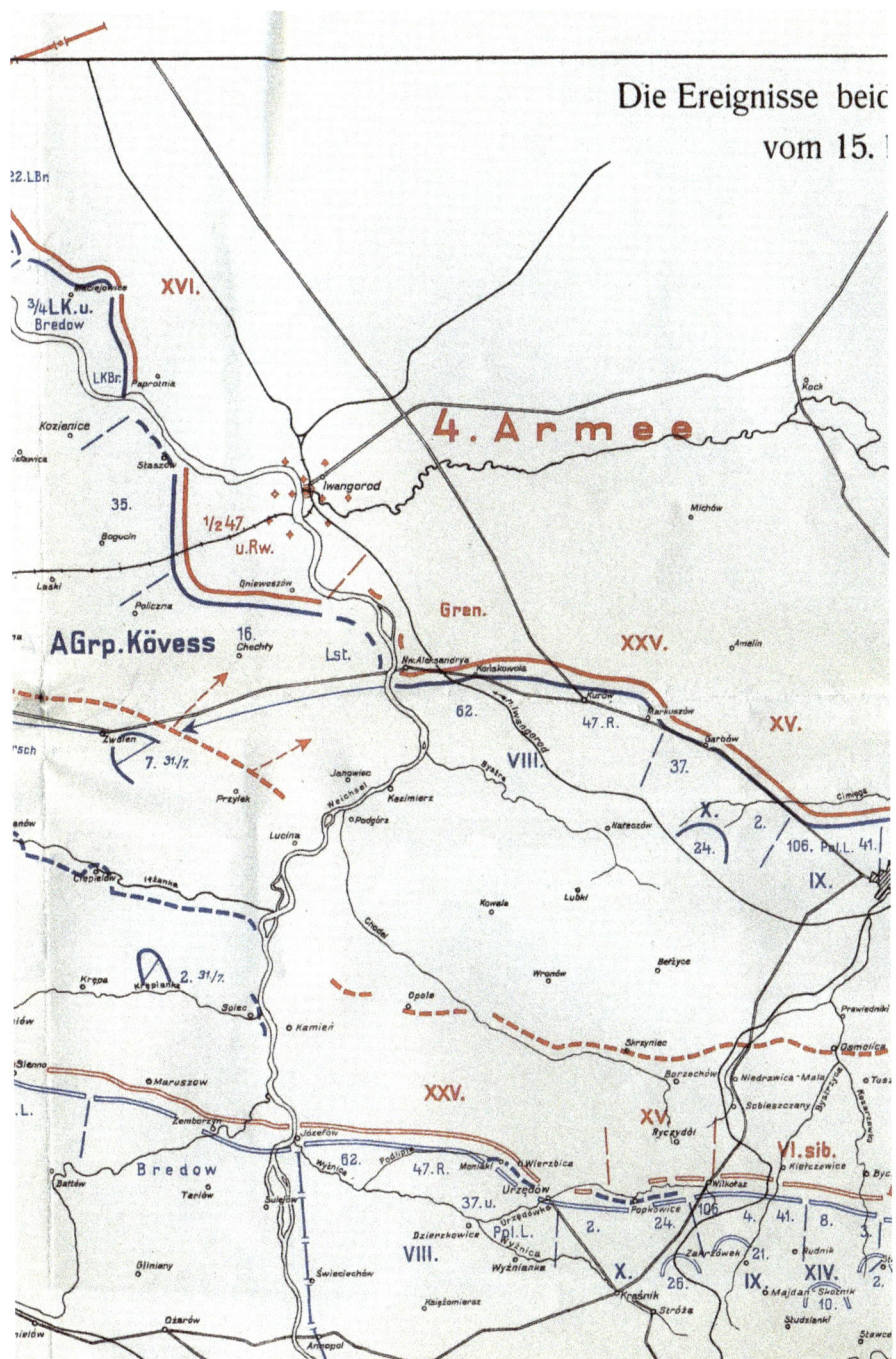

Inset: The Capture of Ivangorod (August 1-4).

The Events on Both Sides of the Vistula, July 15-31.

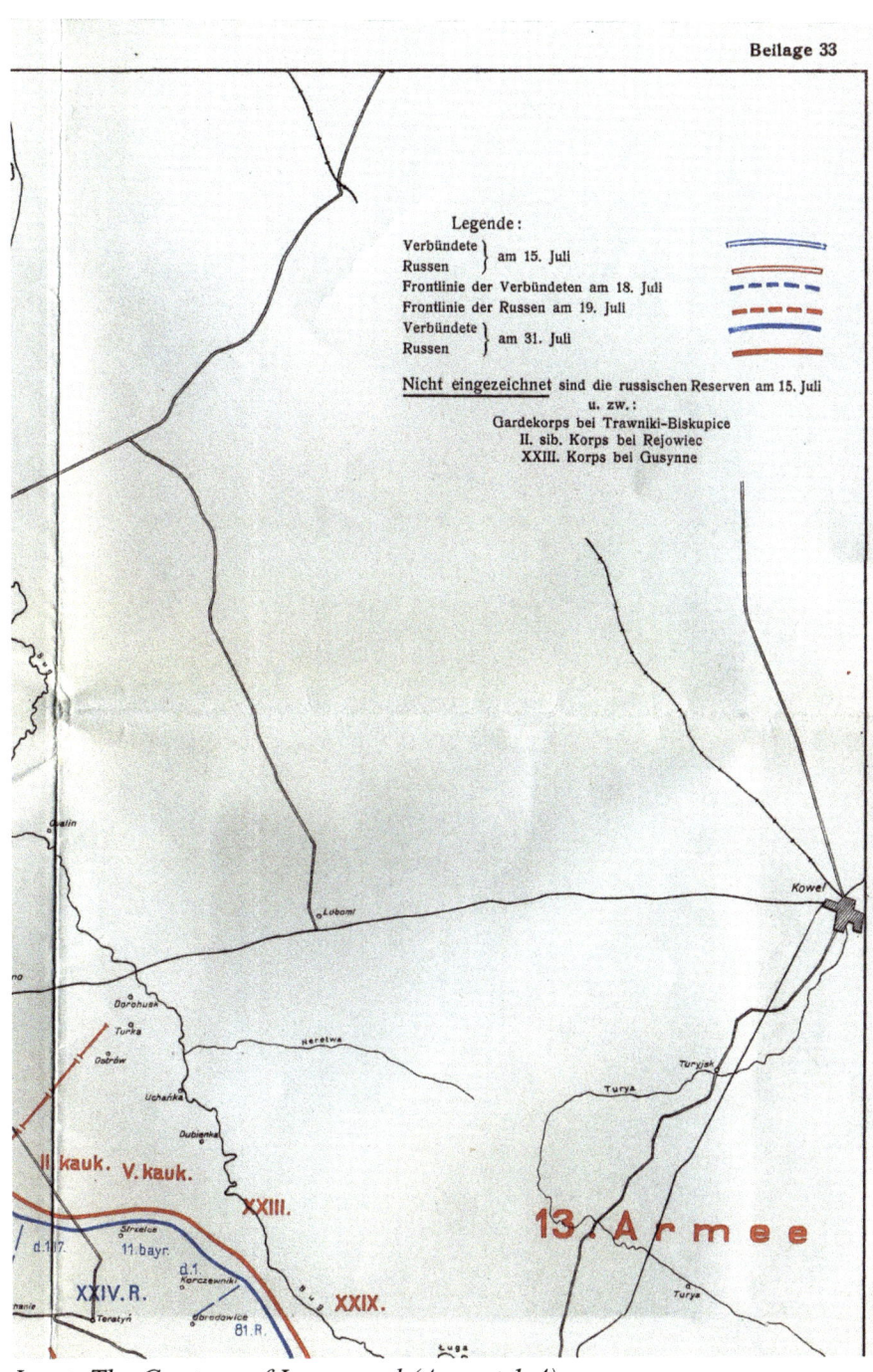

Legende:

Verbündete } am 15. Juli
Russen

Frontlinie der Verbündeten am 18. Juli
Frontlinie der Russen am 19. Juli

Verbündete } am 31. Juli
Russen

<u>Nicht eingezeichnet</u> sind die russischen Reserven am 15. Juli
u. zw.:
Gardekorps bei Trawniki-Biskupice
II. sib. Korps bei Rejowiec
XXIII. Korps bei Gusynne

Inset: The Capture of Ivangorod (August 1-4).

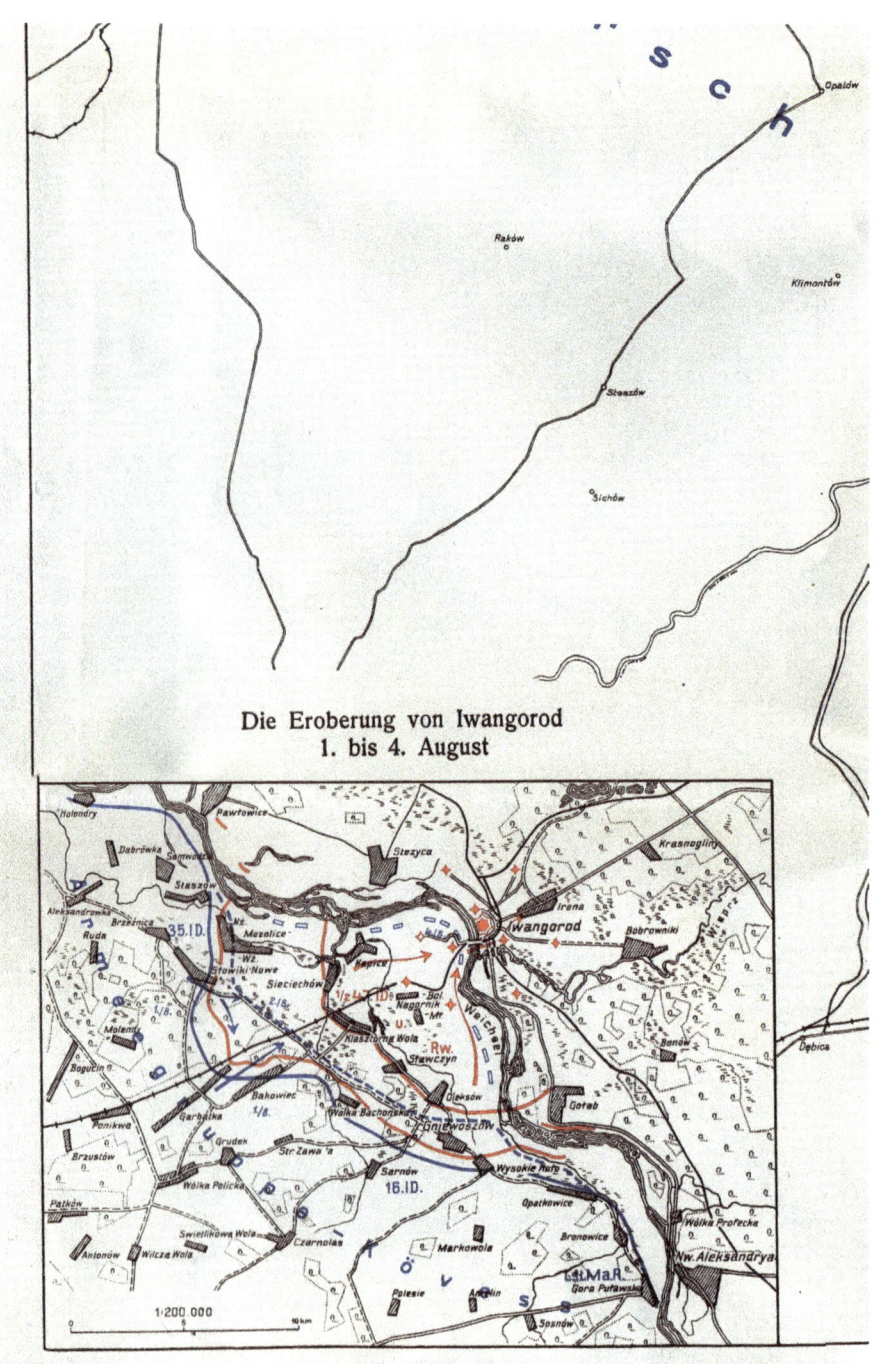

Die Eroberung von Iwangorod
1. bis 4. August

The Events on Both Sides of the Vistula, July 15-31.

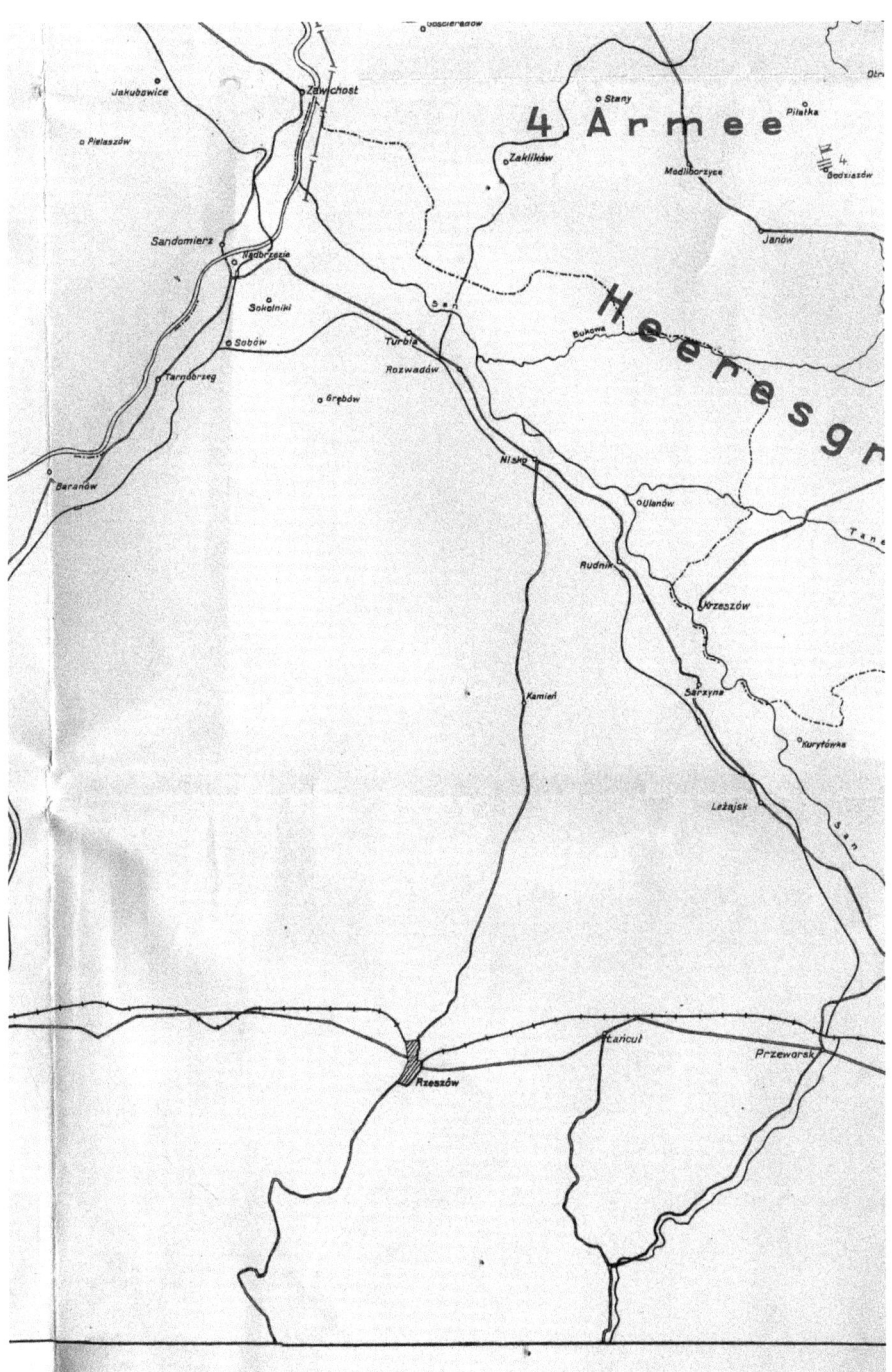

Inset: The Capture of Ivangorod (August 1-4).

The Events on Both Sides of the Vistula, July 15-31.

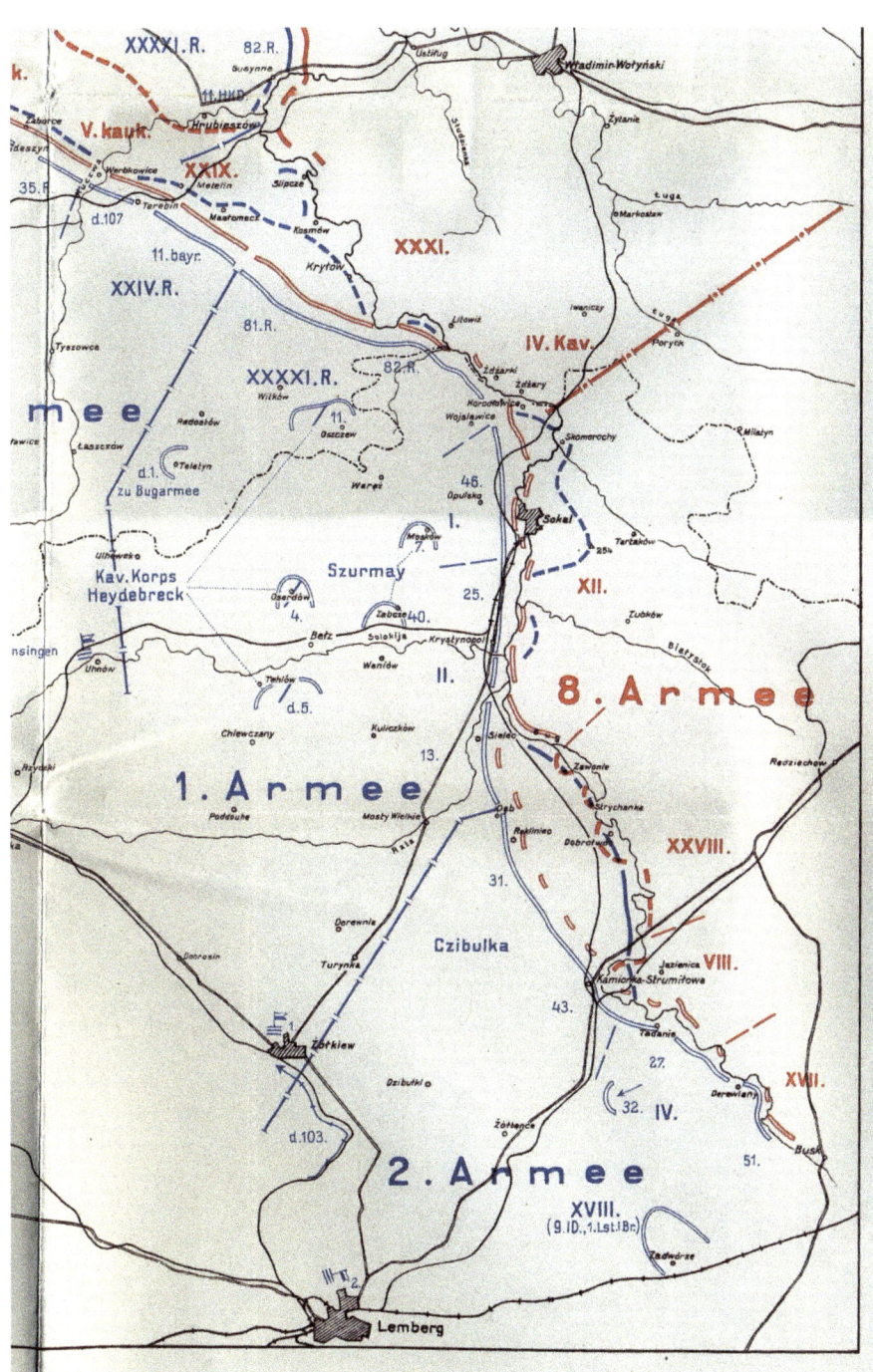

Inset: The Capture of Ivangorod (August 1-4).

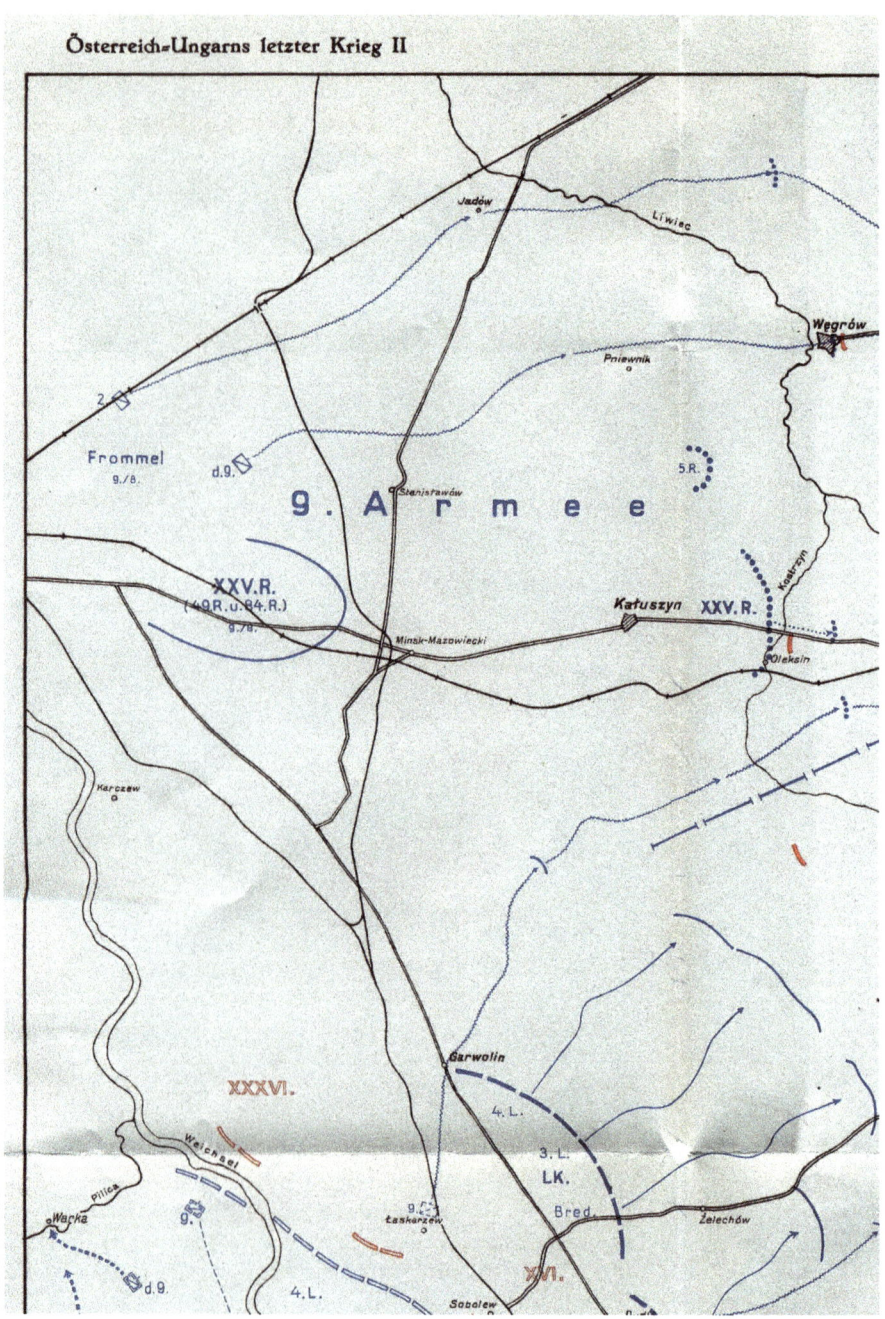

The events of August 6-17 (between

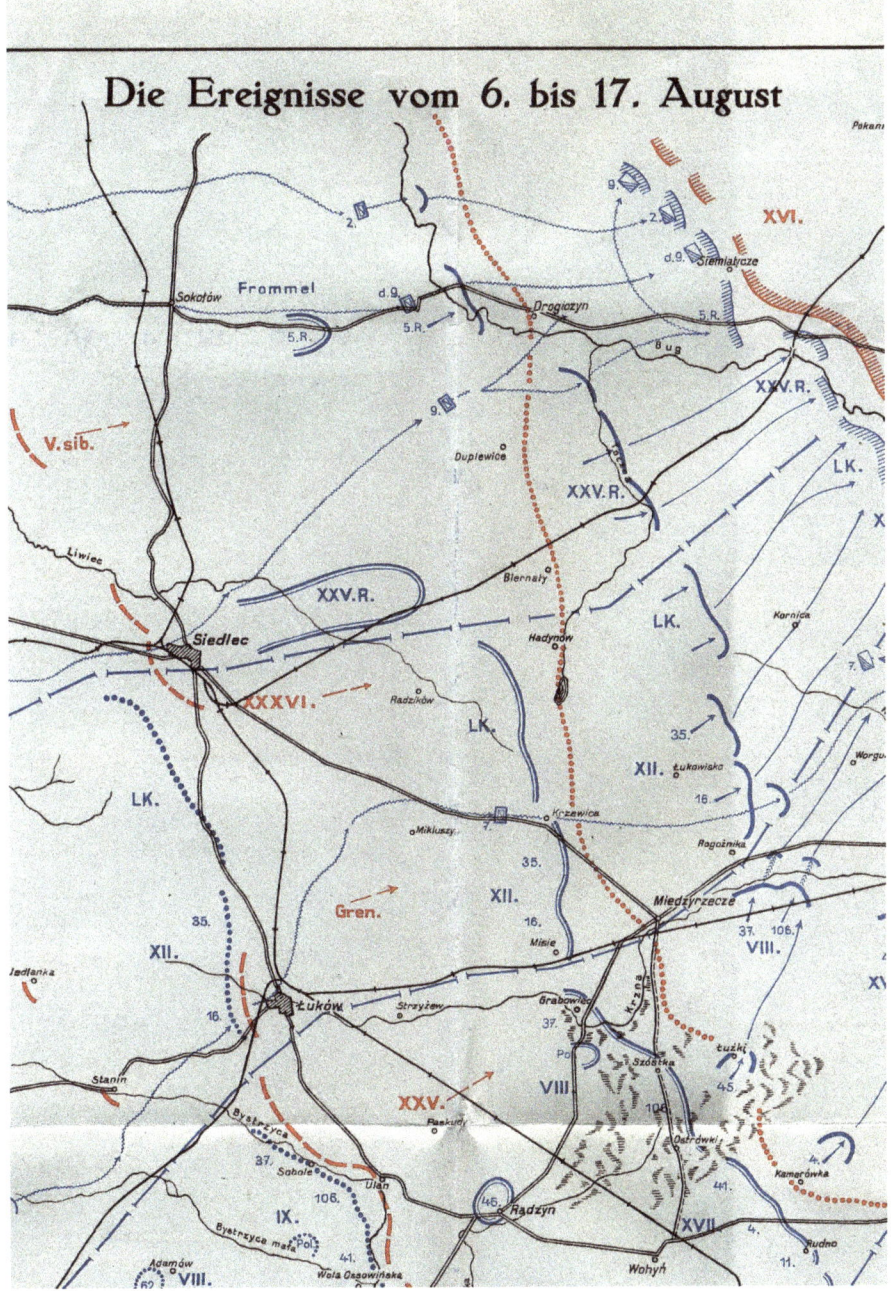

the Vistula and the Bug)

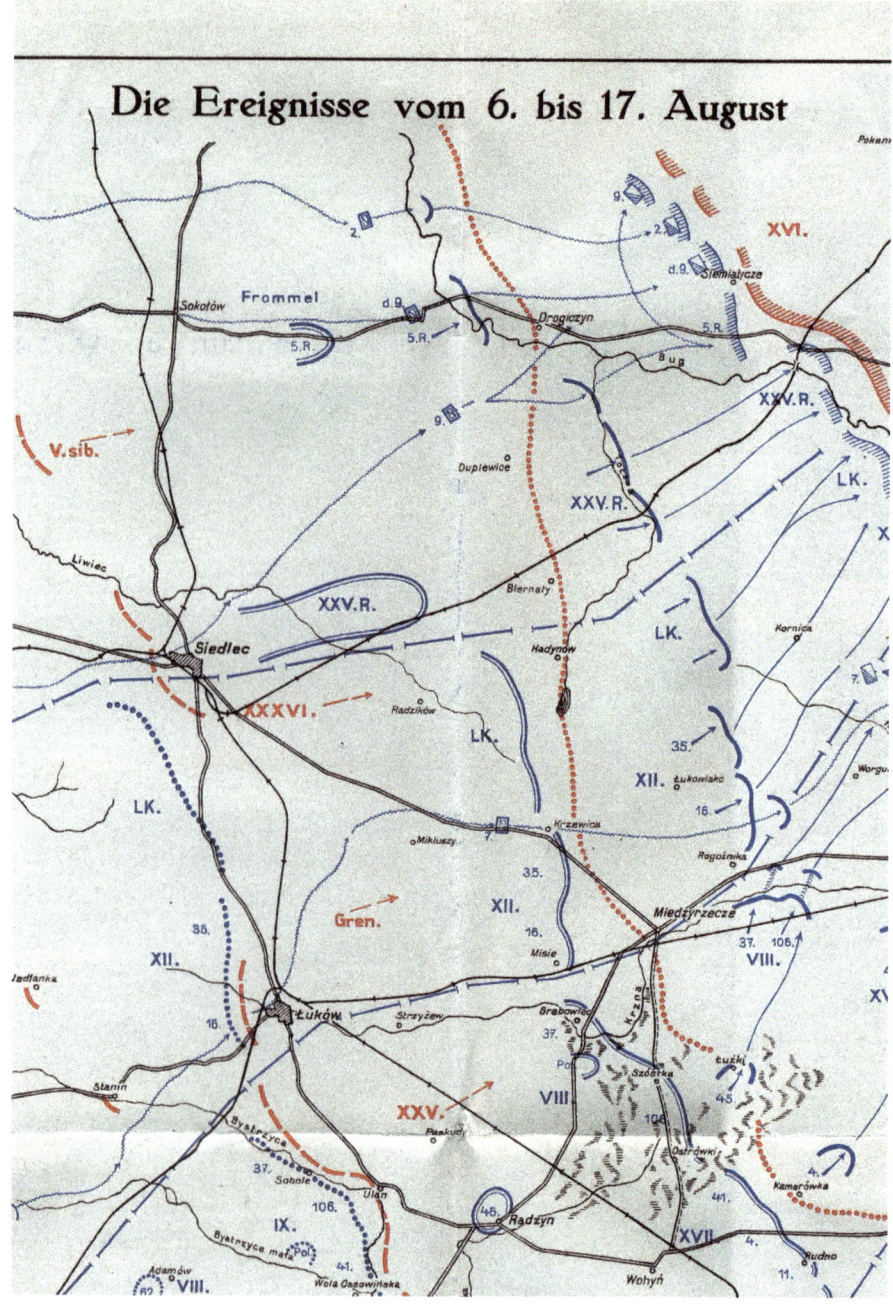

The events of August 6-17 (between

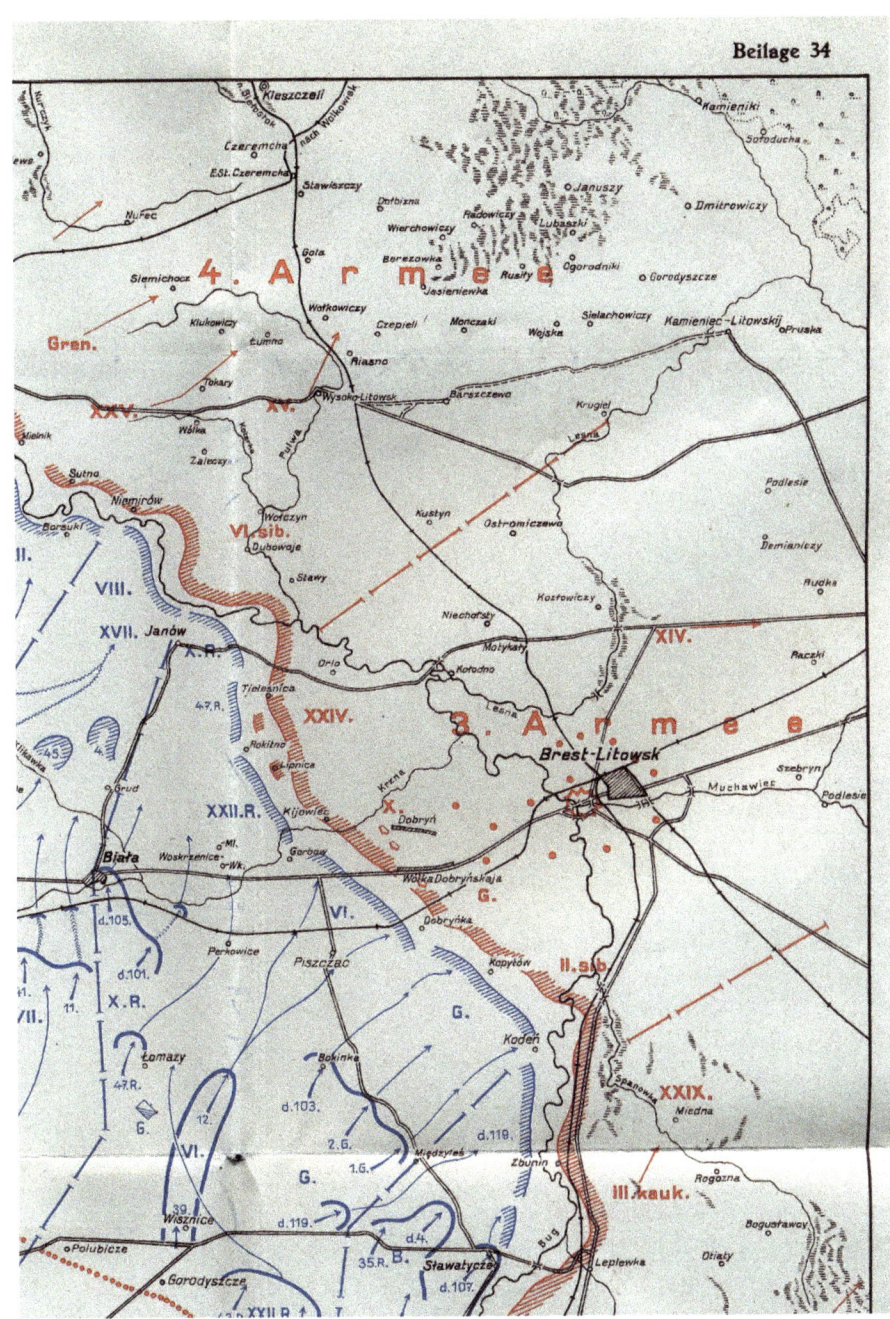

the Vistula and the Bug)

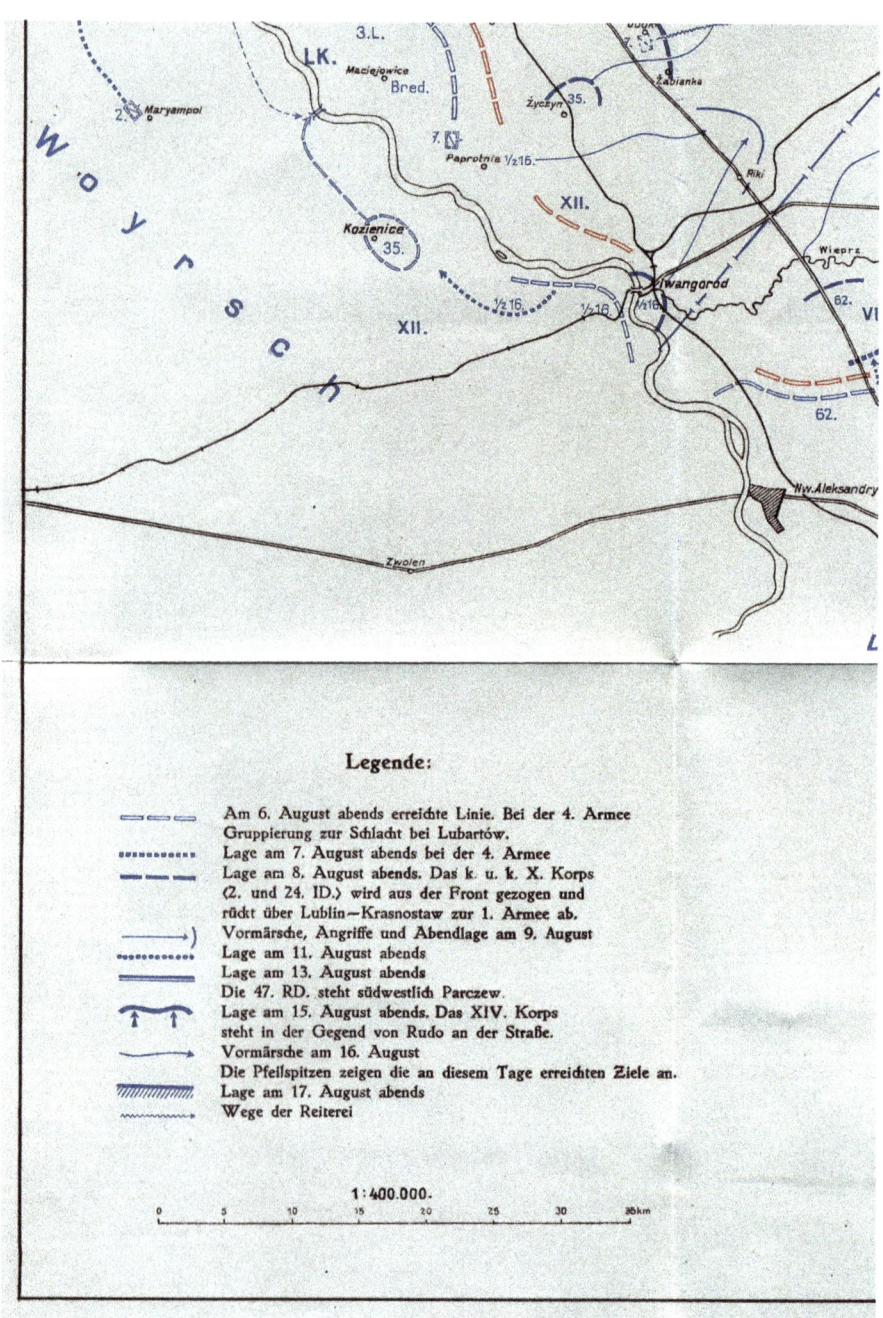

The events of August 6-17 (between

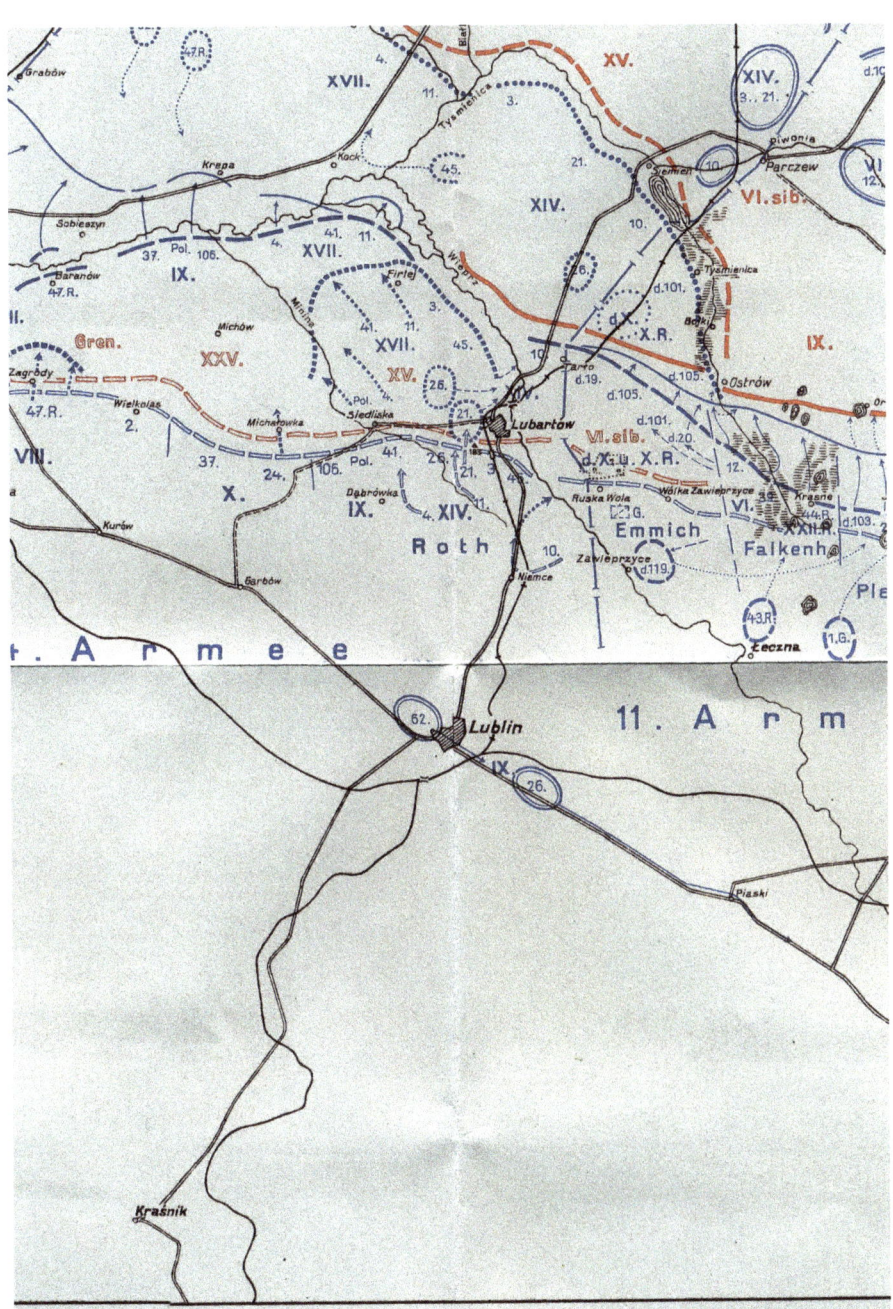

the Vistula and the Bug)

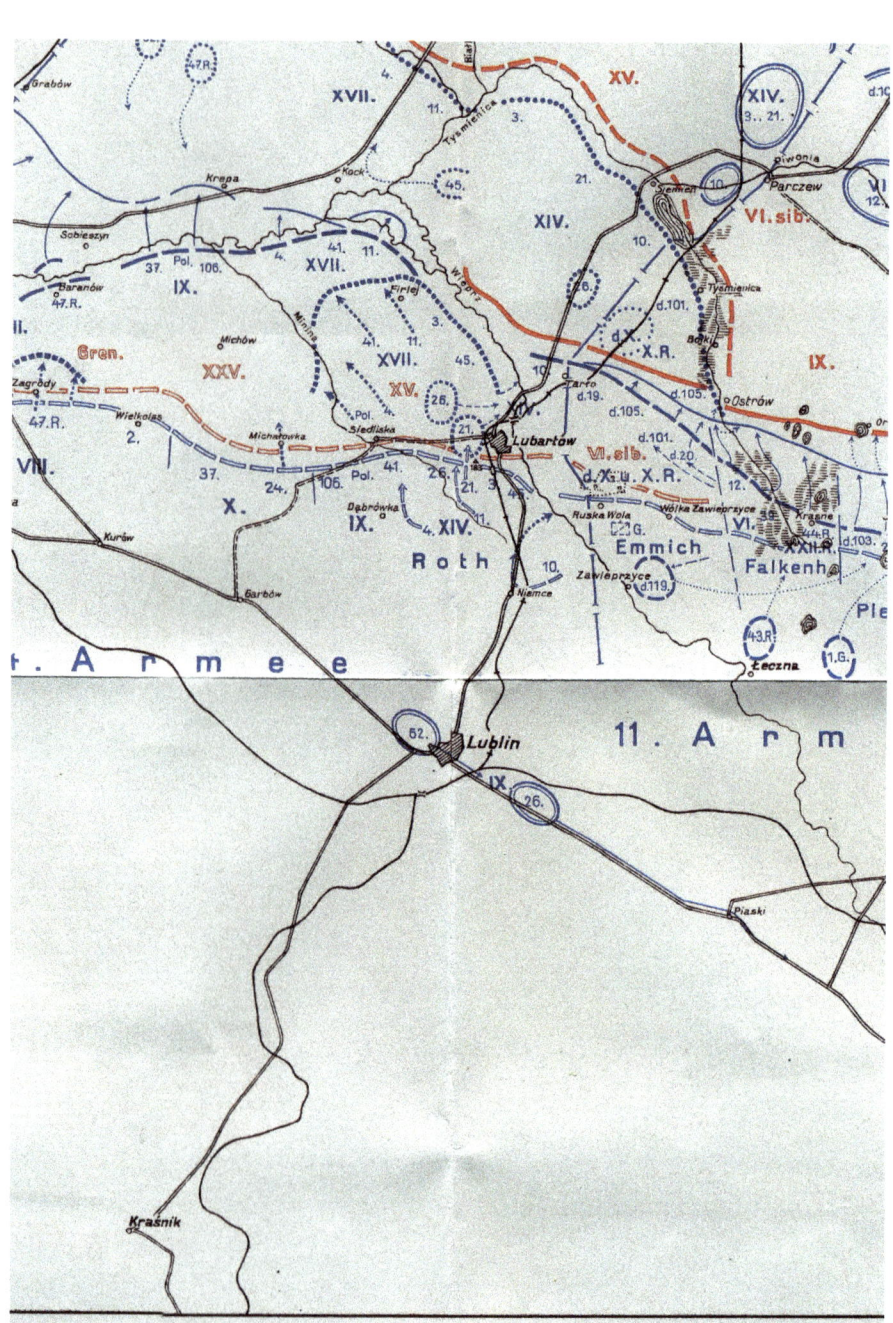

The events of August 6-17 (between

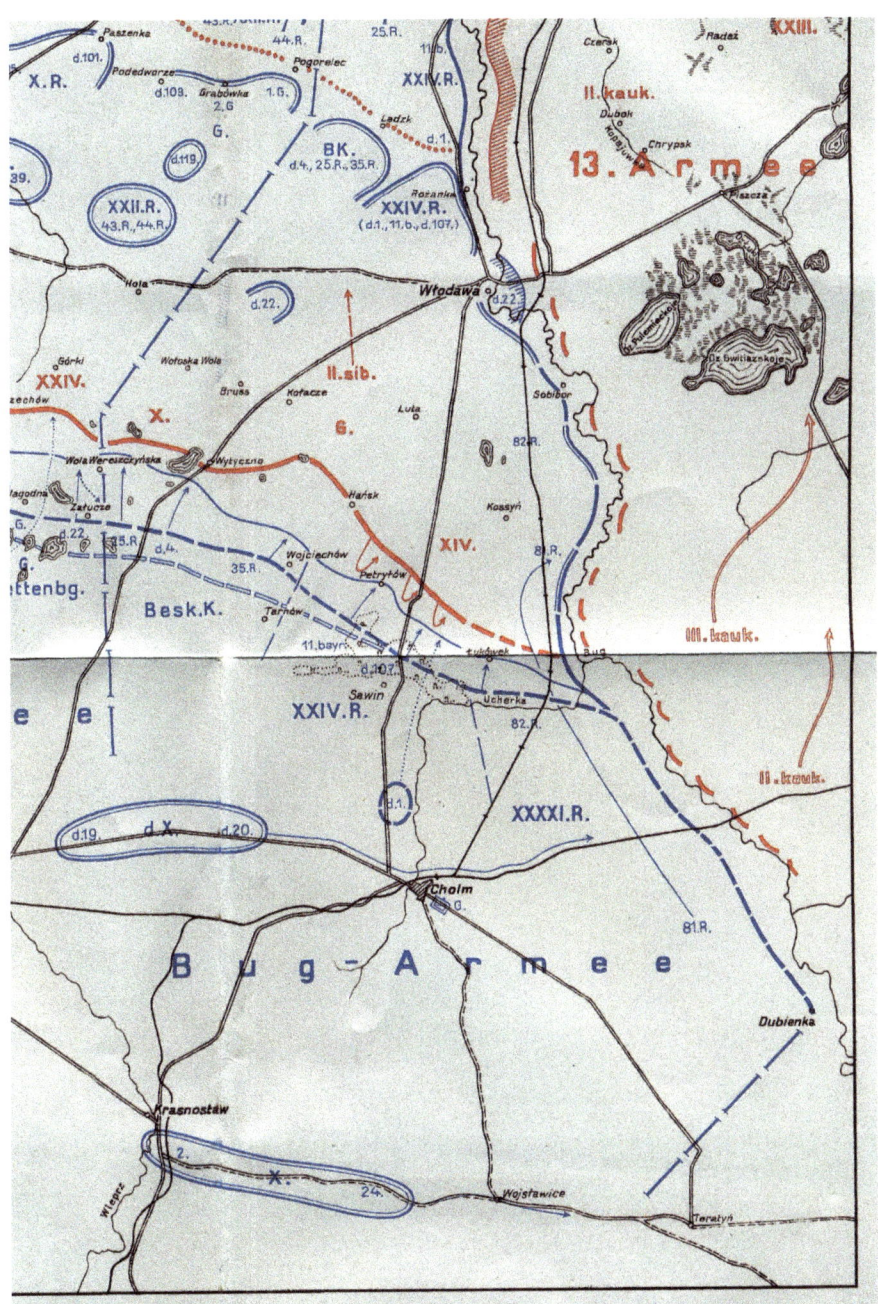

the Vistula and the Bug)

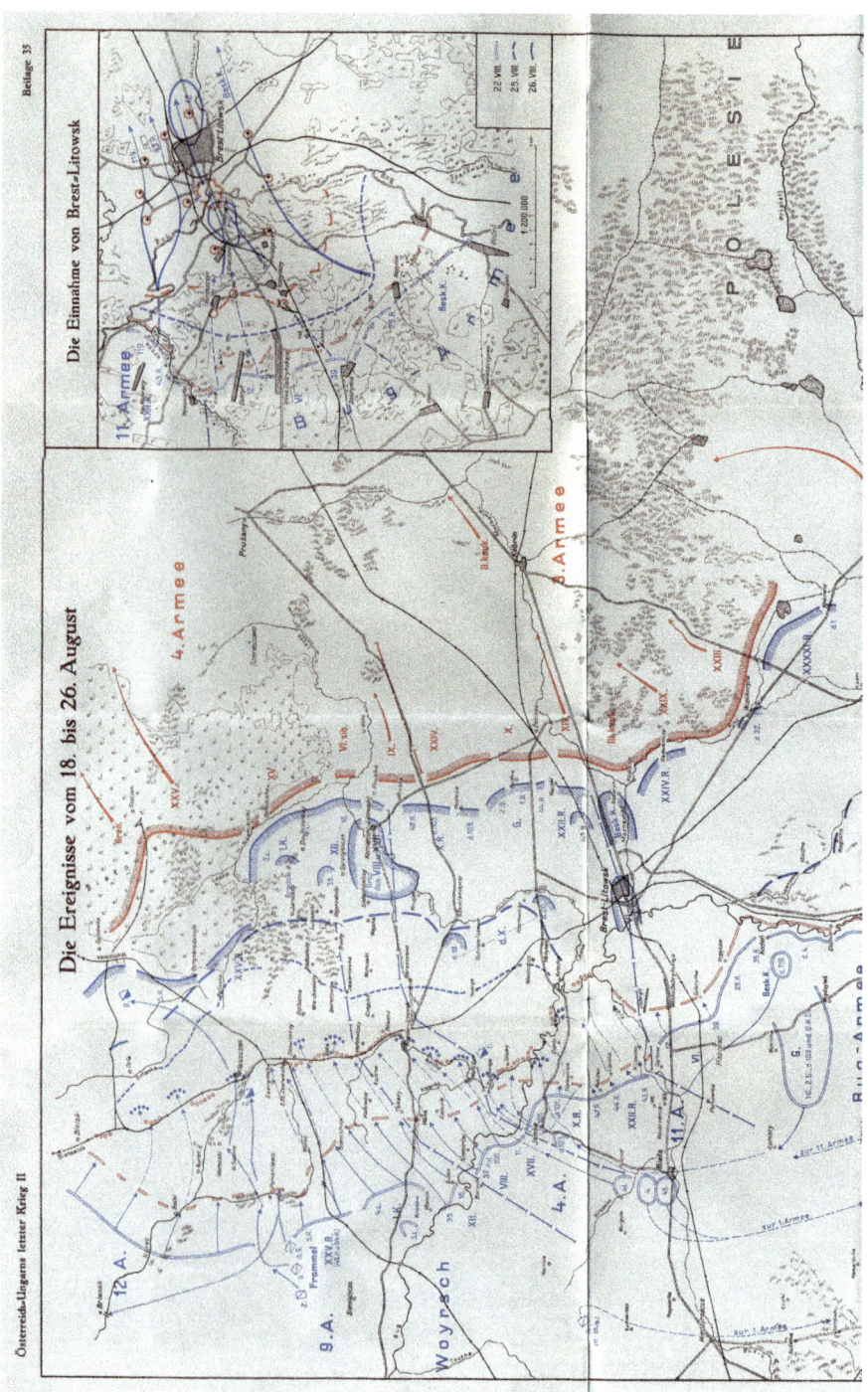

The events of August 18-26 (on the bow).

Side sketch: The taking of Brest-Litovsk

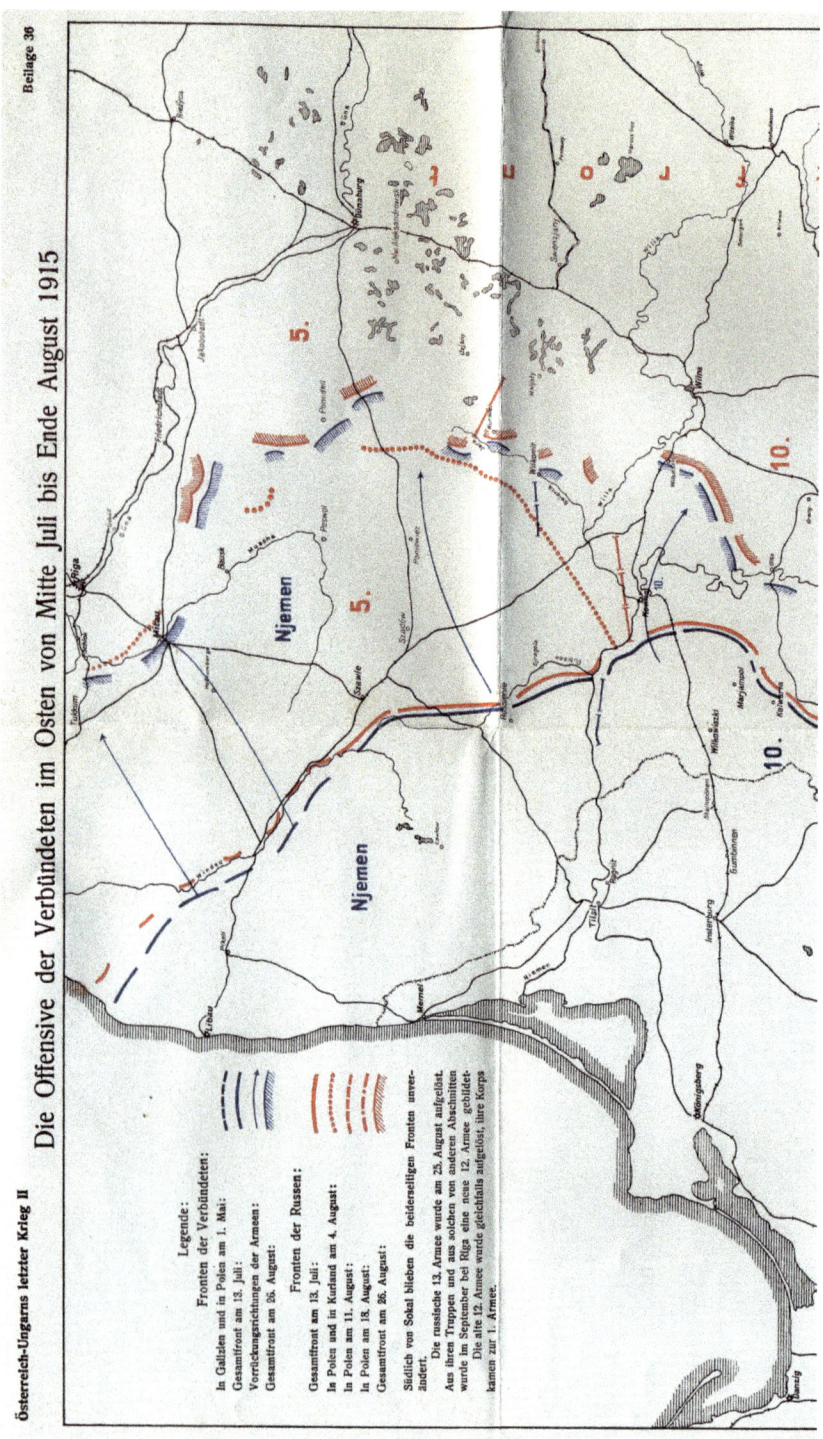

Die Offensive der Verbündeten im Osten von Mitte Juli bis Ende August 1915

Österreich-Ungarns letzter Krieg II

Legende:

Fronten der Verbündeten:

In Galizien und in Polen am 1. Mai:
Gesamtfront am 13. Juli:
Vorrückungsrichtungen der Armeen:
Gesamtfront am 26. August:

Fronten der Russen:

Gesamtfront am 13. Juli:
In Polen und in Kurland am 4. August:
In Polen am 11. August:
In Polen am 18. August:
Gesamtfront am 26. August:

Südlich von Sokal blieben die beiderseitigen Fronten unverändert.

Die russische 13. Armee wurde am 25. August aufgelöst. Aus ihren Truppen und aus solchen von anderen Abschnitten wurde im September bei Riga eine neue 12. Armee gebildet. Die alte 12. Armee wurde gleichfalls aufgelöst, ihre Korps kamen zur 1. Armee.

The Allied offensive in the east from

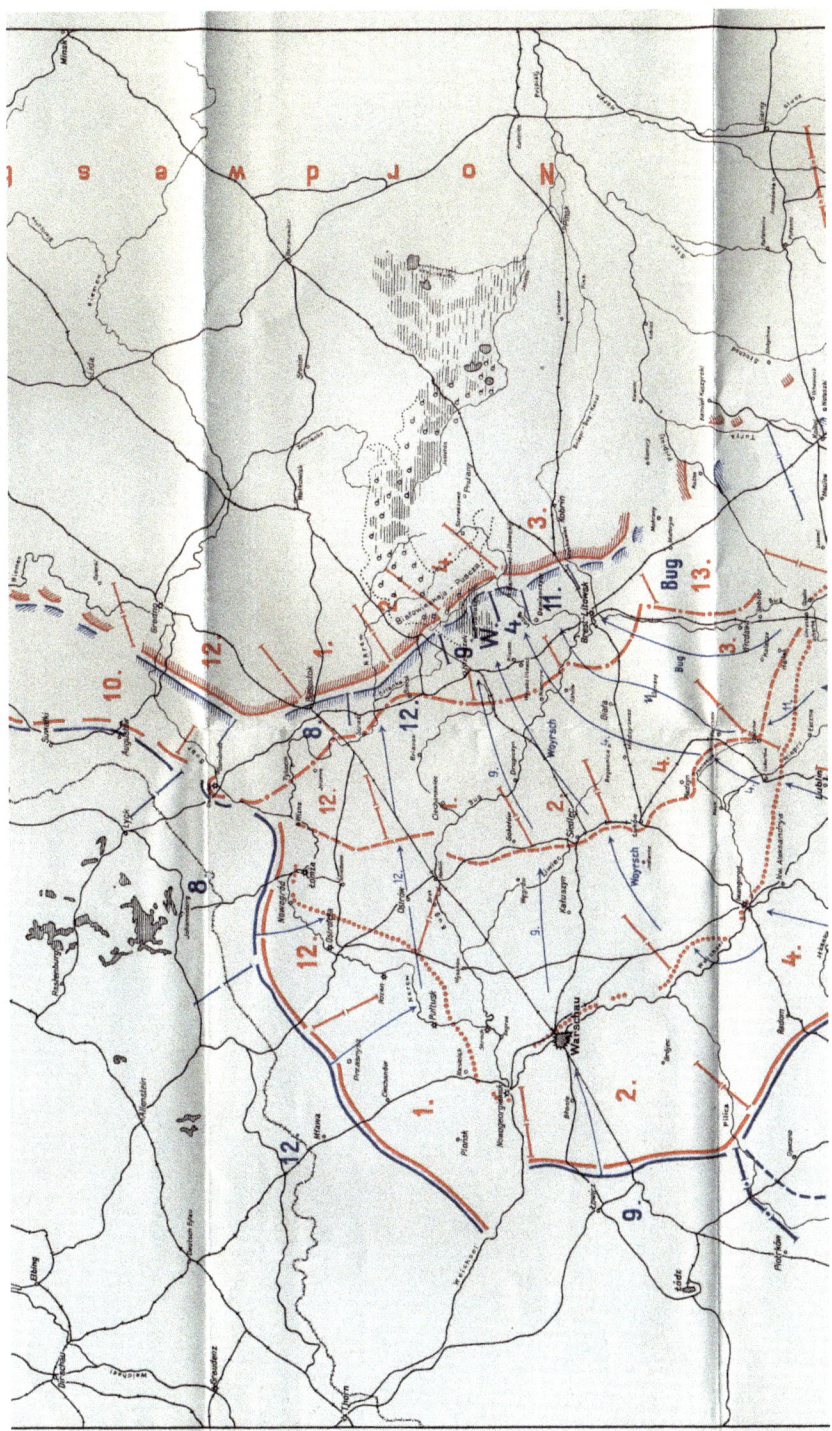

mid-July to late August 1915 (overview)

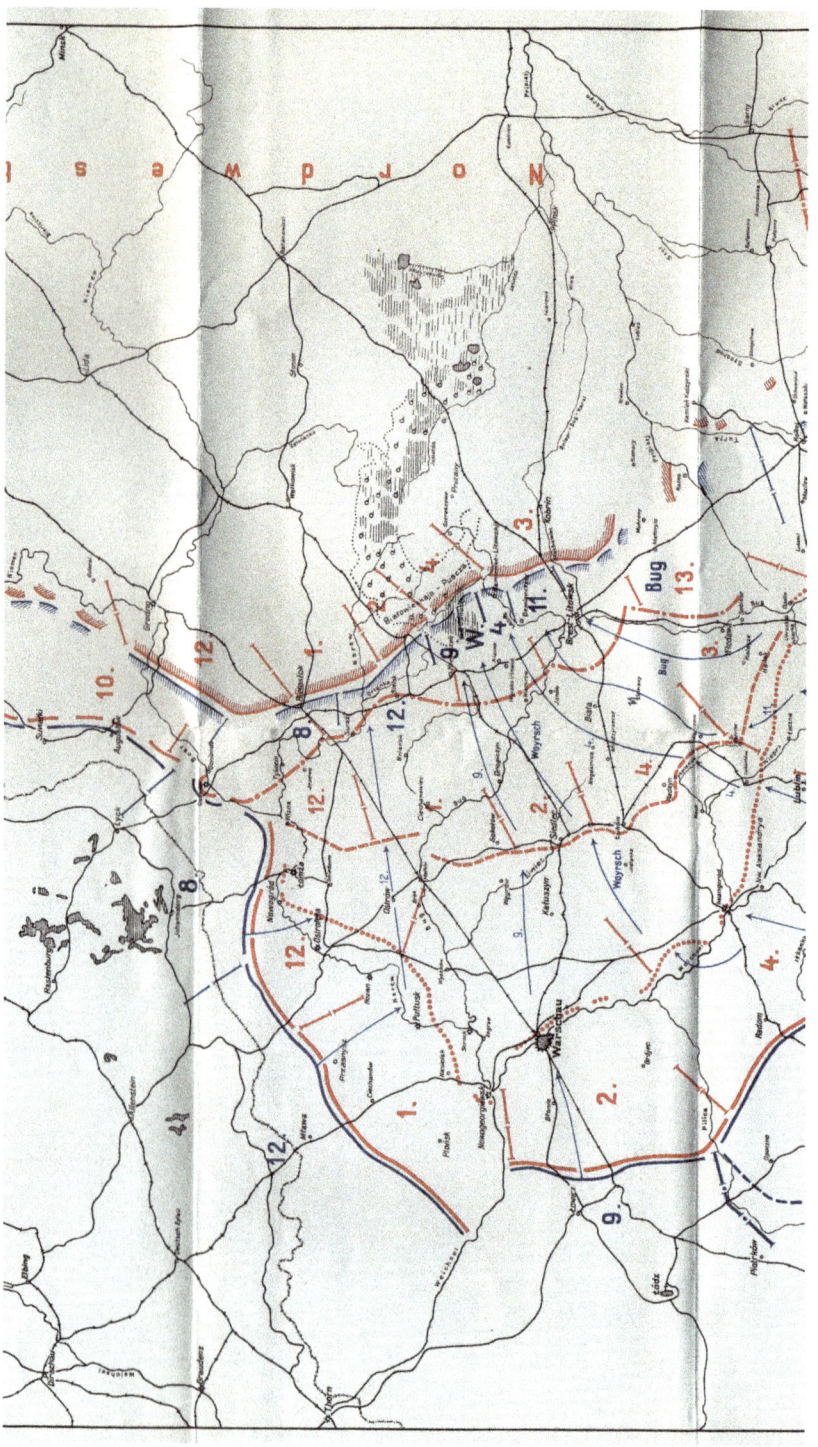

The Allied offensive in the east from

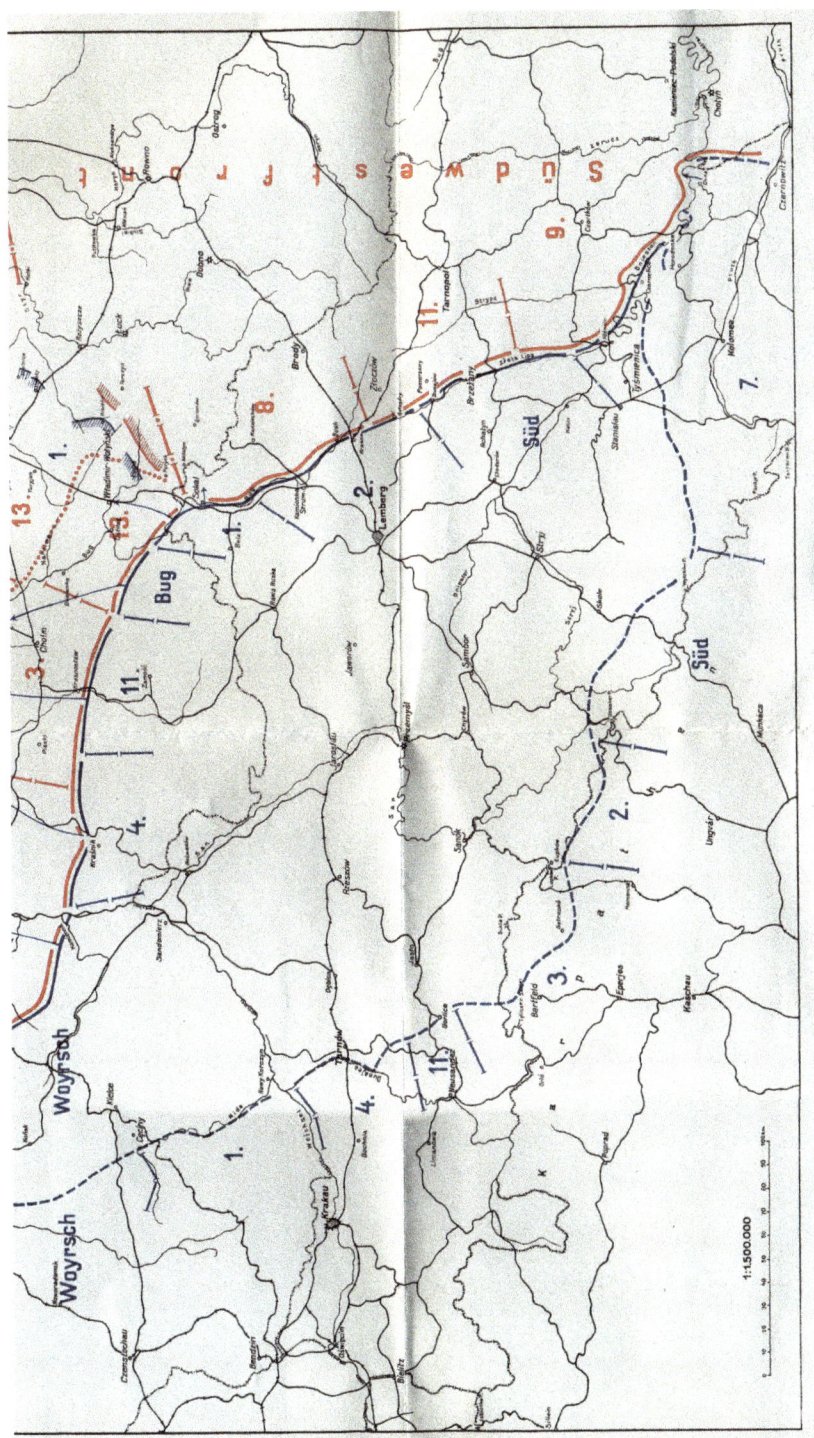

mid-July to late August 1915 (overview)

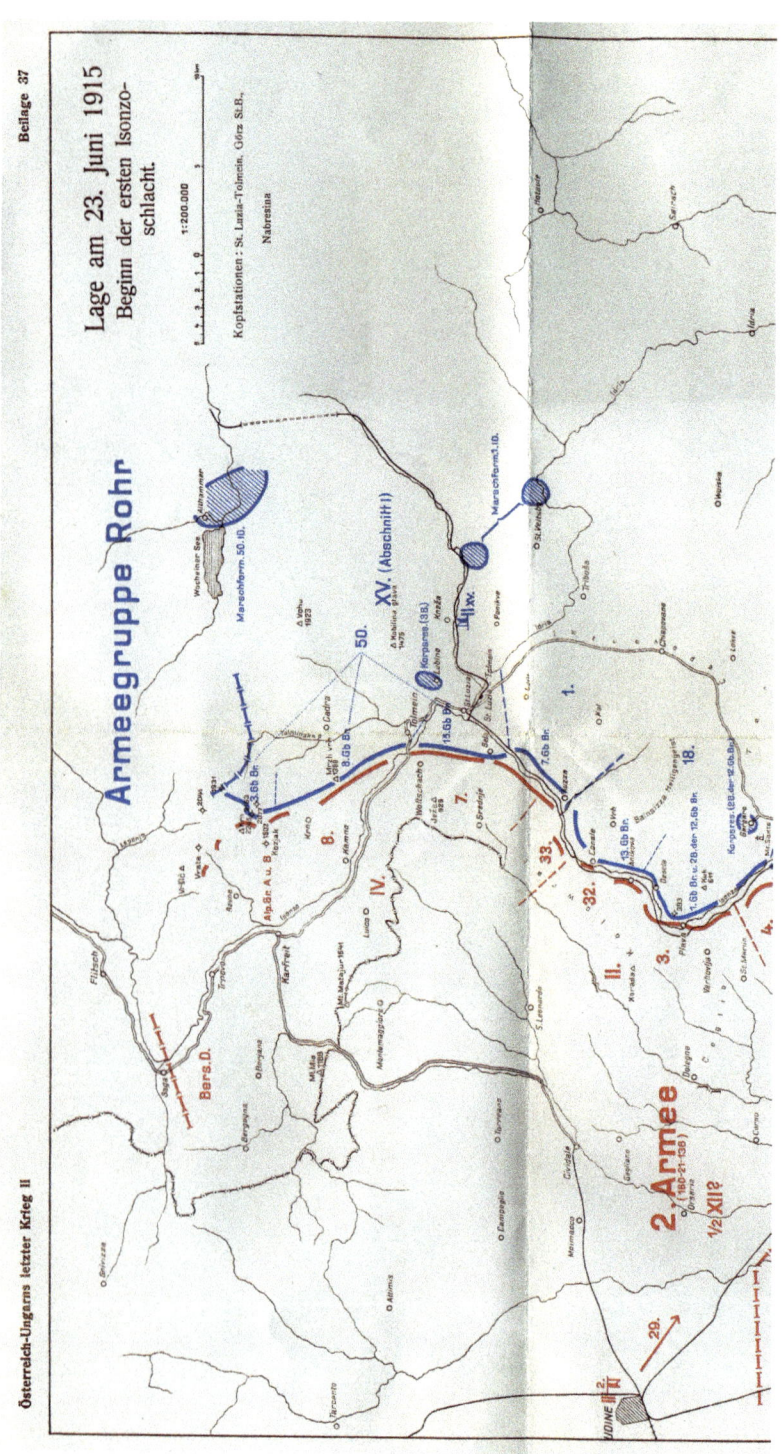

Situation on June 23, 1915. Beginning

of the first Battle of the Isonzo

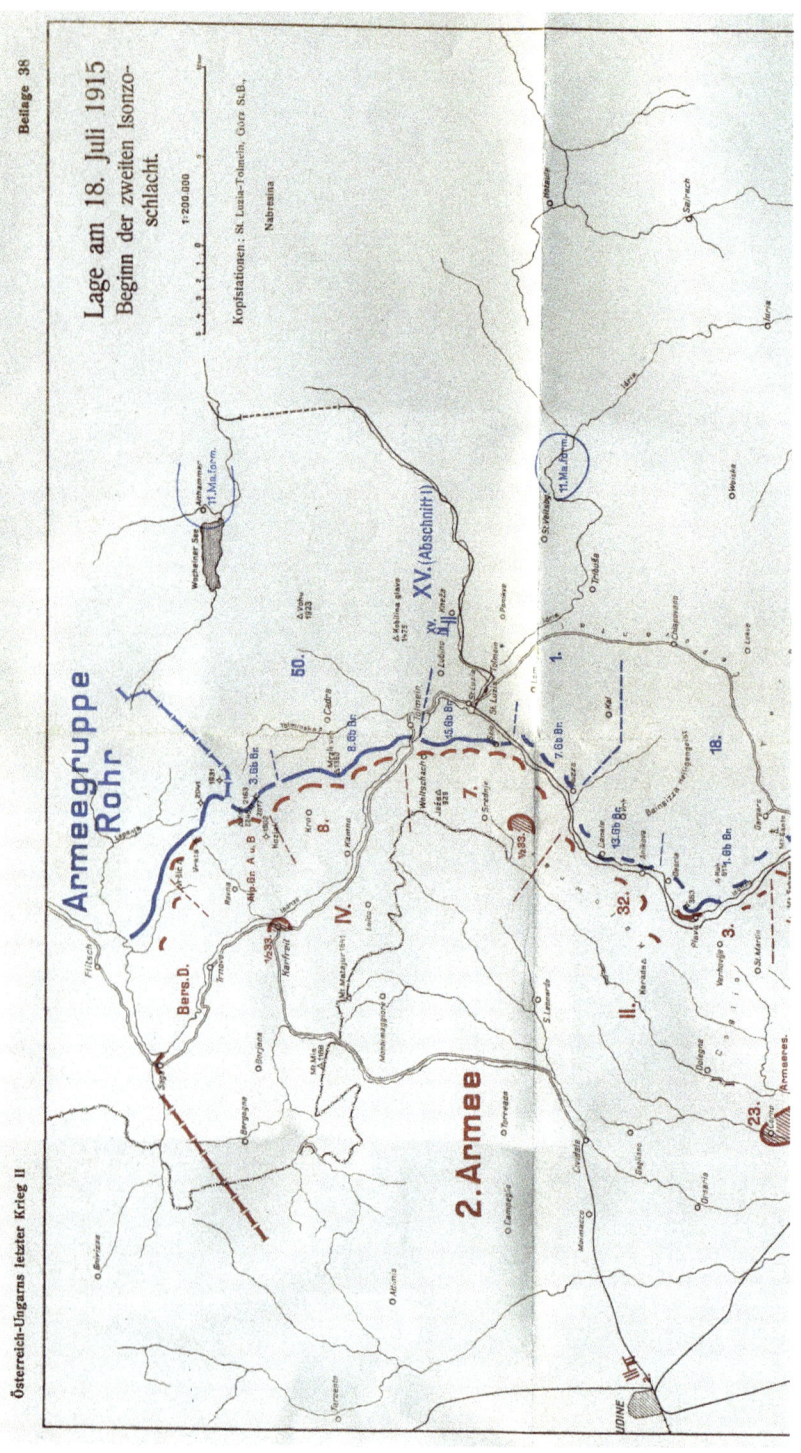

Situation on July 18, 1915. Beginning

of the second Battle of the Isonzo

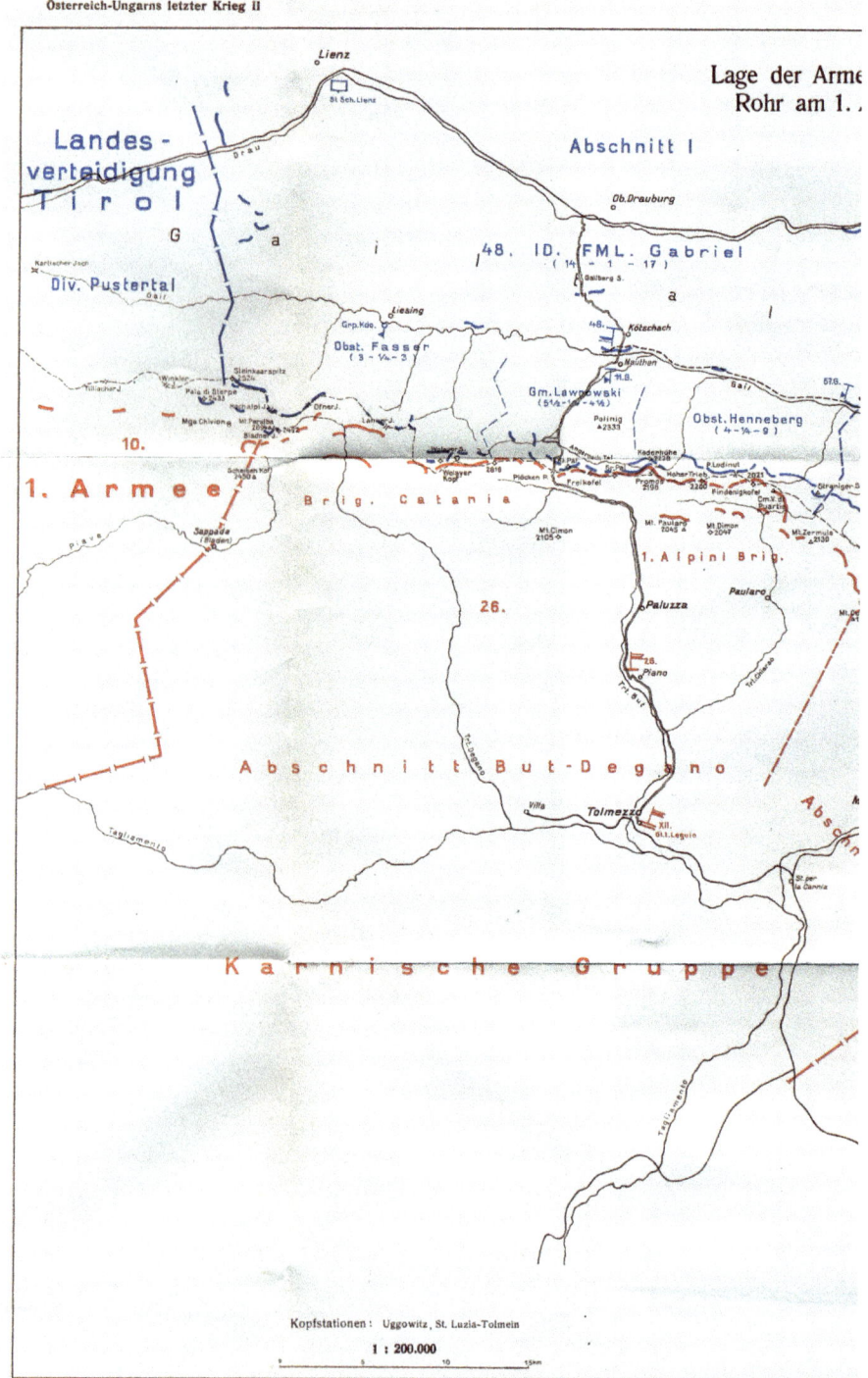

Position of Army Group GdK.

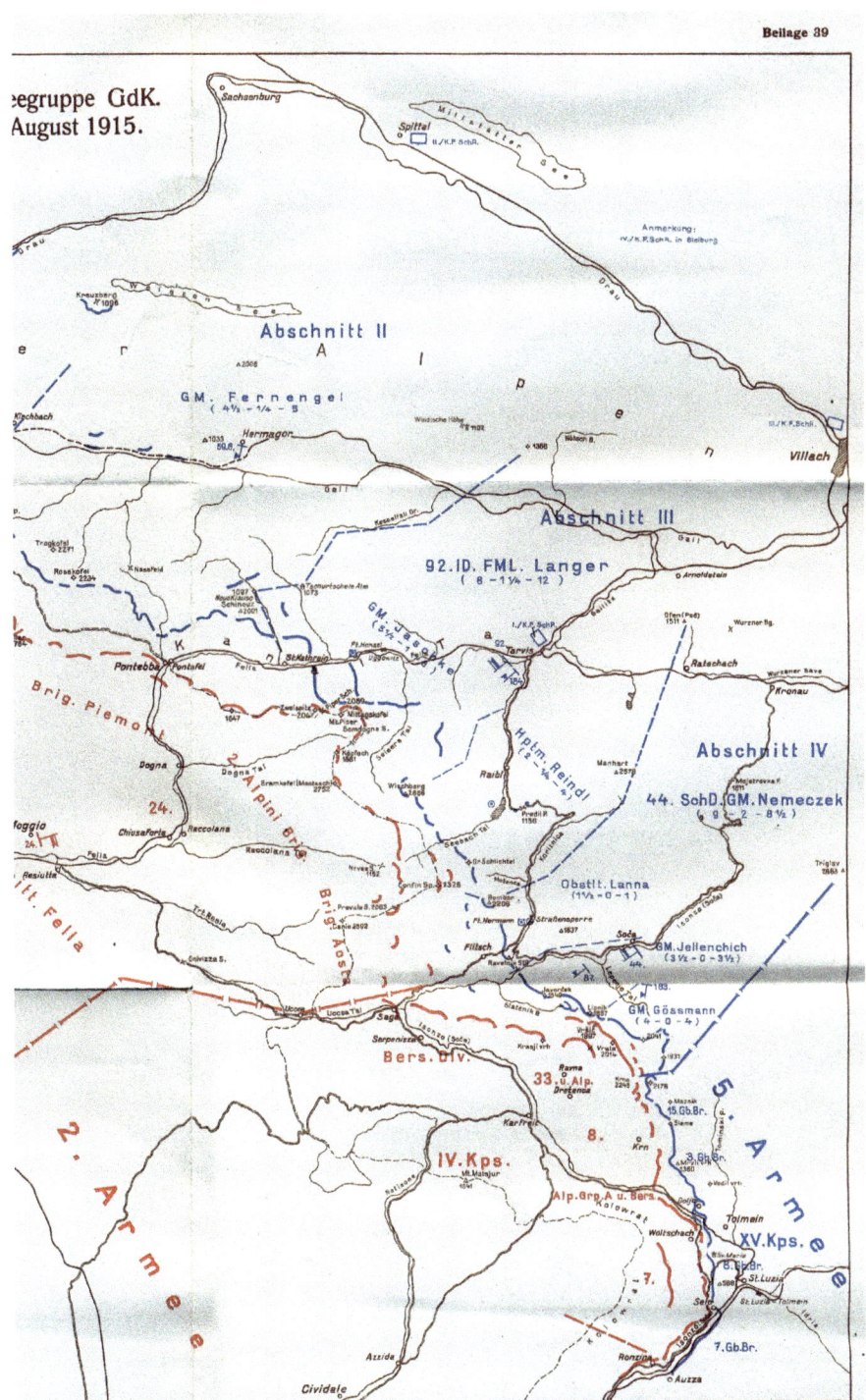

Rohr on August 1, 1915

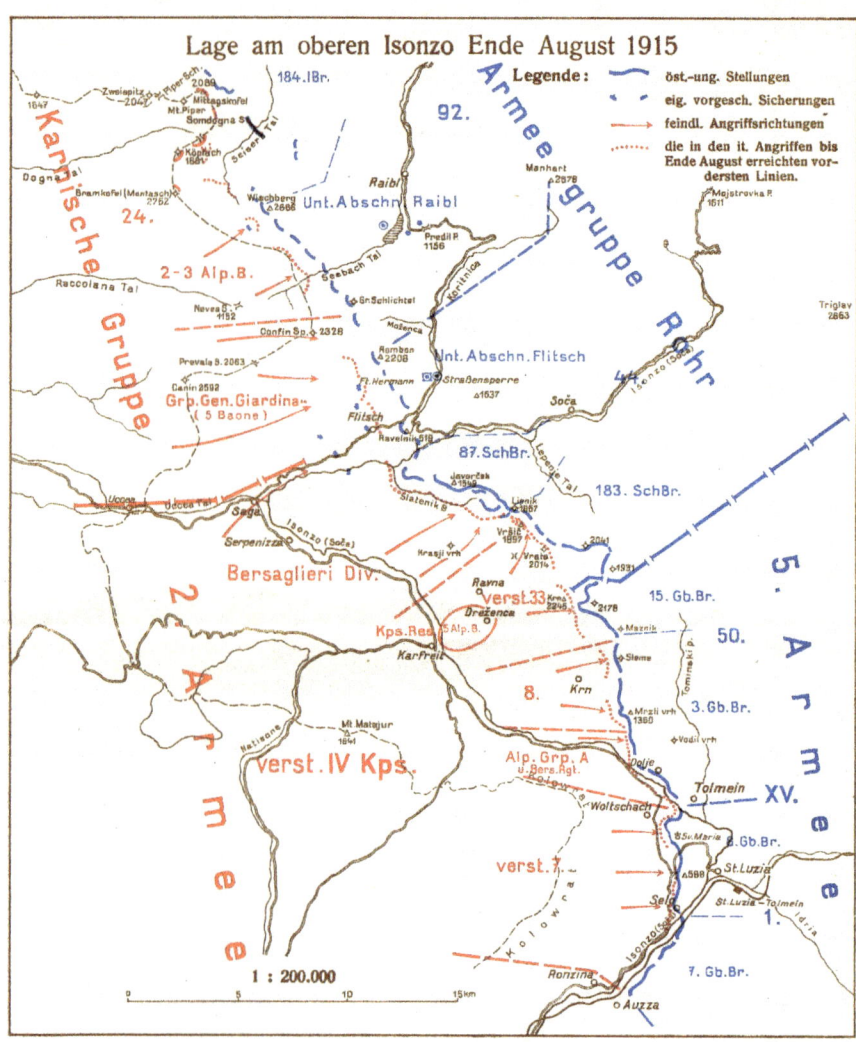

Position on the upper Isonzo at the end of August 1915

Sketches

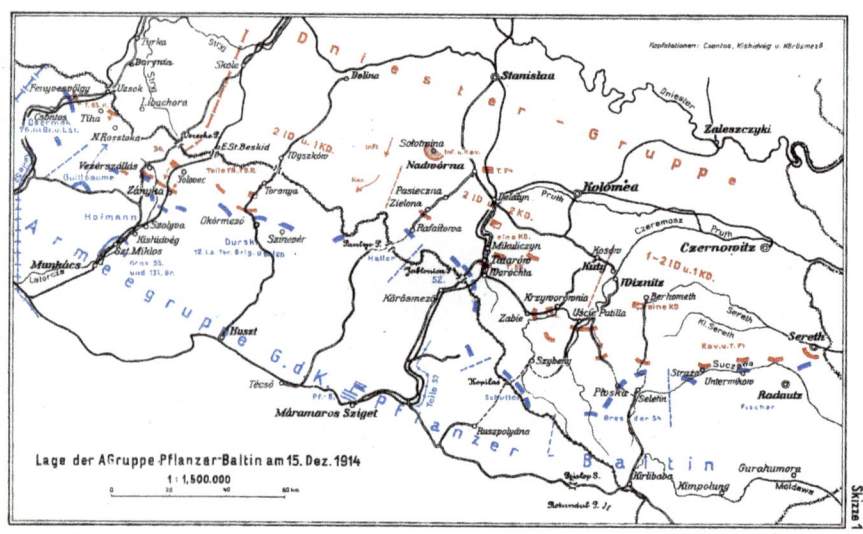

Sketch 1: Position of the Planter-Baltin Army Group on 15 December 1914

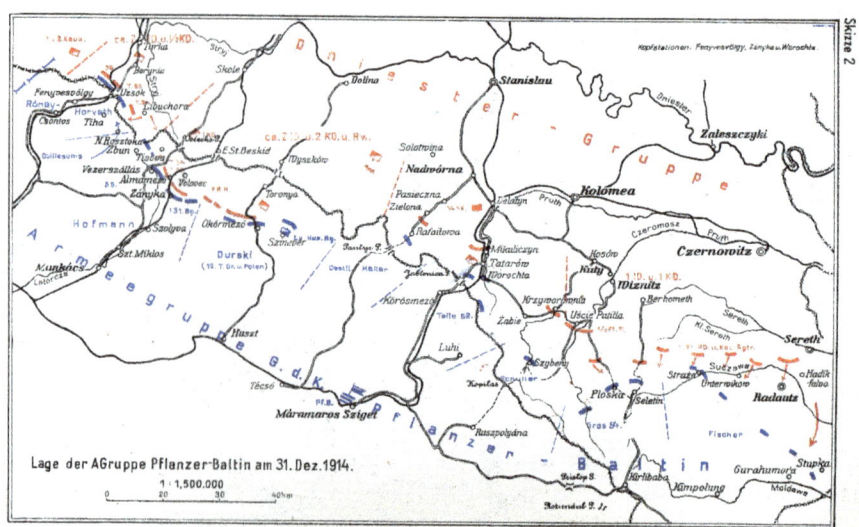

Sketch 2: Position of the Planter-Baltin Army Group on 31 December 1914

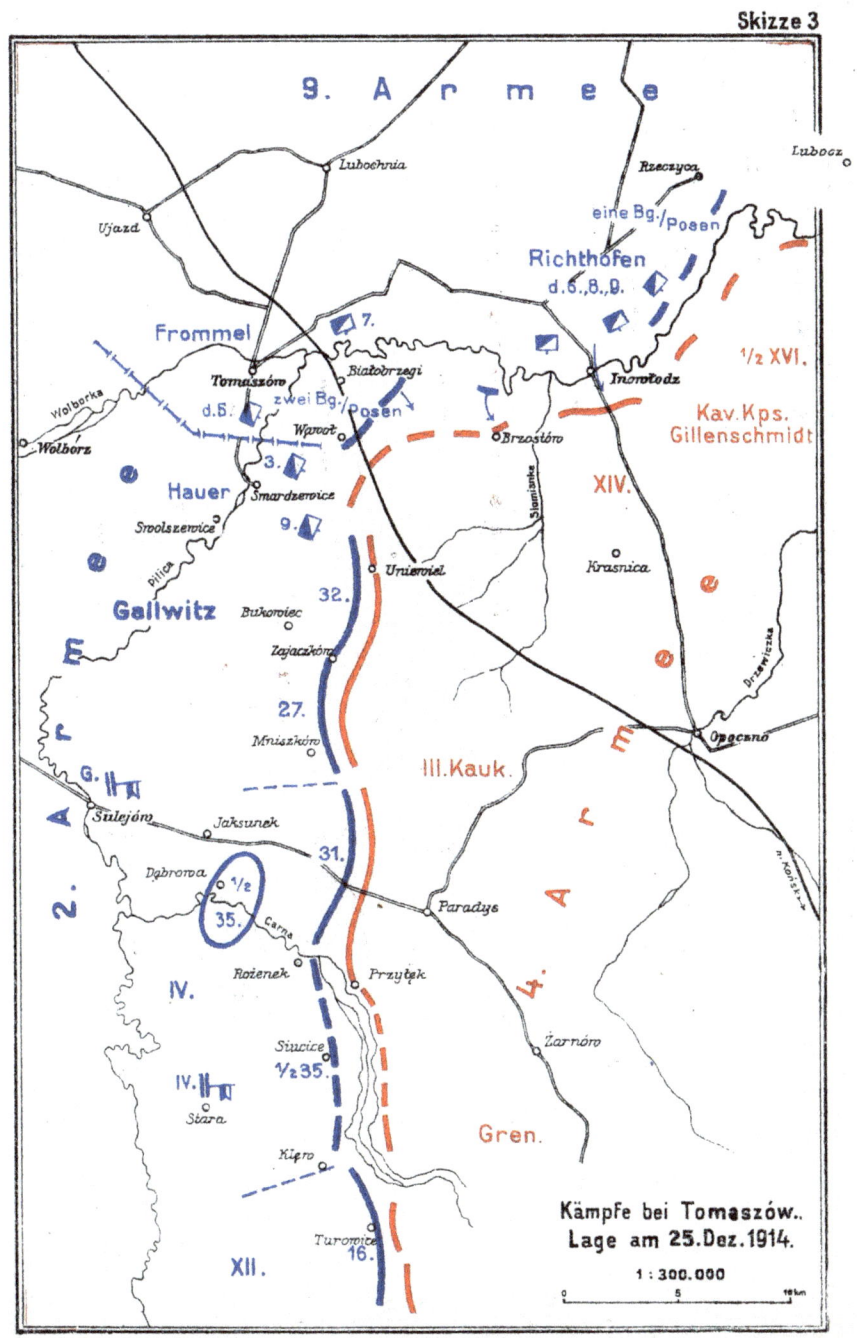

Sketch 3: Battles near Tomaszów. Situation on December 25, 1914

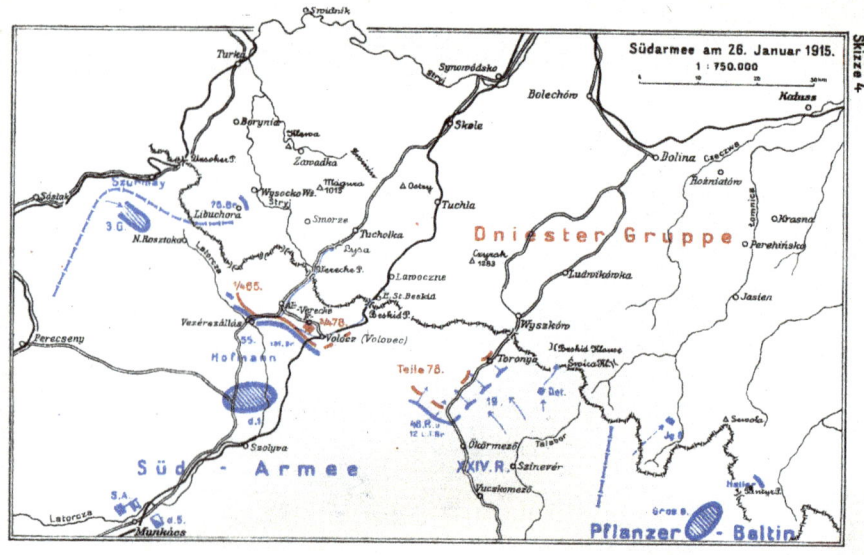

Sketch 4: Southern Army on January 26, 1915

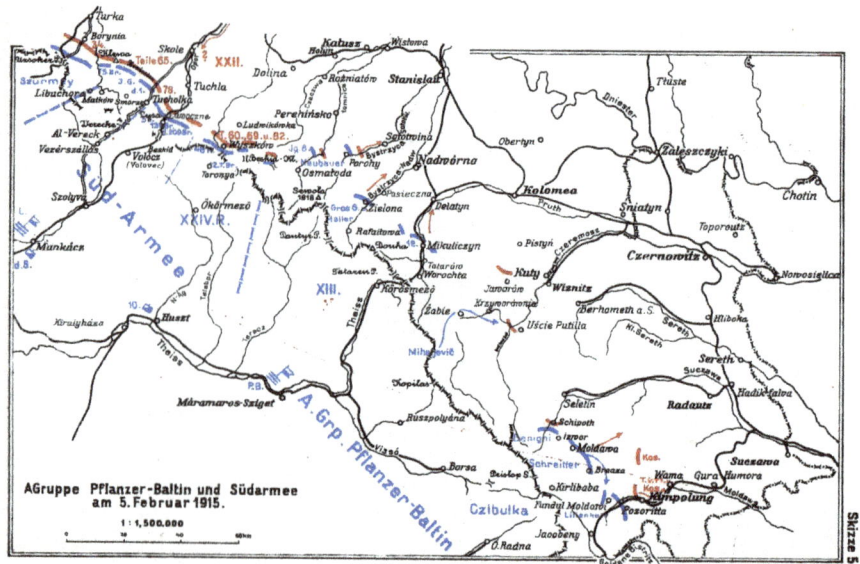

*Sketch 5: Planter-Baltin Army Group and Southern Army on February 5,
1915*

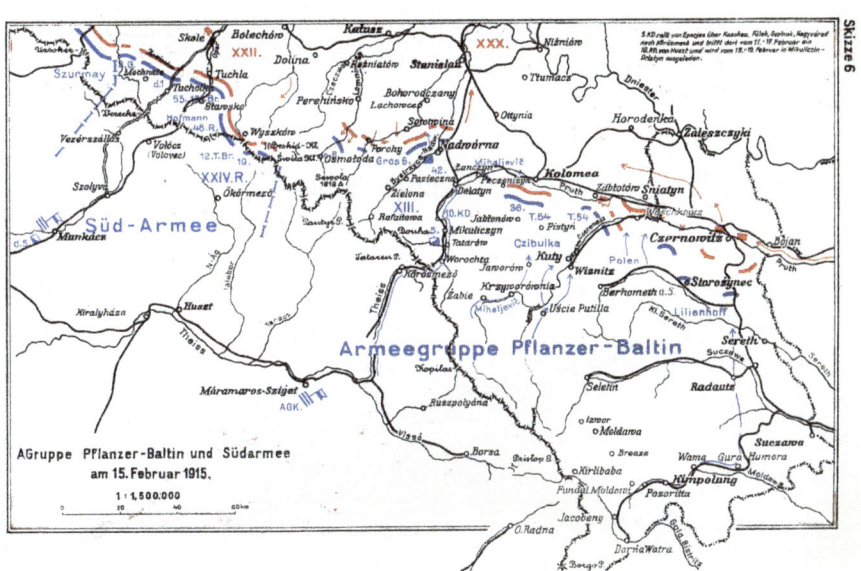

Sketch 6: Planter-Baltin Army Group and Southern Army on 15 February 1915

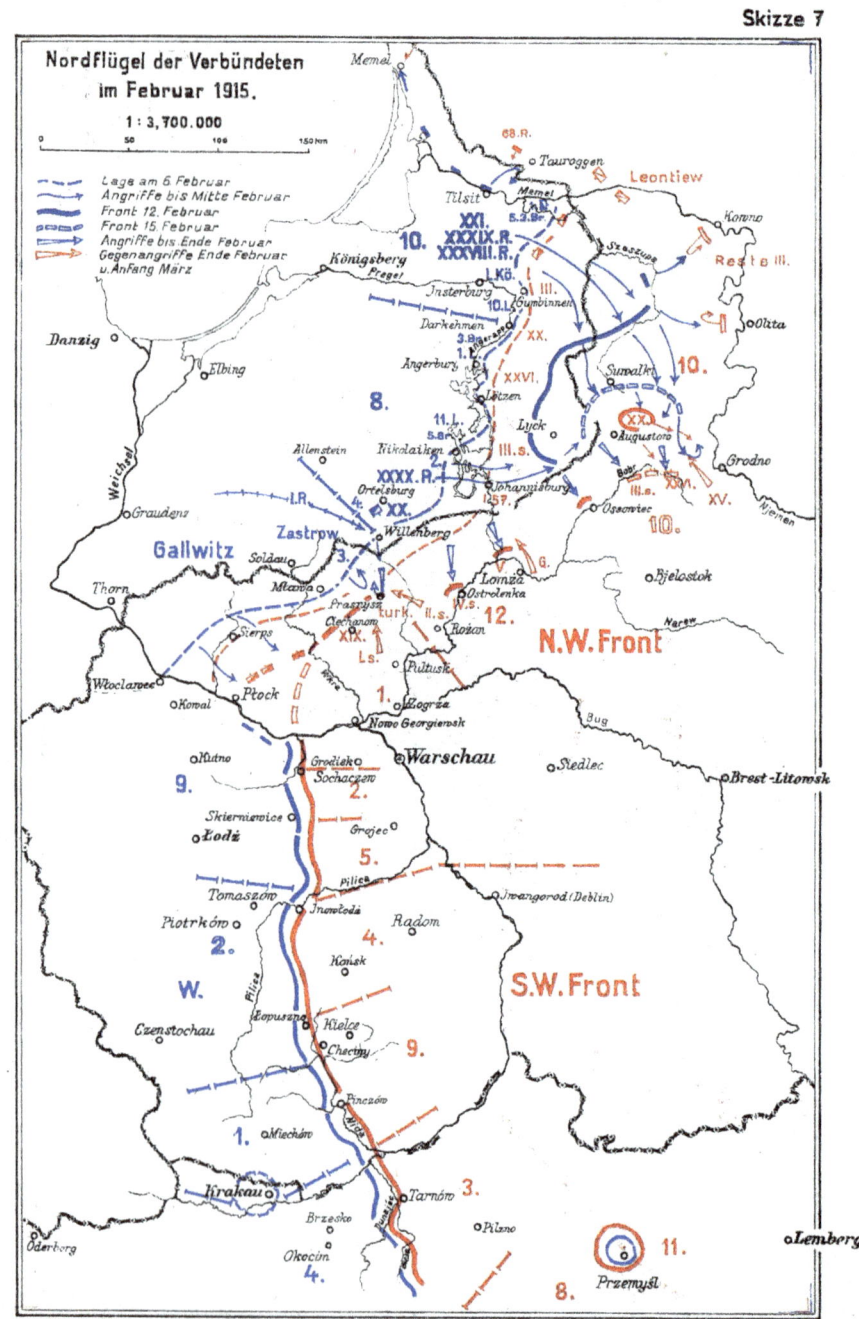

Sketch 7: Allied north wing in February 1915

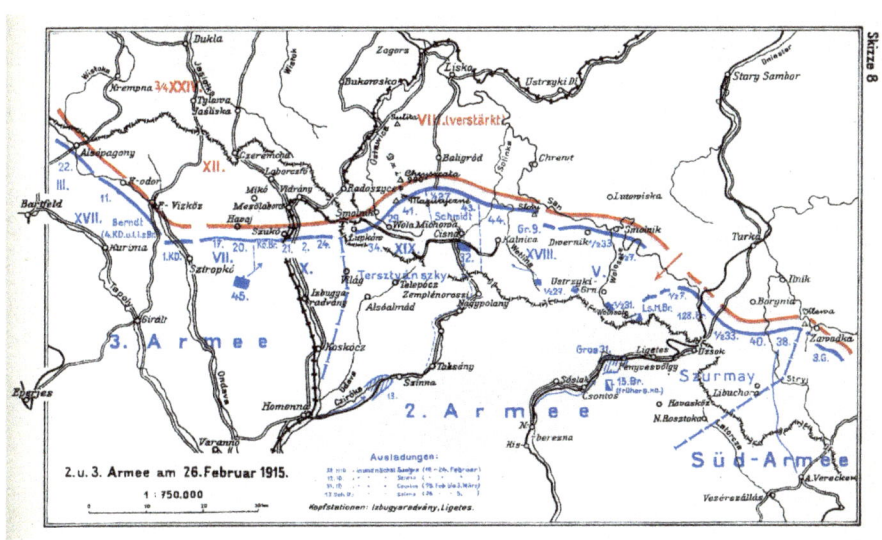

Sketch 8: 2nd and 3rd Armies on 26 February 1915

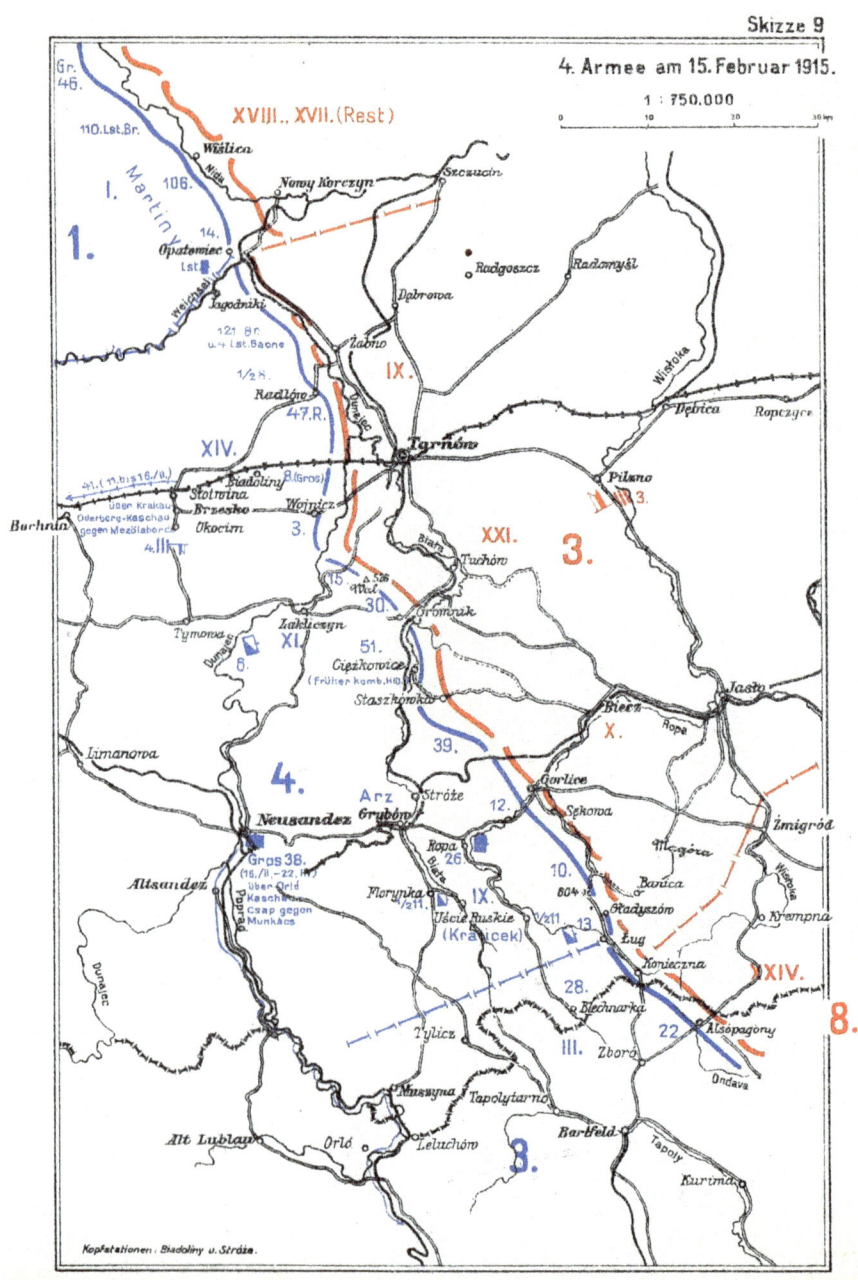

Sketch 9: 4th Army on 15 February 1915

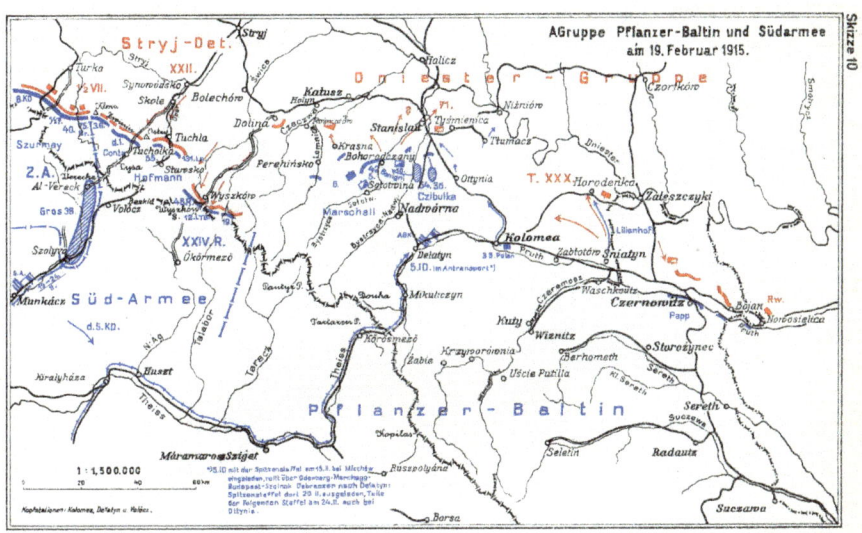

Sketch 10: Planter-Baltin Army Group and Southern Army on 19 February 1915

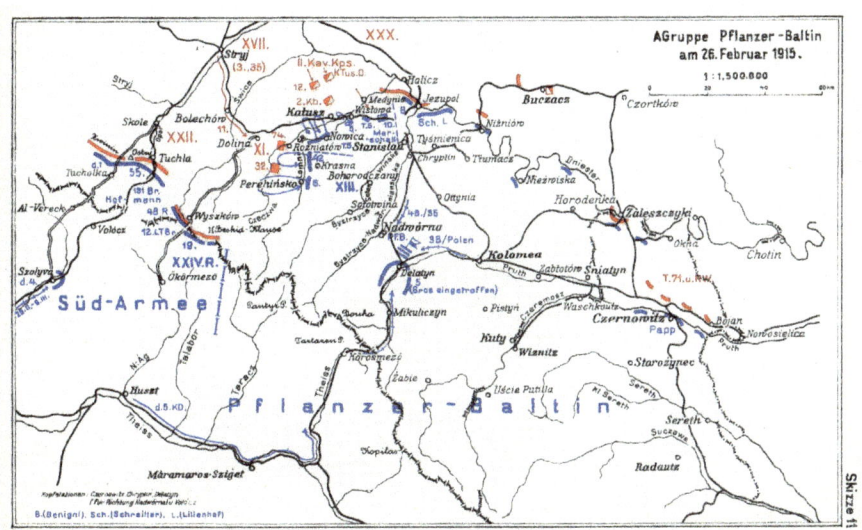

Sketch 11: Planter-Baltin Army Group on 26 February 1915

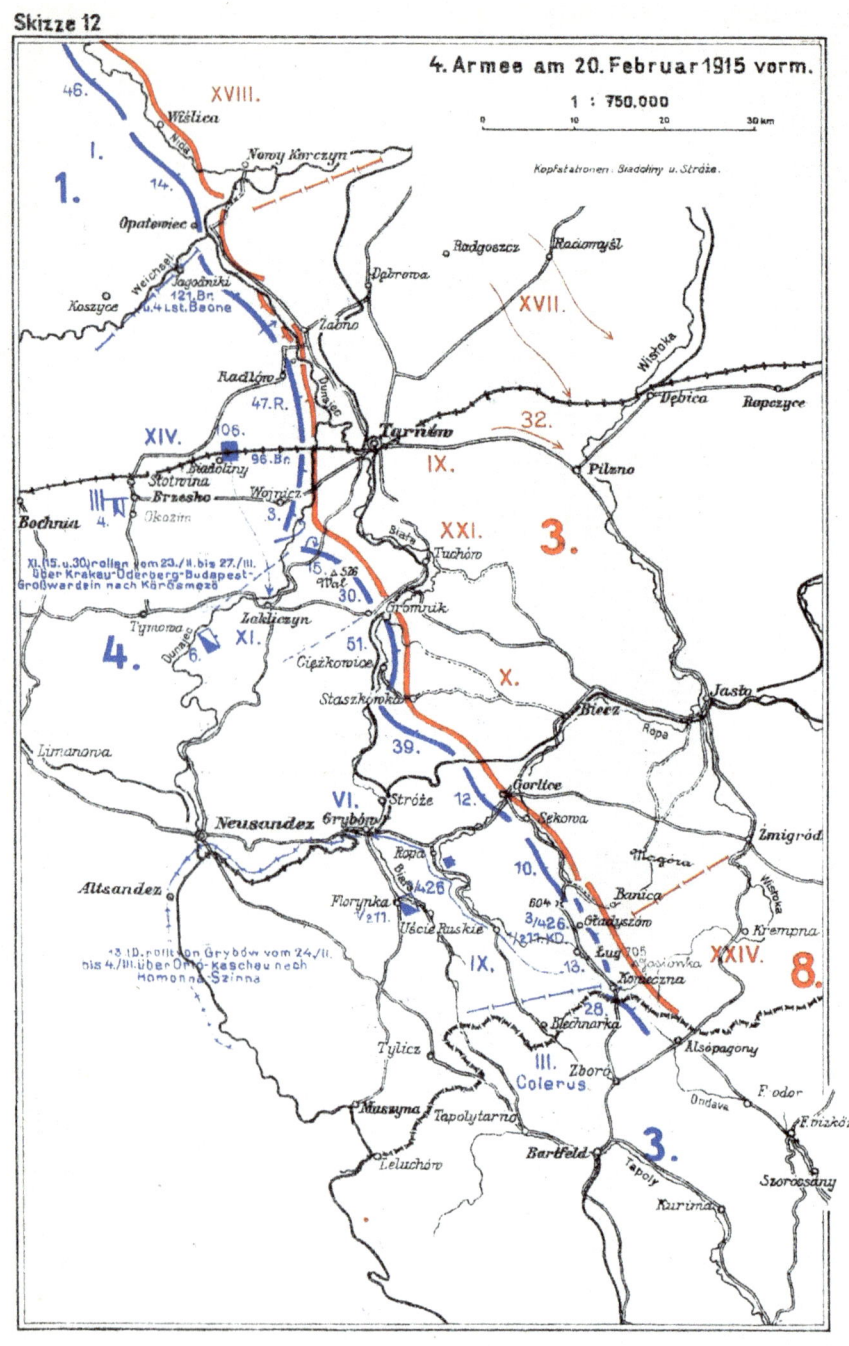

Sketch 12: 4th Army on February 20, 1915 a.m.

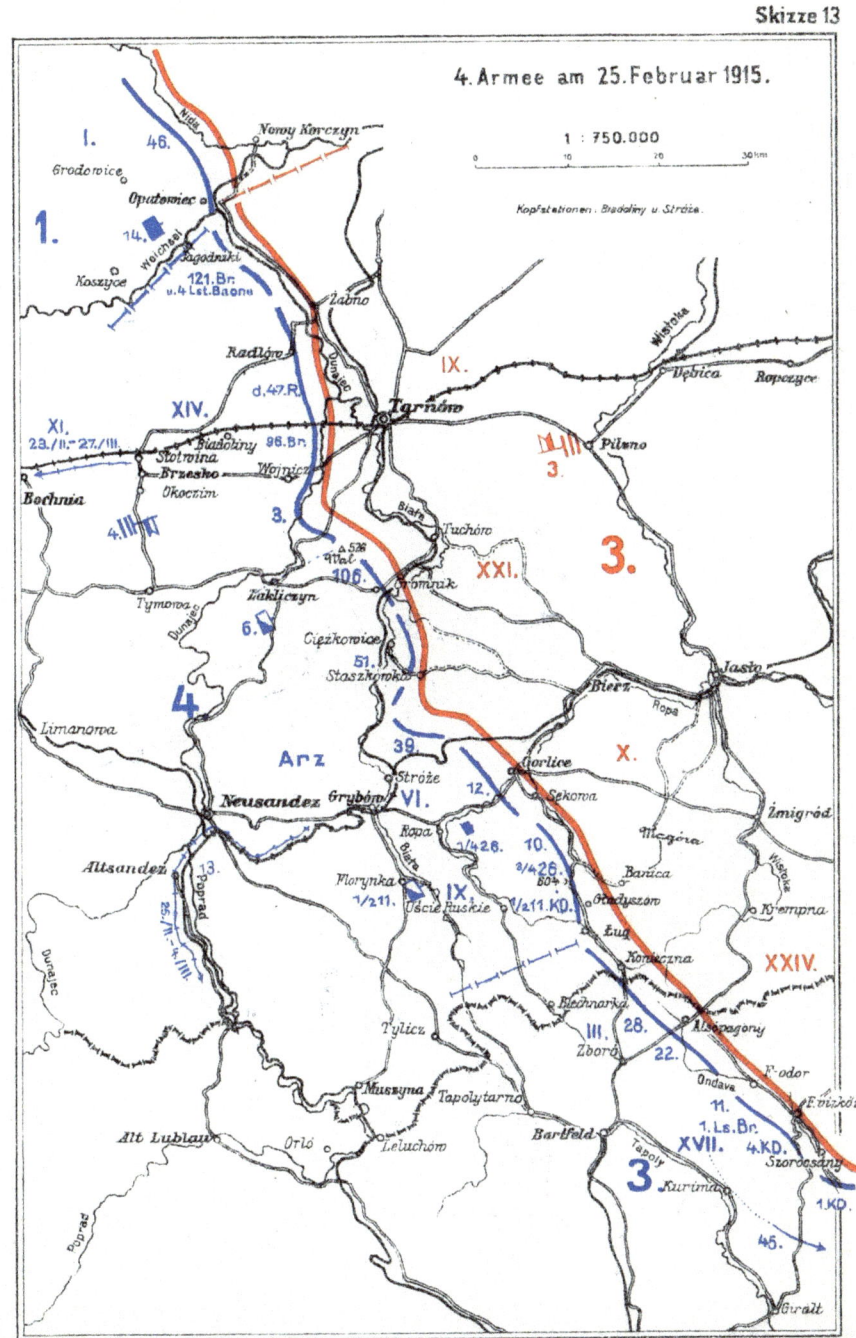

Sketch 13: 4th Army 25 February 1915

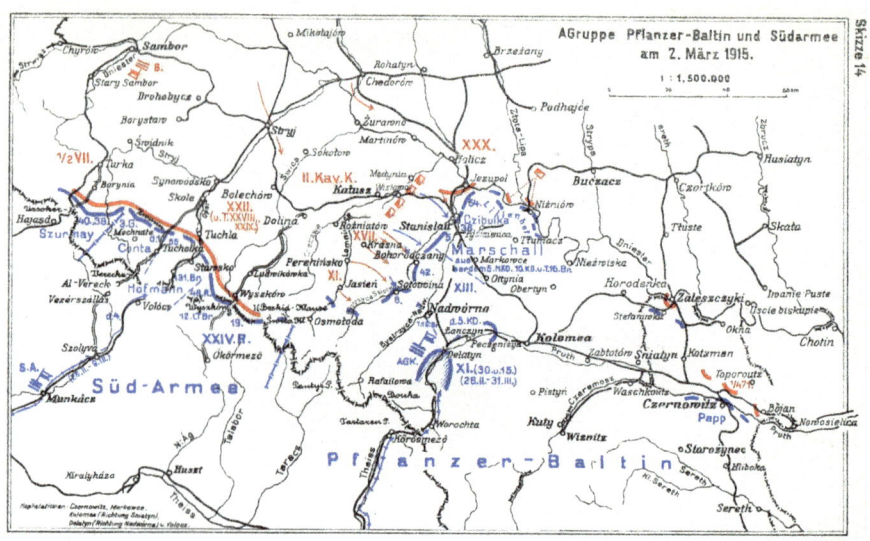

Sketch 14: Army Group Planter-Baltin and South Army 2 March 1915

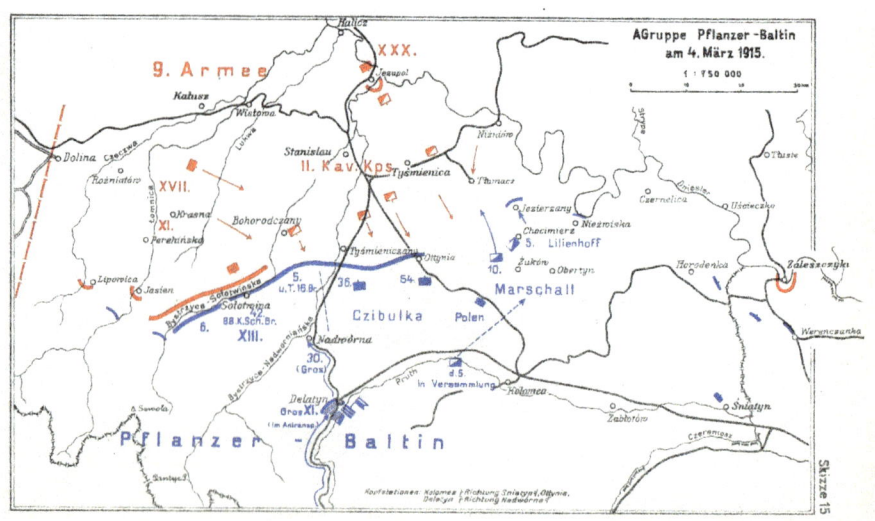

Sketch 15:Army Group Planter-Baltin 4 March 1915

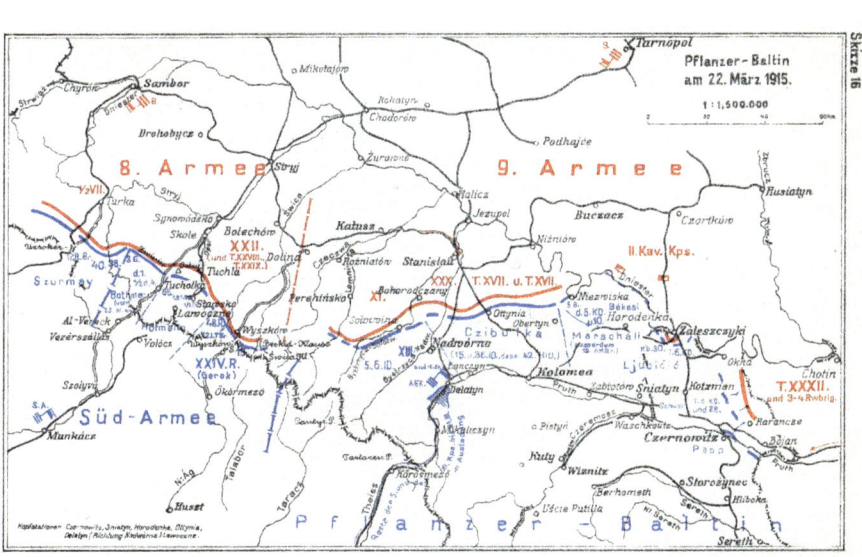

Sketch 16: Planter-Baltin 22 March 1915

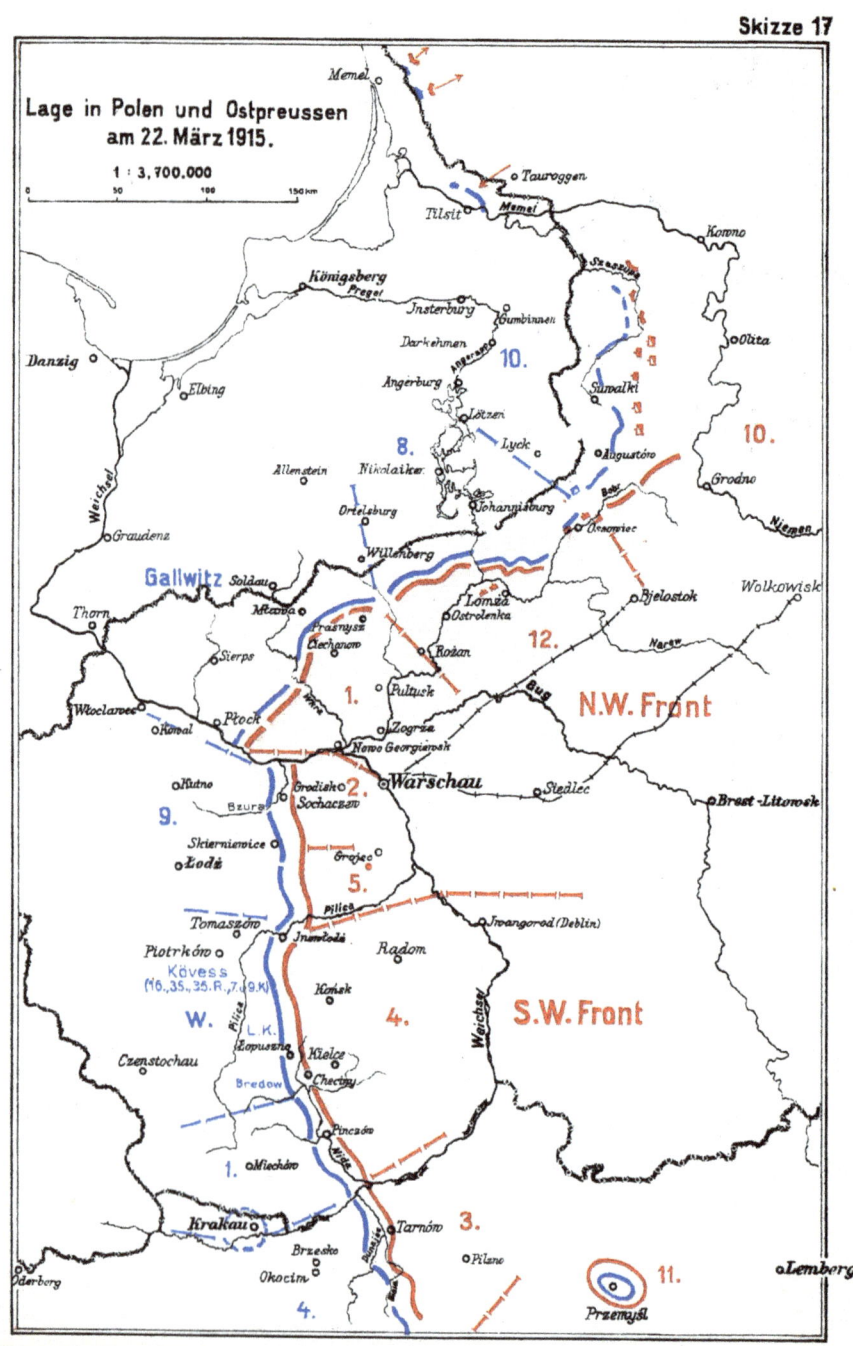

Sketch 17: Situation in Poland and East Prussia on March 22, 1915

Skizze 18

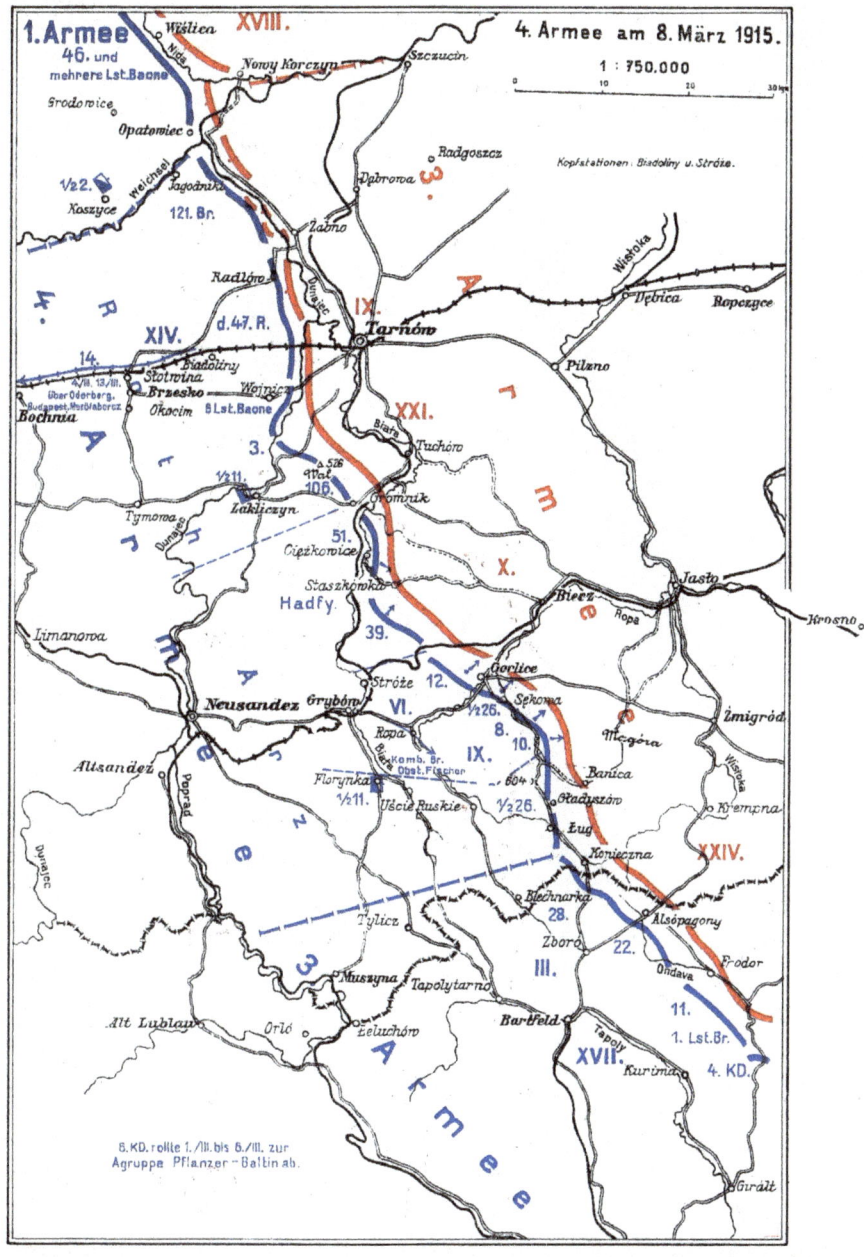

Sketch 18: 4th Army 8 March 1915

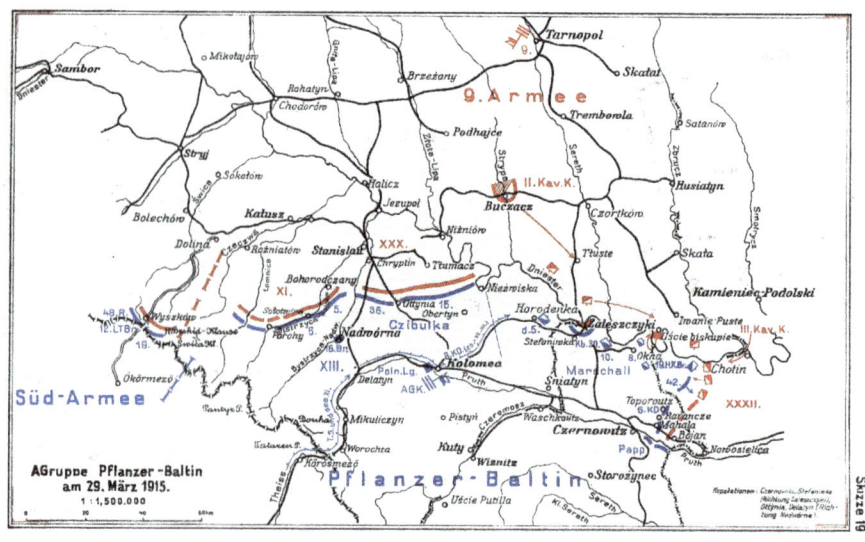

Sketch 19: Army Group Planter-Baltin 29 March 1915

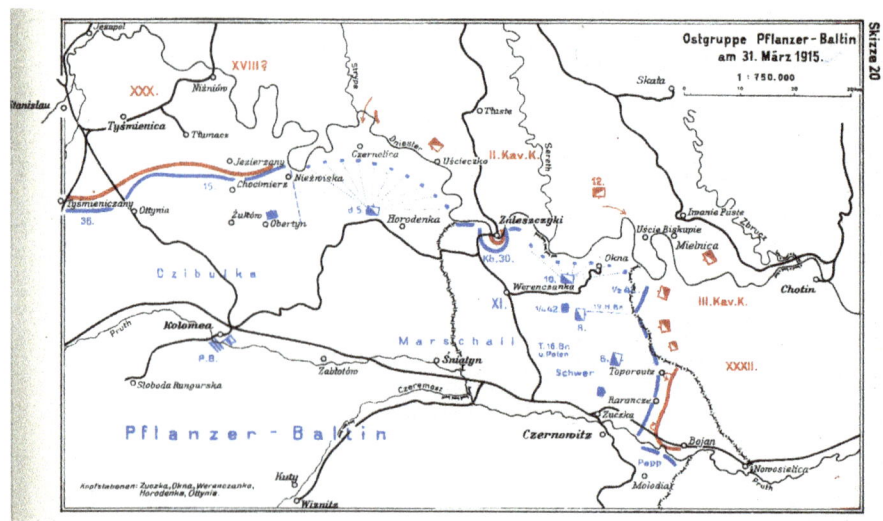

Sketch 20: Planter-Baltin East Group on 31 March, 1915

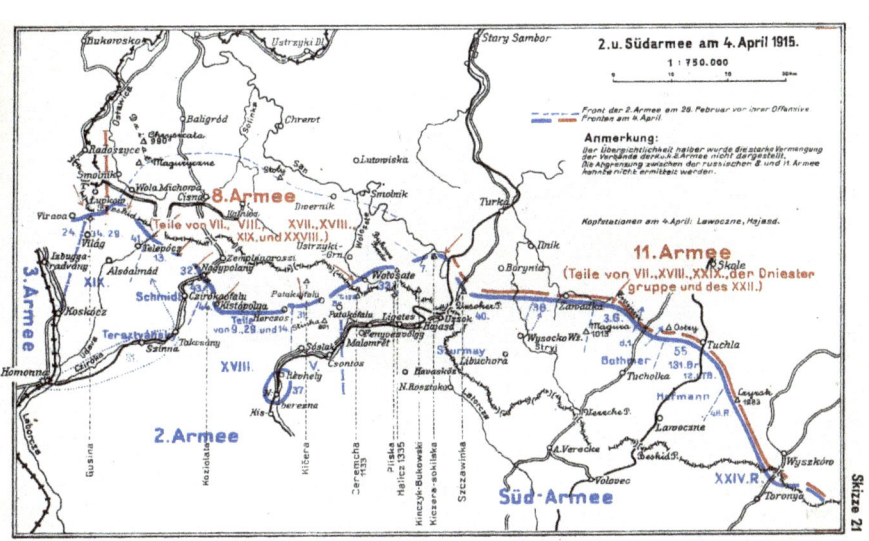

Sketch 21: 2nd and South Army on April 4, 1915

Skizze 22

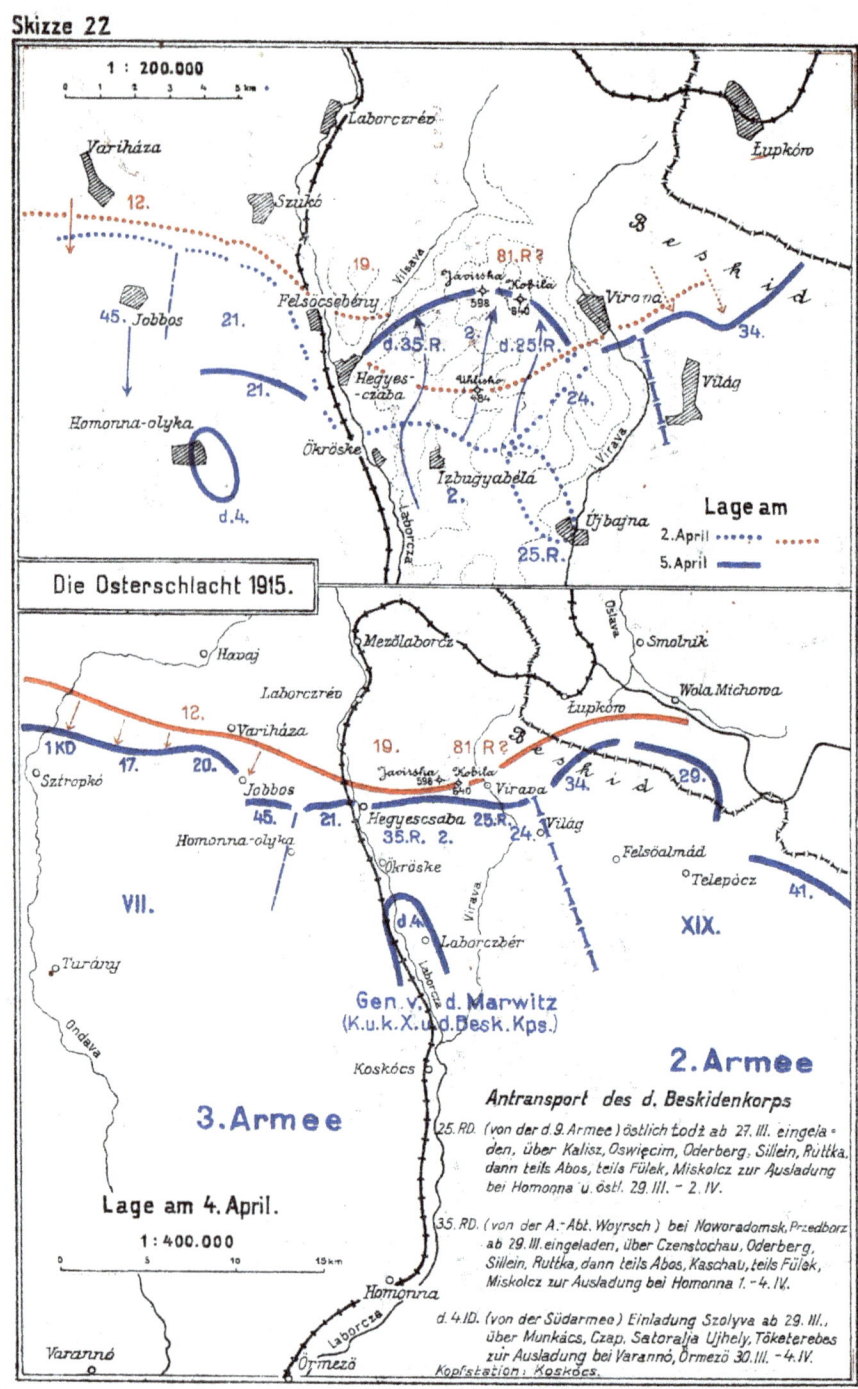

Sketch 22: The Easter Battle of 1915

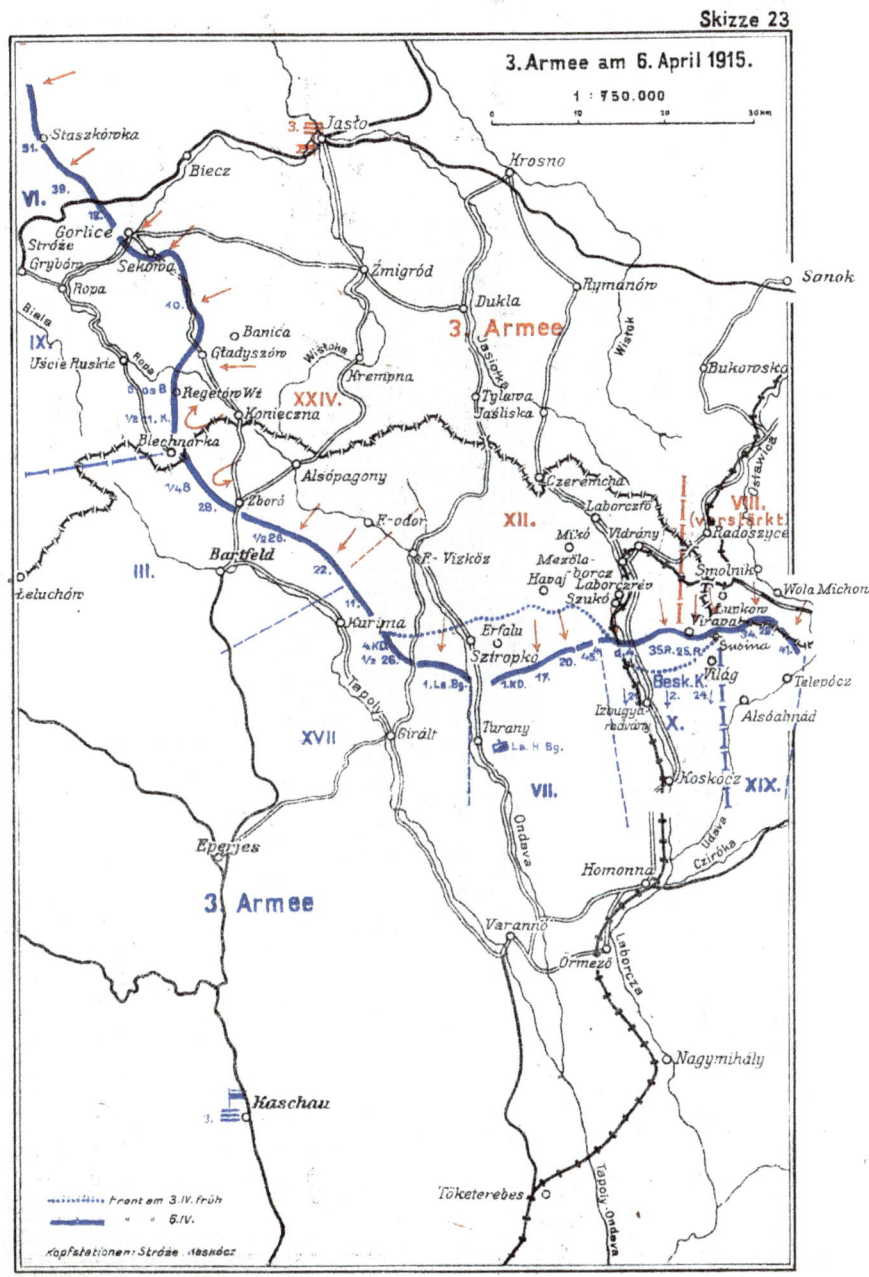

Sketch 23: *3rd Army on 6 April 1915*

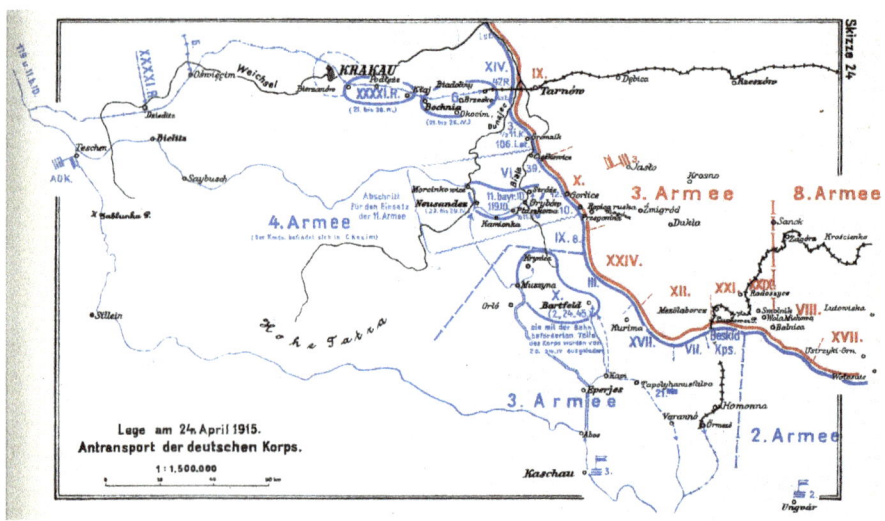

Sketch 24: Position on April 24, 1915. Transport of the German corps

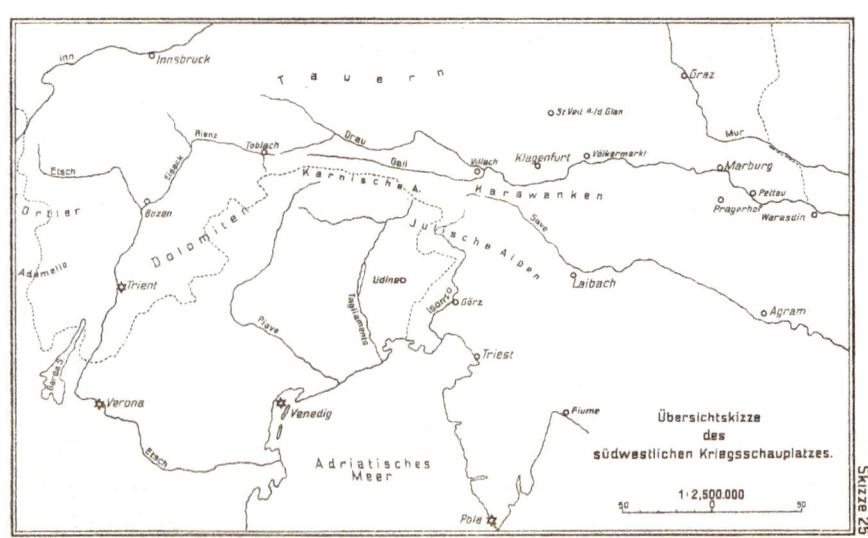

Sketch 25: Overview of the southwestern theater of war

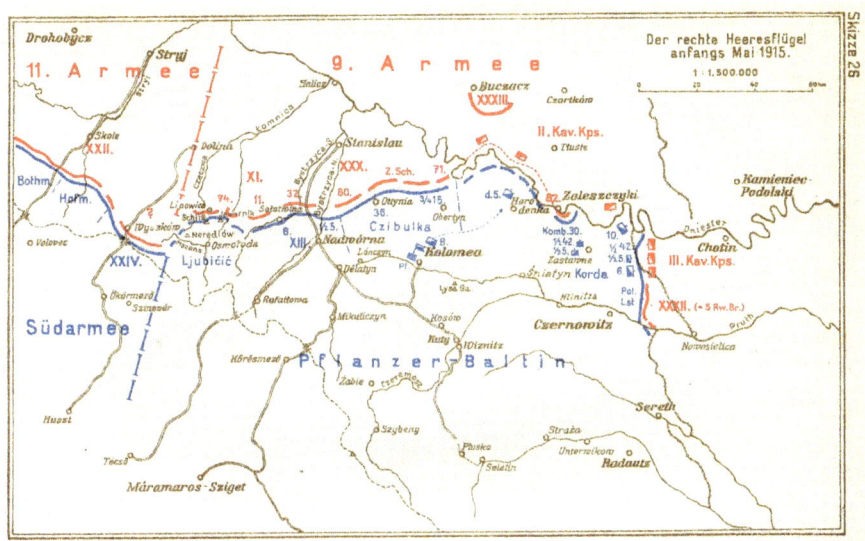

Sketch 26: The right wing of the army in early May 1915 (7th Army)

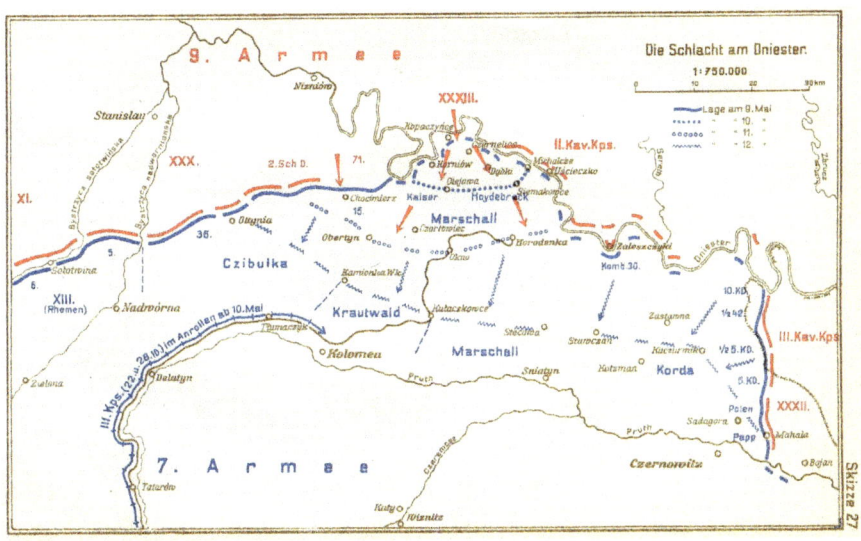

Sketch 27: The Battle of the Dniester

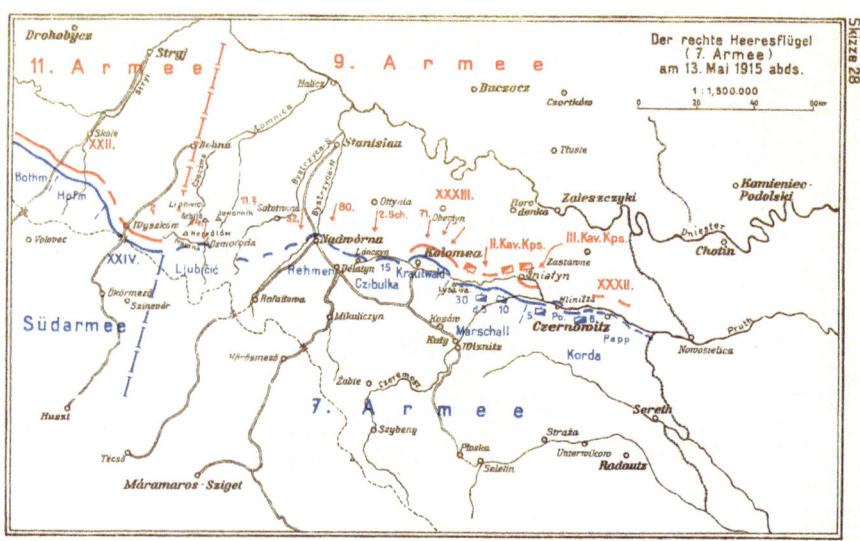

Sketch 28: The right wing of the army (7th Army) on May 13, 1915 in the evening

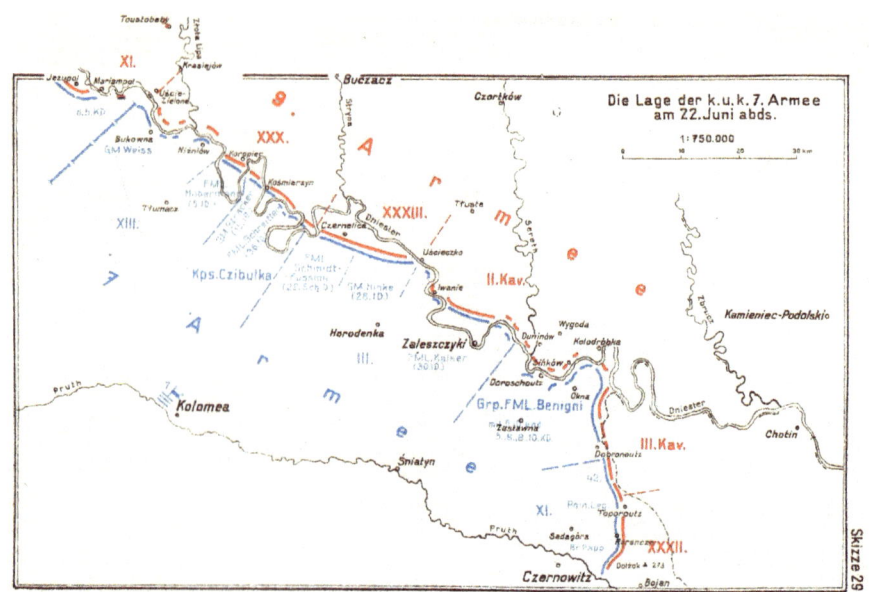

Sketch 29: The position of the k.u.k. 7th Army on June 22 evening

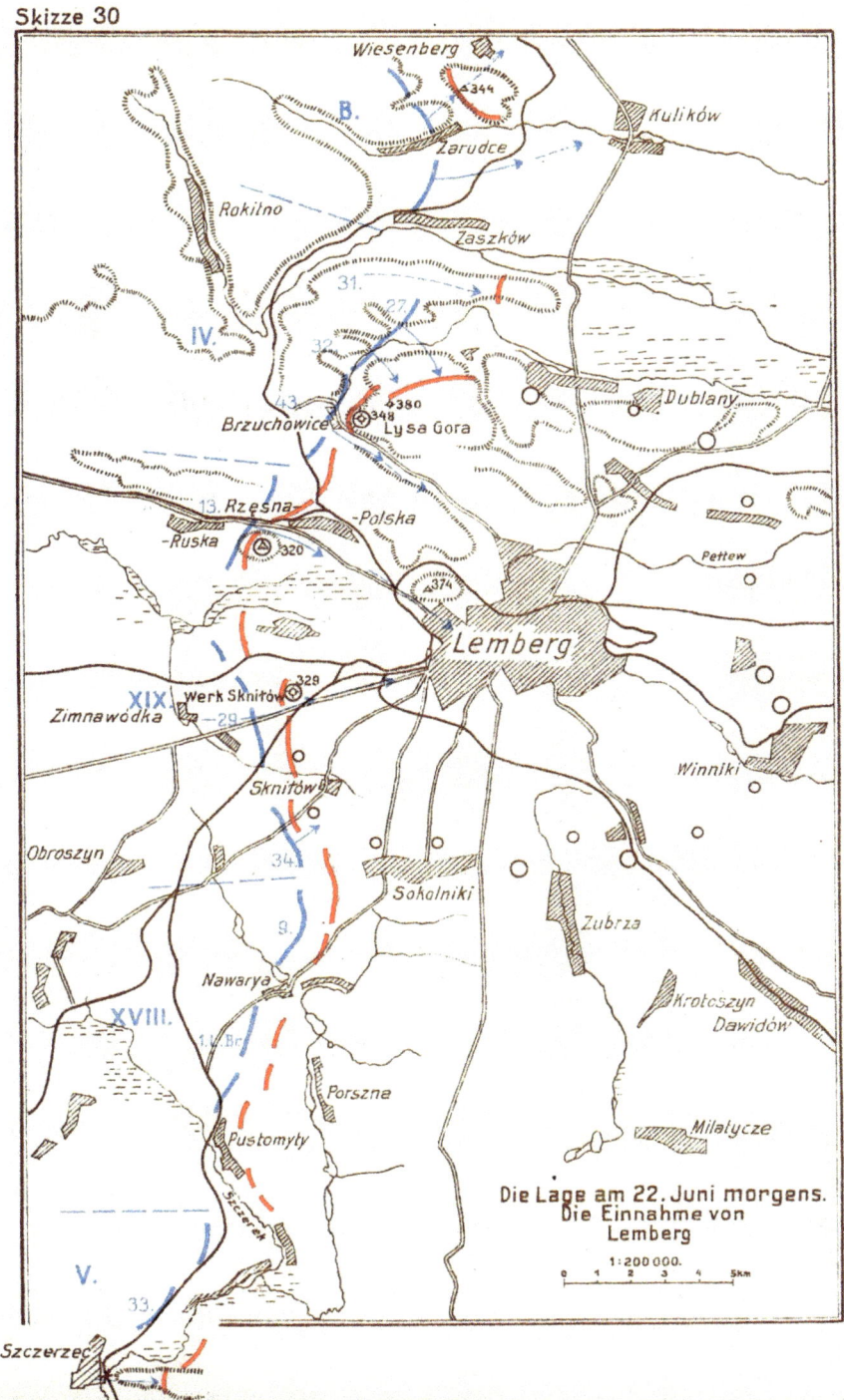

Skizze 30

Wiesenberg
△344
Kulików
B.
Zarudce
Rokilno
Zaszków
31.
27.
IV.
32.
Dublany
43.
△380
Brzuchowice
348
Lysa Gora
13. Rzesna-
-Polska
-Ruska
△320
Pettew
△374
Lemberg
XIX
Werk Sknilów 329
Zimnawódka
29.
Winniki
Sknilów 94
Obroszyn
34.
Sokolniki
9.
Zubrza
Nawarya
Krotoszyn
XVIII.
1. I. Br.
Dawidów
Porszne
Milalycze
Pustomyty
Die Lage am 22. Juni morgens.
Die Einnahme von
Lemberg
Szczerek
1:200 000.
V.
0 1 2 3 4   5 km
33.
Szczerzec

Sketch 30: The situation on June 22 in the morning. The capture of Lviv

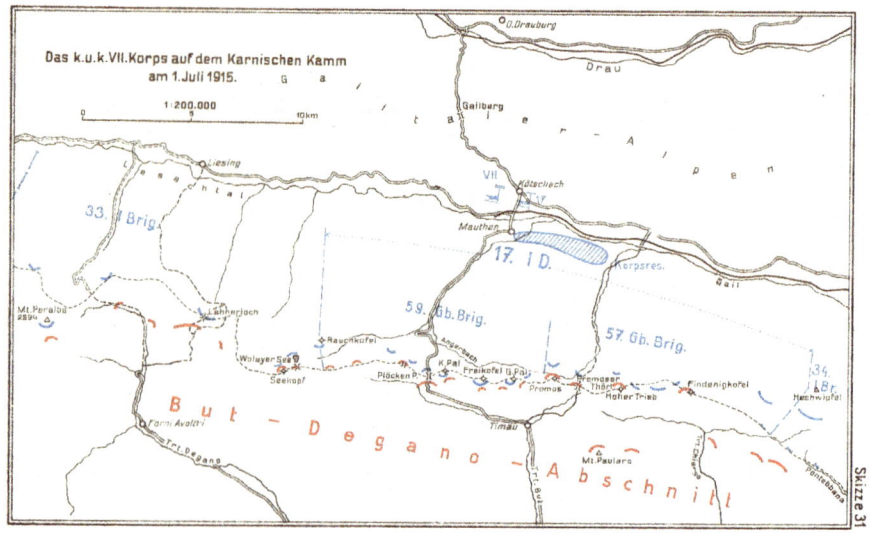

Sketch 31: The K.u.k. VII Corps on the Carnic Ridge on July 1, 1915

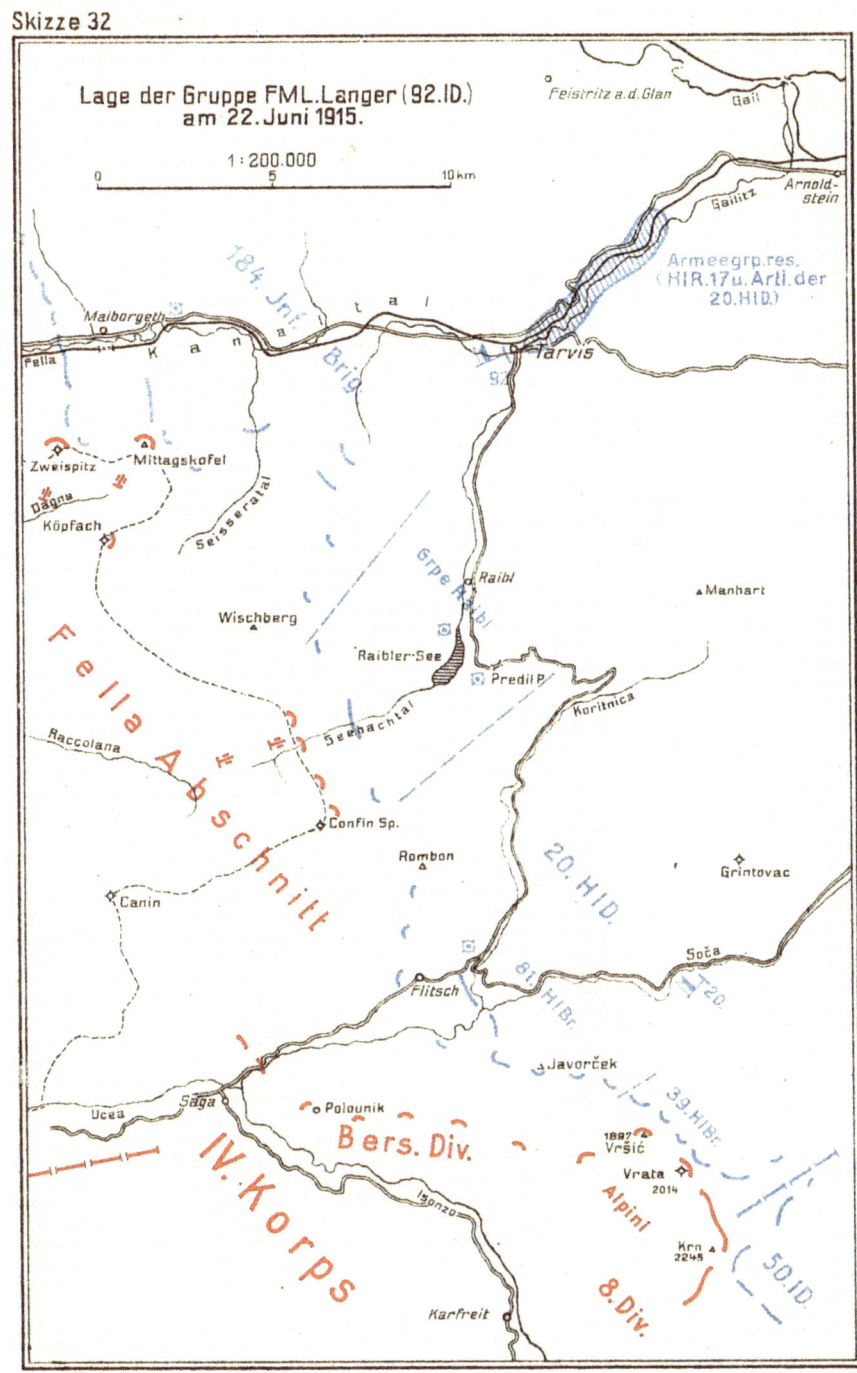

Sketch 32: Position of Group FML. Langer (92 ID) on June 22, 1915

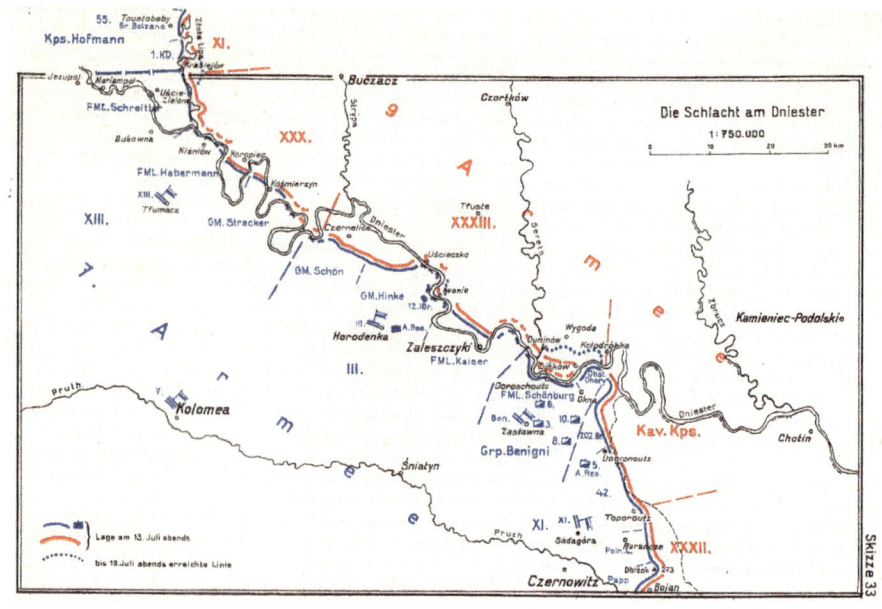

Sketch 33: The Battle of the Dniester

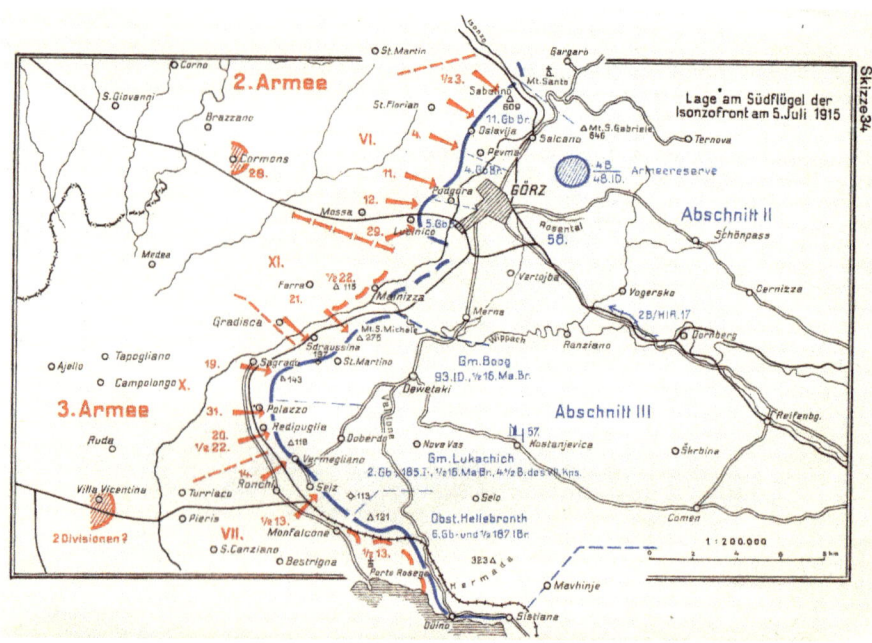

Sketch 34: Position on the southern wing of the Isonzo Front on July 5, 1915

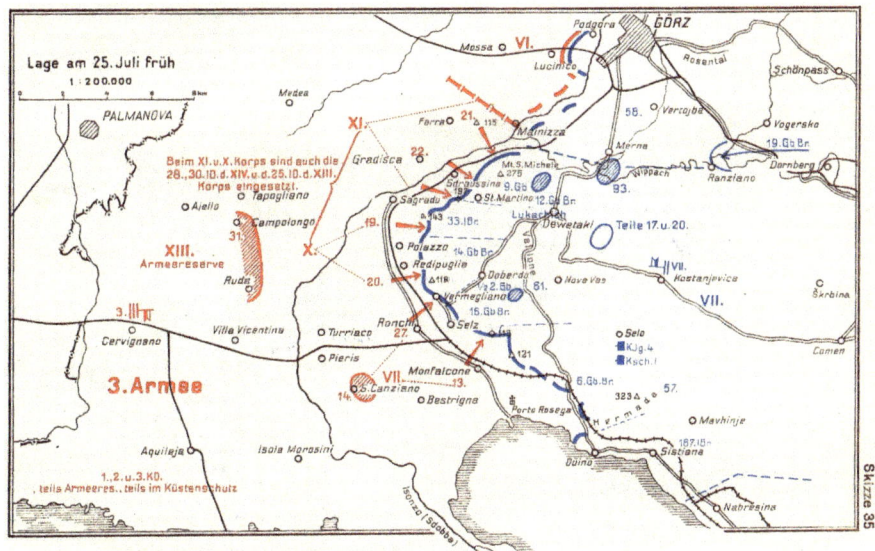

Sketch 35: Situation early on July 25 (on the Isonzo front)

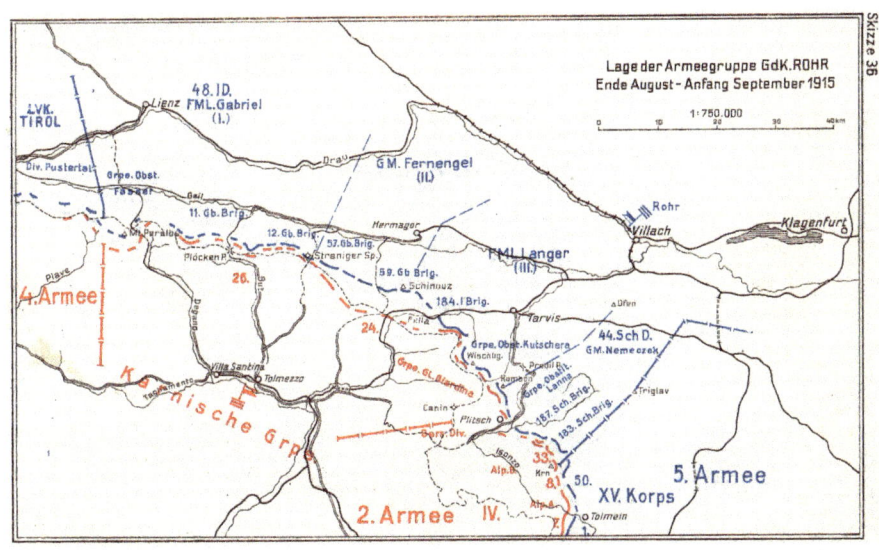

Sketch 36: Situation of Army Group GdK. Pipe late August-early September 1915

Milton Keynes UK
Ingram Content Group UK Ltd.
UKHW050647090424
440793UK00008B/106

9 781927 537855